Why the Democrats Are Blue

Why
the Democrats
Are Blue

How Secular Liberals
Hijacked the People's Party

Mark Stricherz

ENCOUNTER BOOKS
NEW YORK · LONDON

Published by Encounter Books, an activity of Encounter for Culture and Education, Inc., a nonprofit tax exempt corporation.

Encounter Books website address: www.encounterbooks.com

Manufactured in the United States and printed on acid-free paper.

The paper used in this publication meets the minimum requirements of ANSI/NISO Z39.48-1992 (R 1997) (Permanence of Paper).

Library of Congress Cataloging-in-Publication Data

Stricherz, Mark.
    Why the democrats are blue : secular liberalism and the decline of the people's party / Mark Stricherz.
        p.   cm.
    ISBN-13: 978-1-59403-205-9 (hardcover : alk. paper)
    ISBN-10: 1-59403-205-X (hardcover : alk. paper)
    1. Democratic Party (U.S.)—History—20th century.   2. United States—Politics and government—20th century.   3. United States—Politics and government—21st century.   I. Title.
JK2316.S87   2007
324.2736—dc22   2007026662

1 2 3 4 5 6 7 8 9 10

Contents

Introduction

The Democrats limped out of Chicago divided and discouraged, the latest casualties in a culture war that went beyond differences over Vietnam. It would reshape and realign American politics for the rest of the century and beyond, and frustrate most efforts to focus the electorate on the issues that most affect their lives and livelihoods, as opposed to their psyches. The kids and their supporters saw the mayor and the cops as authoritarian, ignorant, violent bigots. The mayor and his largely blue-collar ethnic police force saw the kids as foul-mouthed, immoral, unpatriotic, soft, upper class kids who were too spoiled to respect authority, too selfish to appreciate what it takes to hold a society together, too cowardly to serve in Vietnam. . . . Much of my public life was spent trying to bridge the cultural and psychological divide that had widened into a chasm in Chicago.

BILL CLINTON, *MY LIFE: THE EARLY YEARS*

With the race for the 2008 presidential election under way, it's tempting to conclude that the Democratic Party's candidates can ignore former president Bill Clinton's warning about the culture war. There is a rough consensus that the Democrats are favored to take back the White House; that Democrats will ride in on voter disenchantment with President George W. Bush's handling of the Iraq War, as they did in the 2006 midterms; and that the party's candidates will reach out to culturally conservative religious and blue-collar voters, as Senators Hillary Clinton and Barack Obama already have done.

The conventional wisdom is reasonable enough. If Iraq continues to haunt the Republicans, the economy nosedives, or the Democratic presidential nominee makes a major concession to social conservatives, the Democrats probably will win the White

House. There will be joy in Berkeley and Oakland, Evanston and Chicago, Cambridge and Boston.

But the conventional wisdom is shortsighted. Should the news from Iraq improve, the economy stay strong, and the Republicans nominate a cultural conservative, more voters will be likely to make their choices around issues like abortion and homosexuality. In the past five presidential elections, the percentage of Americans who vote on social issues has swung between one-seventh and one-third of all voters. Given that the vast majority of "values voters" choose the more culturally conservative candidate, the Democrats might well lose the presidency. Again.

"The social issue" has played a major role in keeping a Democrat out of the White House in six of the last nine elections. When Ben Wattenberg and Richard Scammon coined the term in their 1970 classic, *The Real Majority,* "the social issue" comprised race, crime, and values. Although President Clinton helped diminish the importance of the first two, Democrats continue to stumble over values issues, as David Carlin, former Democratic majority leader in the Rhode Island Senate, has argued:

> As the Civil War approached, the Democrats took the wrong position on slavery, and they found themselves, except for a few episodes of prosperity, America's minority party from the election of Abraham Lincoln in 1860 until the election of Franklin Roosevelt in 1932. At the time of the Great Depression of the 1930s, the Republicans took the wrong position on the social and economic welfare responsibilities of the federal government, and they remained America's number-two party until the coming of Ronald Reagan and Newt Gingrich in the 1980s and '90s. Today the Democrats are taking the wrong position on morality and religion, which may doom them to remain America's minority until well into the twenty-first century.

The wrong position that national Democratic leaders have taken is that of secular liberalism. They oppose extending any legal protections to an unprotected class of human beings— unborn infants. And they favor granting public benefits to homosexual couples. Considering that the national party was known as "the party of the little guy" and was led by Catholic big-city and state bosses, the post-1968 party's support for secular liberalism qualifies as a revolution, not an evolution.

So why did the national Democratic Party side with secular liberals ("the kids and their supporters," as Bill Clinton said in his autobiography) rather than religious traditionalists ("the mayor and his largely blue-collar ethnic police force")? The question is of more than historical interest. To political observers, it should affect how they evaluate the Democratic presidential candidates. To those disgruntled with the national Democratic leadership, it should affect how they seek to reform the party.

I got a chance recently to pose this question to Bill Clinton, when he attended a funeral service at the National Cathedral in Washington for Eugene McCarthy. Clinton had delivered a eulogy for the former Minnesota senator, who in his 1968 campaign ran against the "immoral" Vietnam War and the "autocratic" Democratic bosses like Mayor Daley. After the service, Clinton stopped to chat with people in the crowd, smiling and laughing and having pictures taken. Spotting a lull in his repartee, I asked the former president if he thought the McCarthy movement was the transition between the old party, which was formed into the New Deal or Roosevelt coalition, and the current party. He paused for seven or eight seconds, looked away briefly, and pursed his lips.

"Yes and no," Clinton said plainly. "I think that he reflected the beliefs that Democrats had in the sixties. He didn't want to give up the old members of the party, the blue-collar workers. He was someone who, as you heard today, had grown up in a small town. He didn't think that because blue-collar workers favored the war, they would leave the party. And I think he would have been *appalled* at the massive cultural change that took place between the two parties. A lot of the things that happened in '68 caused that."

When I tried to ask a follow-up question, he tapped me on the wrist with his large left hand. "I'm fixin' to say something," he said. "I lived through that time, and I loved Bobby Kennedy, but if you look at what he was doing to get the support of blue-collar workers, he was making very emotional appeals and speeches. See, what McCarthy was trying to do was to get them off the farms. I think they understood that he was from Minnesota and had worked a combine. So they could oppose the war just like the kids were. He tried to talk to them in more of a calm tone [than did Kennedy]." Clinton then got around to addressing the culture wars: "I think he would have been repulsed—I think it would have made him sad—that urban, rural, and suburban voters were voting on guns, gays, and whatever. It all started in the late sixties."

Clinton is right to focus on the McCarthy movement and the culture war. When political observers discuss the revolution in the national Democratic Party, they focus on the defection of the South in response to the passage of civil rights legislation in the 1960s. Their explanation isn't crazy, but it's only half the picture. Like them, Clinton failed to identify the real reason that the party sided with secular liberals instead of religious traditionalists. That is ironic, because in the summer of 1969 Clinton visited a friend in Washington who was interning for the McGovern Commission and made the acquaintance of a commission member.

Officially known as the Commission on Party Structure and Delegate Selection, the commission was approved by a majority of delegates at the very convention that Clinton deplored, the 1968 Democratic National Convention in Chicago. The twenty-eight-member panel is best known for creating the modern presidential nominating system, in which primary and caucus voters rather than big-city and state bosses choose the party's nominee. It is also known for its first chairman, Senator George McGovern, who won the party's nomination in 1972.

Otherwise, the McGovern Commission has been all but forgotten, its notoriety minuscule in comparison with the Warren Commission or the 9/11 Commission. This is understandable. The McGovern Commission was overlooked during its four-year existence (1969 to 1972) and sank into obscurity afterward. It has not been re-examined by journalists and historians since the early 1980s. This book is the first account of the McGovern Commission in a generation. It draws on interviews with nearly all the active participants. The book is also based on extensive archival material, featuring memos, personal notes, and oral history interviews from the collections of Harry Truman, John F. Kennedy, Hubert Humphrey, Lyndon Johnson, George McGovern, and Jimmy Carter.

The most significant consequence of the McGovern Commission is that the Democratic Party's coalition changed and shrank. The New Deal or Roosevelt coalition had included white Southerners, Catholics, union members, blacks, and intellectuals. Under this coalition, the national party was a majority party, and its presidential candidates won seven of the ten elections from 1932 to 1968.

The McGovern Commission destroyed this old electoral alliance and replaced it with a Social Change coalition led by secular liberals. The commission pushed through a rules change that required informal delegate quotas for women and young people. The proposal had three major consequences. First, while the Democratic coalition added feminists and secular professionals, it drove away blue-collar workers and Catholics, many of whom became Reagan Democrats. Second, it broke the Democratic Party's longstanding alliance with the Roman Catholic Church. Third, it reduced the number of Democratic constituents. According to the party strategists William Galston and Elaine Kamarck, only 21 percent of the electorate regard themselves as liberal, while 34 percent call themselves conservative.

The fourth consequence of the McGovern Commission is that the Democratic Party's nominating system reduced the clout of traditional Democrats. Under the old boss system, big-city and state politicians chose the nominee based on the candidate's perceived ability to help the local ticket back home. While the boss system was undemocratic as a procedure, it was democratic in substance, nominating candidates from almost every wing of the party between 1932 and 1968.

Demolishing this system was a top goal of several commission aides. The aides created a nominating process that would ensure the nomination in 1972 of a candidate committed to ending the Vietnam War. Under this new activist system, college-educated and upscale Democratic voters and activists vote for a nominee on the basis of ability to win and conformance to their ideological preferences. To be fair, the activist system is procedurally more democratic than the boss system. But it is internally undemocratic, relying on gender and racial quotas for the party's presidential delegates—those who attend the national convention. The activist system is also less democratic in substance. Not since 1972 has a major Democratic presidential candidate run as a social conservative.

The fifth consequence of the McGovern Commission is that secular, college-educated professionals hijacked control of the party machinery and imposed their own secular, college-educated agenda. The old presidential or national wing of the Democratic Party had been in the hands of Northern Catholic bosses. Although an elite group, they regularly delivered for their cross-racial, working-class constituents, helping make possible the legislation of the Fair Deal, the New Frontier, and the Great Society. In contrast, the party's new presidential wing—while decreasing the likelihood of American troops fighting overseas and stopping the GOP from repealing most federal social programs—has not passed any major domestic initiatives, has allowed Republicans to advance their economic agenda of turbo-capitalism (e.g. lowering of the capital gains tax and taxes on the wealthiest Americans), and has excluded socially conservative Democrats from the national stage.

To millions of Americans devoted to the old Democratic Party, the story of the McGovern Commission and its legacy is a tragedy—a classic tale of *understandable* motives along with an ends-justify-the-means mindset, hypocrisy, rationalization, and hubris.

Chapter One explores the moral and cultural alienation of many Catholic and blue-collar workers from the Democratic Party. Focusing on several voters in one county in western Pennsylvania, it tells the stories of these "Caseycrats"—so named after the late pro-life governor Robert P. Casey—who favor liberal or populist economic policies along with conservative cultural policies. They once sided with Democrats on the basis of economic issues, but they oppose the national party's secular liberalism. The alienation of voters like the Caseycrats has cost

Democratic presidential candidates at least the last two elections, as the party's own pollsters confirm. Although the national party's commitment to cultural liberalism continues to attract upscale voters, it also continues to alienate downscale voters, who represent nearly three-fifth of all those who vote in presidential elections. Why did the national party repel such voters? The standard answers are appealing but fail to explain the magnitude of the change.

The second chapter examines the main virtue of the boss nomination system: It was democratic in substance. David L. Lawrence, as mayor of Pittsburgh and governor of Pennsylvania, was known as "Mr. Democrat" in western Pennsylvania. He sought to extend legal protection to an unprotected class of human beings, black Americans, by playing a key role in passing the civil rights plank at the 1948 Democratic convention. He also was instrumental in choosing every presidential nominee from Truman to Johnson. Along with Lawrence, Mayor Richard J. Daley of Chicago and John M. Bailey, boss of the Connecticut state party, exemplified the strengths of the boss nomination system. They were more ethical and less sectarian than their predecessors; they still retained patronage, which kept them close to voters; they delivered for their cross-racial, working-class constituents; they went beyond their base to choose the party's presidential nominees; and they had no litmus test other than the candidate's perceived ability to win.

Chapter Three assesses the main defect of the boss nomination system: It was undemocratic as a process. The Lawrence Commission (1965–68) did make the boss system more democratic, but antiwar Democrats were marginalized in 1968. Consequently, young aides to Eugene McCarthy's campaign succeeded in passing a minority report at the Chicago convention that sought to democratize the nomination process.

It was secular activists who overthrew the party bosses, as Chapter Four shows, by acting like old-style bosses themselves. The young McCarthy aide Eli Segal feared that his efforts in 1968 to reform the party's nomination system would fail. Although party officials appointed a successor to the Lawrence Commission, which came to be known as the McGovern

Commission, Segal believed that party regulars would undercut the commission. So he created a small executive committee within the McGovern Commission to control its agenda. Rather than make the executive committee broadly representative of the party, he stacked it with supporters of the New Politics. While Segal and other former McCarthy aides were drawing up their preferred rules changes, they gave the appearance of having consulted with the other wings of the party. In truth, they flew ideologically sympathetic commissioners in for key votes, coached Representative Allard Lowenstein of New York on his testimony before a commission hearing, and misleadingly claimed that Democrats endorsed their version of party reform.

The true motives of the activists in wresting control of the party machinery are examined in the fifth chapter, which focuses on Fred Dutton, the chief designer and builder of the post-1968 Democratic Party. While serving on the Board of Regents of the University of California in the 1960s, Dutton believed that baby-boomers and college students were the future of American politics. Unlike the founders of the Democratic Party and Robert F. Kennedy, whose 1968 campaign he managed, Dutton wanted to reduce the party's ties with working-class whites. Like theoreticians of the New Left and New Politics, Dutton believed that the cultural agenda of students should outweigh the economic agenda of blue-collar workers. The chapter also shows how Segal, Anne Wexler, and Ken Bode sought to scrap the boss system in favor of an activist system based on participatory democracy, in which voters discussed the candidates. Segal, Wexler, and Bode were motivated by their opposition to the Vietnam War specifically and the military-industrial complex in general. Bode and possibly others proposed informal delegate quotas for women and young people, the two groups most likely to oppose the war.

Chapter Six looks at the first result of the McGovern Commission's rules changes: Liberation feminists entered the Democratic coalition. In November 1971, leaders of the National Women's Political Caucus, a newly formed nonpartisan group, met with DNC officials in Washington. The women demanded that they enforce the quotas passed by the McGovern Commission. DNC officials complied. At the time, it was unclear whether the emerging feminist movement would side with the Republicans or the Democrats, or form a third party. An upper-class and secular group, the feminists immediately sought to remove legal protection for a class of human beings, lobbying for an abortion plank at the 1972 Democratic convention.

The second result of the commission's rules changes, as detailed in the seventh chapter, is that McGovern won the party's presidential nomination in 1972. He had faced long odds in his bid. He had thin or frayed relations with union leaders, Catholics, and blacks; and his main issue, opposition to the war, was losing steam politically. But McGovern recognized that the party's nomination system had been revolutionized. So he became the candidate of liberal activists; used his chairmanship of the McGovern Commission to tell party leaders that he would not form a third or fourth political party; and ran on Dutton's Social Change coalition. His strategy worked, in a way. On the one hand, McGovern won the party's nomination. On the other hand, Catholics and white working-class voters defected to the Republican Party in November.

The eighth chapter details the third result of the commission's rules changes: secular liberals completed their hijacking of the national party. No individual Democrat could stop them. DNC chairman Robert Strauss, a staunch party regular, was unable to release their grip on the party machinery in the 1970s. Jimmy Carter, as president, was unable to prevent secular feminists from controlling the party platform in 1980. And Bill Clinton, as the party's presidential nominee in 1992, could not prevent feminists from denying a speaking slot at the national convention to Governor Robert Casey of Pennsylvania. As a result of this takeover, support for a once-great national party has dwindled to "blue states" on the coasts and in the Great Lakes region.

The Democratic Party can return to being a People's Party, the afterword argues. To do so, party officials will have to shift power to the people. State caucuses and conventions, which reward highly motivated activists rather than ordinary voters, should be abolished. Independent voters should be allowed to participate in state primaries. Demographic quotas for delegates should be repealed. Super-delegates should be eliminated. And swing states should hold the first primaries in the nation. Enacting this package of reforms would dilute the power of party activists, but it could revive a once-great party.

ONE

The Ghost
of Bob Casey

Irmo Antonacci used to vote for Democratic presidential candidates. The son of a local bar owner and Italian immigrant, Irmo grew up and lives in Jeannette, Pennsylvania, a dying industrial town once famous for making glass and producing natural gas. After dropping out of college in 1950, he got a job with Bell Penn installing telephones. He registered as a Democrat and became a big fan of John Kennedy. In the early and mid 1990s, as the Democratic committeeman of the town's Fifth Ward, he attended the local party's monthly meetings and helped elect candidates. He campaigned for Representative John Murtha when his district covered Jeannette. "They were for the working man," he says of the party. "They were trying to do things for the people."

On the Sunday after the 2006 midterm elections, Antonacci was trimming an ornamental pear tree in front of his one-story brick house on Birch Street. He wore a crimson USC baseball cap and a large white sweatshirt with an image of a smiling Jayhawk, the mascot for Jeannette High School. On his front lawn were a one-foot statue of St. Francis and another of the Virgin Mary. As you may guess, Antonacci is a social conservative. His turn away from the Democrats has everything to do with the national party's liberation-minded stands on cultural issues. "I'd seen the time, from where the party used to be and where the party is now accepting abortion and gay rights, and I didn't go for that," he said.

Betty Nemchik turned away from her ancestral party, too. Her father worked for fourteen years in the Keystone coal mine in Salem Township, one of the vast number of bituminous coal mines in western Pennsylvania. Betty graduated from Greensburg-Salem High School in 1958 and took a few computer classes at a local community college before dropping out to get married and raise three sons. For the past twenty-six years she has worked part-time as a bookkeeper for St. James Catholic Church in New Alexandria, Pennsylvania. She registered as a Democrat in 1960 and voted for John Kennedy, Lyndon Johnson, and Hubert Humphrey ("something about him I just liked," she said).

Nemchik is no devotee of the free market or big business. (Her father, who is now eighty-eight, never received a pension after years working in the coal mines and on the highways.) But she changed her party registration after traveling to Washington in 1997 for the annual March for Life. Many times since then, like thousands of western Pennsylvanians, she has arisen at the break of dawn to hop on a bus with other members of her church, ride for five or six hours, march for five or six hours, and ride home again. Speaking of the Clinton administration, Nemchik said, "They were so liberal. I'm basically a conservative person."

Bob Petersen ought to be a reliable Democrat, too. He's a forty-six-year-old construction worker in Greensburg, Pennsylvania, supervising the building of new homes in the area. In front of his house on Zellers Street was a mustard-colored sign saying HEMPFIELD HIGH GRADUATE, five months after his son Daniel graduated from the school. Petersen's own education never went beyond high school, and he expressed pride that his eldest son, after going to Triangle Tech Community College, might be accepted into the architecture school at Penn State. When I talked to Petersen one Sunday evening, he wore faded blue jeans with a hole in the left knee, wire-rim glasses, and a white March of Dimes T-shirt. He looked the very image of a white, working-class voter.

Petersen is a registered independent. Though independents nationally broke for the Democrats in 2000 and 2004, Petersen voted for George W. Bush each time. His reason wasn't Bush's strong stand on terrorism, though Petersen's father was a career Army officer. "Everybody wants our troops back safe," he said. His reason was that he admired Bush's experience and values: "He comes from a good family, and he's been affiliated with the White House for a long time because his father was president." Although Bush's personal image and character factored in, Petersen said that values issues were important, too. Raised a Baptist, Petersen has a frequent Bible study with some of the men in the neighborhood.

Antonacci, Nemchik, and Petersen are what John Rosso-mando has called "Caseycrats": voters who support a conservative stance on cultural issues and a liberal stance on economic issues. At the same time that they favor government protections for the unborn, the traditional family, and guns, they back government assistance in providing health care and education. These views formed the political outlook of Robert P. Casey, who was governor of Pennsylvania from 1987 to 1995. Casey wrote in his autobiography, *Fighting for Life,* "I do not believe that every moral duty can or should be entrusted to government. But I am dead certain that when people are in serious trouble—unemployed, exploited, forgotten by the rest of society—it is government's duty to protect them. And those people should not be viewed as a burden to the rest of us: they are our neighbors, our fellow citizens." Casey's philosophy of Christian humanism finds its greatest support among the working classes and traditional Christians, especially Roman Catholics and Orthodox Christians. In fact, Casey kicked off his 1986 gubernatorial campaign in Westmoreland County, the southwestern Pennsylvania hometown of Antonacci, Nemchik, and Petersen. Although not well known nationally, Casey is still remembered as an admired and courageous figure in his native state. "I voted for Bob Casey," Nemchik said, echoing Antonacci. "He was a good man."

In the last two presidential elections, the opposition of most white Catholic and working-class voters to a relativist stance on cultural issues has helped defeat the Democratic Party's nominees. In 2000, these voters played a key role in costing Al Gore the presidency. "Voters turned away from Al Gore, in the first instance, on cultural concerns, followed by concerns with trust and the role of government," concluded Stanley Greenberg, formerly a pollster for President Bill Clinton, in a post-election analysis. "But the cultural minefield made the most damage, moving non-college white women and younger non-college white men to Bush and unraveling the larger progressive majority in the country." White Catholics voted 52 to 45 against Gore. Overall, the three biggest doubts about Gore centered on cultural issues: abortion, gay rights, and guns.

In 2004, these same voters cost John Kerry the presidency. "Large sections of downscale America shifted, opting to vote their values rather than their economic worries," Greenberg concluded. "That produced a cultural surge at the end, an intensified polarization that took down many Democrats in rural states and the South, that diminished their blue-collar support generally and that allowed George Bush to get a national majority from red America." In an analysis months later, Greenberg and his colleague Matt Hogan emphasized that "[t]he drop in Catholic support is a big part of the 2004 election story," especially among blue-collar Catholics, who "differ from Democrats" on abortion, gay marriage, and the gun issue.

As recently as 1968, both Catholics and blue-collar workers voted heavily Democratic. Catholic voters favored Humphrey over Nixon 59 percent to 33 percent, while "manual workers" went for Humphrey 50 percent to 35 percent. "The 1968 election upset no longstanding political patterns. It created no new alignments of interest groups. Nixon won on the protest vote and so 1968 must be considered a temporary deviation from the normal pattern of Democratic Party dominance," concluded Angus Campbell, director of the well-respected Survey Research Center in Ann Arbor, Michigan, in a post-election analysis. Blue-collar workers gave a majority of their votes to every Democratic presidential nominee stretching back before the New Deal. "The Democrats, despite the Agnew hoopla about Democratic elitist establishmentarians, are those 'plain people who work with their hands,'" wrote Richard Scammon and Ben Wattenberg in *The Real Majority*. Catholics were an even more reliable Democratic constituency, having voted for Democrats since large numbers of them first came to the United States in the 1830s. As the historian George Marlin has noted, "Catholic voters overwhelmingly supported the presidential ambitions of Andrew Jackson, Samuel Tilden, Al Smith, Franklin D. Roosevelt, Harry Truman, and John F. Kennedy." Catholic voters even gave a majority of their ballots to Adlai Stevenson in 1952 and 1956.

But after 1968, both white Catholics and working-class whites moved away from the Democratic Party. Even Catholic women have de-aligned from the Democratic Party. White Catholic voters have cast a majority or plurality of their ballots for Democratic presidential nominee only three times—once for Jimmy Carter and twice for Bill Clinton—and even then at levels not approaching those before 1972. Working-class whites—defined as those with a high school degree or some college education—have moved even more sharply against the Democrats. In the nine presidential elections since 1972, they have given a majority of their ballots to the Democratic presidential nominee only once, to Clinton in 1996. The 2004 election was a good example of this phenomenon. Bush won 54 percent of those with some college education and 52 percent of those with a high school diploma.

Why, after decades of voting for Democratic presidential candidates, have white Catholics and working-class whites defected? The question is tied to the breakup of the party's New Deal or Roosevelt coalition—the electoral alliance of white Southerners, Northern Catholics, blacks, intellectuals, and laborers, or as the presidential chronicler Theodore White put it, the coalition of "Southern white–big city–big labor–ethnic minority." A couple of hypotheses have been proposed by journalists and academics, but none explains the magnitude of the change. After all, Democratic presidential candidates continue to lose elections regularly. In the last thirty-five years, only two Democrats have been elected. The party's record of six losses in the previous nine presidential elections is its worst since the pre–New Deal era of 1896 to 1928. In short, national Democrats have become a blue party, not just in the political sense of representing the blue states in the red-state/blue-state divide, but in the Louis Armstrong/Miles Davis sense as well.

—⟋⟋—

THE OLDEST THESIS about why white working-class and Catholic voters defected is racial, maintaining that whites have left the party in response to the influx of blacks and the party's adoption of the civil rights platform. The thesis was popular among such analysts and journalists as Kevin Phillips in *The Emerging Republican Majority* (1969); Peter Brown in *Minority Party: Why Democrats Face Defeat in 1992 and Beyond* (1991) and Thomas Byrne Edsall and Mary D. Edsall in *Chain Reaction: The Impact of Race, Rights, and Taxes on American Politics* (1991). The Southern-racial explanation maintained that until the mid-to-late 1960s, most working-class white voters had every reason to vote Democratic. They received benefits, in the form of Social Security, Medicare, and the right to bargain collectively; they did not compete with black Americans in the marketplace; and because of racial segregation, they did not have to worry about blacks taking the party away from them. Then the Democratic Party embraced the civil rights movement and President Johnson pushed his Great Society programs. In Phillips' version of the thesis,

> The principal force which broke up the Democratic (New Deal) coalition is the Negro socioeconomic revolution and liberal Democratic ideological inability to cope with it. Democratic "Great Society" programs aligned that party with many Negro demands, but the party was unable to defuse the racial tension sundering the nation. The South, the West, and the Catholic sidewalks of New York were the focal points of conservative opposition to the welfare liberalism of the federal government; however, the general opposition which deposed the Democratic Party came in large part from prospering Democrats who objected to Washington dissipating their tax dollars on programs which did them no good. The Democratic Party fell victim to the ideological impetus of a liberalism which had carried it beyond programs taxing the few for the benefit of the many (the New Deal) to programs taxing the many on behalf of the few (the Great Society).

In the late 1960s, trying to capture votes from supporters of George Wallace, the former governor of Alabama, Republicans embarked on a "Southern strategy" to woo Southern whites. As late as the 1980s and early 1990s, racial issues continued to move white Democrats away from their ancestral party. Stanley Greenberg in 1985 wrote a famous report about Macomb County in Michigan, a former Democratic stronghold that turned Republican in the 1980s primarily because of race-related concerns such as forced busing and welfare. Peter Brown criticized Democratic leaders for failing to recognize the concerns of white voters. "Although most Democrats cringe at any racial analysis, it is impossible to avoid the math," he said. "No party can win the presidency without a majority, or near majority, of whites, who are 80-plus percent of the electorate."

The Southern-racial thesis is persuasive in some ways. Mississippi and Alabama have not given a single presidential elector to the Democrats since 1960, while Oklahoma has not been in the Democratic column since 1964. Many Northern states, such as Illinois and Michigan, voted for the Republican Party partly out of racial concerns. The overall white vote has not gone Democratic since 1964. In 2005, the chairman of the Republican National Committee, Ken Mehlman, apologized to African Americans on behalf of the party for playing to white voters' racial fears.

The weakness in the Southern-racial case, however, is that the white backlash isn't as powerful as it once was. In national politics today, racial animosity has largely run its course. Racially loaded issues—forced busing, crime, welfare, prison furloughs— have been largely swept from the table, especially since President Clinton moved to the center and signed on to welfare reform. Moreover, George Wallace and his ghost never haunted many precincts of the North. It is true that Macomb County in the 1980s moved toward the Republican Party partly out of racial concerns, but plenty of other counties continued to vote Democratic. Nowhere was this truer than in the Rust Belt, including southwestern and northeastern Pennsylvania, Ohio, and West Virginia.

Consider Westmoreland County in Pennsylvania. Voters there stayed in the Democratic column in every presidential election from 1932 to 1996, except in 1972, and usually the Democrat won with more than 55 percent of the vote. West

Virginia is another example. Save the Republican landslide years of 1972 and 1984, voters in this heavily white state went Democratic in every election from 1960 to 1996. But in 2000 and 2004, both Westmoreland County and West Virginia voted for the Republican candidate, George W. Bush. In 2006, Westmoreland County went for the Republican gubernatorial candidate, Lynn Swann, a black pro-lifer, over incumbent Ed Rendell, a white pro-choicer. It goes against all common sense to argue that white voters in the North are now voting against blacks more than ever, when racial issues have become much less divisive.

The second major thesis about why Catholics and working-class whites left the Democratic Party is socioeconomic, stressing the difference between the old social order of industrial society and the relatively recent postindustrial society. This argument has been voiced by academic historians and journalists, such as Everett Carll Ladd Jr. and Charles D. Hadley in *Transformations of the American Party System: Political Coalitions from the New Deal to the 1970s* (1975) and John B. Judis and Ruy Teixeira in *The Emerging Democratic Majority* (2002).

Ladd and Hadley contend that most white Catholics and working-class whites no longer support social change. Having reaped the benefits of the affluent society, they argue, both groups oppose governmental efforts to aid others:

> Urban whites, manual workers, Catholics, and Southern whites were change-demanding groups in the agenda of the New Deal. And they supported the more change-initiating or liberal of the two major parties, the Democrats. In the post-industrial setting, these groups are relatively conservative—not in the New Deal sense of the term, of seeking to bring back the ascendancy of business nationalism and to dismantle the managerial state, but relatively resistant to components of social and cultural change, to extensions of equalitarianism. And it is because the Democrats are the prime partisan custodian of the new liberalism in national politics that they can no longer count upon the new white bourgeoisie for a high measure of electoral sustenance.

Judis and Teixeira offer another version of the postindustrial argument, maintaining that only rural and Southern members of the white working class oppose "extensions of equalitarianism." Those who live in and around "ideopolises"—metropolitan areas that include central cities and suburbs, and in which ideas and services have supplanted the production of goods—continue to vote Democratic. As Judis and Teixeira explain,

> Democrats did best among white working-class voters who had been most dramatically affected by the experience of the sixties and by the transition to postindustrial society. These included not only working women, but men and women who lived in large metropolitan areas that have been transformed over the last four decades from manufacturing centers to centers for production of services and ideas. A white working-class voter in Seattle's King County or in the Boulder-Denver area is likely to support the right to abortion and the need for environmental regulation and to place some importance on being racially tolerant.

The postindustrial thesis has appeal. Pocketbook issues don't pack the punch they once did. Working-class voters are materially better off today and therefore have less incentive to vote for economically liberal Democratic candidates. As the journalist David Brooks has pointed out, Americans with an annual household income of $30,000 to $50,000 express a fair degree of satisfaction with their circumstances; 85 percent say they are satisfied with their housing, almost seven in ten with their car, and two-thirds with their ability to go out for an evening. What's more, the liberal-centrist group Third Way released a study showing that the economic tipping point for white voters to go Republican was only $23,700 in annual income. Not surprisingly, Bush beat Gore among white voters in the $30,000 to $50,000 income group by 15 percentage points and lost among *all* voters of this income group by only one point in both 2000 and 2004. As the Pew Research Center in 2001 concluded, "this sense of deprivation tends to be concentrated in a relatively small segment of the population." Even among whites with household incomes of $15,000 to $30,000 a year, Bush received 55 percent of their votes compared with 42 percent for Gore. John Kerry fared even worse among this group, nationally and in Westmoreland County. Two days after the Democratic National

Convention ended, Kerry and his running mate, Senator John Edwards of North Carolina, staged a rally in the rain outside a converted train station in downtown Greensburg. They hit the economic issue hard, but failed to make much headway. In contrast to Gore, who received 45.8 percent of the county's vote, Kerry got 43.5 percent.

Despite the strengths of the postindustrial thesis, this argument, too, is flawed. The problem with Ladd and Hadley's case is that white working-class and Catholic voters are not nearly as resistant to social change as alleged. Both groups do want social and cultural change. It's just not always the change that those in the professional classes want. Take greater protections for unborn children. According to the Voter News Service data from the 2000 election, a slight majority (52 percent) of whites with high school diplomas or less believed that most abortions should be illegal. By contrast, only 37 percent of whites with college and postgraduate degrees said they wanted the same. White working-class voters also want a higher minimum wage and more health-care coverage.

As for Judis and Teixeira, their argument makes no sense in the case of Westmoreland County. In the last fifteen years, the county has undergone a dramatic transition to postindustrial society; yet at the presidential level of voting, the county has changed from Democratic to Republican. Trying to understand this apparent paradox, I drove to Westmoreland County again, this time five days after the 2006 election.

Perhaps nowhere else was the transformation in the county's economy more evident than in Jeannette, the hometown of Irmo Antonacci. The hilly city used to boast more than half a dozen manufacturing plants, including the Pennsylvania Rubber Company, Jeannette Glass, and the Victor Brewing Company. Due to the organizing efforts of the AFL and the CIO during the Great Depression, the jobs in the factories were stable and paid well. After the war, Jeannette's population soared to 20,000. Antonacci remembers going out on Saturday night and having his pick of nightclubs and theaters. "This town used to be jumping on Saturday night!" he said. Then, starting in the late 1970s and ending in the mid-1980s, the plants and factories closed down. A couple of the factories, such as Pennsylvania Rubber and Elliott Turbines, are still there, though their combined employment has shrunk from around 4,000 to 400. The other plants have been demolished or shuttered. On Seventh Street is the rusted-out, hollowed shell of the old McKee Glass factory. As the plants closed, Jeannette lost population and many of its other businesses. The town now has only about 9,800 residents. The downtown area is pockmarked with storefronts for sale or lease—Planet Fitness, Sara Ellen Candies—and homes with doors ajar and only darkness inside.

Jeannette's story is not unique in western Pennsylvania. The region's other manufacturing industries—mining, steel, bituminous or hard coal—have declined as well. Tom Balya, a Democrat who serves as a city councilman in Greensburg, sketched the recent economic history of the county this way:

> Historically, this was heavily industrial. Alcoa in the north end of the county. Big steel plants in Latrobe. Allegheny and Kisk Valley. Monongahela Valley had TV and steel companies leave. Since I've been a child all that has disappeared. What's happened are real demographic changes. The small towns have lost populations, so power shifts to more service- and white-collar jobs. Mining is most definitely not around. In my time, 35 to 40 years ago, my dad quit school in the eighth grade. Now it's all mined out. When the factories shut down, they didn't have anyone leave. So when a big employer moves in, a lot of old people and young people moved in, no baby-boomers.

Light manufacturing and service companies have replaced the old industrial order. In towns such as Latrobe, Greensburg, and Jeannette, the emergence of these postindustrial businesses is obvious. In contrast to the old manufacturing plants, which usually are located downtown, the light manufacturing and service industries moved to the outskirts of town, into a mall or industrial park. In the early 1990s, Sony built a plant in Greensburg that makes 36-inch TVs and employs about 3,500 workers. Timken operates a ball-bearing plant on the outskirts of Latrobe. The malls also reflect the growth of exurbs in former farmland areas, such as Hempfield, Washington, and Unity townships, in the central part of the county. Former residents of Pittsburgh and surrounding Allegheny County have decamped to those exurbs in search of bigger lots with homes that are as much as 20 percent cheaper. The light manufacturing and service companies came mostly in the 1990s, the outgrowth of legislation by local Democratic lawmakers to attract business. Their arrival affected county politics in two ways. First, the county stopped hemorrhaging population. After losing around 20,000 residents in the 1980s, the county's population remains at 370,000, the same figure as in 1990. (The county is now the eighth largest in the state.) Second, the new residents voted Republican. "People making in the mid-30s, mid-40s sort of vote against Pittsburgh," said Allen Kukovich, a Democrat who was a Pennsylvania state senator but lost his re-election race in 2004. "They built homes on larger lots and they don't like anything Pittsburgh has done."

The major political change in Westmoreland County is not so much the economy as the decline of unions. In 1964, almost two in five Pennsylvania workers (38 percent) were unionized. In 2000, fewer than one in five were (17 percent). When the manufacturing plants began to falter in the late 1970s and 1980s, Democrats tried to revive them and the attendant union jobs. In 1986, Robert Casey began his third, and ultimately successful, gubernatorial bid in Monessen, an old steel town at the southwest end of the county. His autobiography, *Fighting for Life,* recounts how he pledged, if elected, to "go to Monessen to dramatize my resolve to help struggling people there and all across the state." But Casey's efforts, as well as those of other Democrats, failed to stem the tide. "No one lives in Monessen anymore," says Rosemary Trump, chairwoman of the county Democratic Party. "It's a ghost town." Over the last three decades, the numbers of card-carrying union members have plunged. Today about 18 percent of the state's workers are unionized. The biggest union remaining in Westmoreland County is the Service Employees International Union, which has only 800 to 900 members. The unions' influence clearly "has diminished over time," as Tom Balya notes.

Contrary to Judis and Teixeira, the transition to postindustrial society has a downside for Democrats. The party adds upper-class voters but loses working-class voters. To paraphrase Stanley Greenberg, Democrats win it upscale but lose it downscale.

If unions had remained robust in Westmoreland County, voters there may well have continued to vote for Democratic presidential candidates. Despite the frequently heard remark that the rank and file no longer follow the leadership, they often do so at the voting booth; union members gave 59 percent of their votes to Clinton and Gore in both the 1996 and 2000 elections. But the unions' disintegration has loosened the ties of white working-class voters to the Democratic Party. For Republicans, this means it is easier to appeal to blue-collar voters. For working-class voters, it is easier to vote for Republicans on the basis of cultural issues; in essence, they can vote against Hollywood and Planned Parenthood, rather than against Wall Street.

A good example of this type of working-class voter is Bill Cain, whom I ran into one Friday afternoon in Greensburg while he was running errands. Born in 1923, Cain supported his wife and six kids on the wages of a unionized factory worker. "I've been a Democrat all my life," he says in a deep bass reminiscent of the actor Bob Mitchum. But after voting twice for Bill Clinton, he went for George W. Bush in 2000 and 2004. Cain is a near-daily communicant at Blessed Sacrament Cathedral downtown, and he supports the Republican Party's stands on social issues. When I talked to him again in early 2004, he said his vote would be based not on Iraq or the economy, but rather opposition to homosexual marriage. "I'm not bigoted, but the whole damn thing is that the good Lord didn't mean marriage to be for this sort of thing. He wanted marriage to be between one man and one woman, so they could procreate."

Cain's comments lead us to the third major theory about why white Catholic and working-class voters have defected from the Democratic Party: the culture war. This culture-war hypothesis has been enunciated by E. J. Dionne Jr. in *Why Americans Hate Politics* (1991); by Ronald Radosh in *Divided They Fell: The Demise of the Democratic Party, 1964–1996* (1996); by Samuel G. Freedman in *The Inheritance: How Three Families and the American Political Majority Moved from the Left to the Right* (1996); by Jules

Witcover in *The Year the Dream Died: Revisiting 1968 in America* (1997); and by Thomas Edsall in *Building Red America: The New Conservative Coalition and the Drive for Permanent Power* (2006). The culture-war school holds that working-class white and Catholic voters fell away in response to the party's embrace of the antiwar, youth, and feminist movements of the late 1960s and early 1970s. The Democratic Party was once identified with patriotism and family values; Democratic administrations presided over World War II and supported programs that allowed the breadwinner to feed and clothe the family. Then came the late 1960s and the counterculture movement. The Democratic Party came to be identified with protesters, hippies, drugs, and sex. As Dionne put it:

> The politics of the 1960s shifted the balance of power within the liberal coalition away from working-class and lower-middle class voters, whose main concerns were economic, and toward upper-middle class reformers mainly interested in cultural issues and foreign policy. Increasingly, liberalism is identified not with energetic intervention in the economy, but by its openness to cultural change and its opposition to American intervention abroad. The rise of the cultural issues made the upper-middle class reformers the dominant voices within American liberalism.

The culture-war thesis makes sense. The American electorate is split along cultural lines, between blue states along the coasts and in the upper Midwest, and red states in the heartland and the South. In 2000 and 2004, weekly churchgoers, married couples, and small-town and rural voters all went heavily for George W. Bush, while secular voters, singles, and big-city residents went heavily for Al Gore and John Kerry. Indeed, two of President Clinton's pollsters in 1996, Dick Morris and Mark Penn, discovered a polling technique that proved to be a more accurate predictor of voting behavior than any other factor except party affiliation and race. Voters were asked their attitude on five issues—homosexuality, pornography, adultery, premarital sex, and religion. Those who gave a liberal answer on at least three of the five questions voted for Clinton overwhelmingly, while those who gave a conservative answer on three of the five went heavily for Bob Dole. Voters in Westmoreland County have supported local pro-life Democrats, such as the state representative Tom Tangretti. In 2004 they went heavily for Robert Casey Jr., son of the legendary former state governor, in his race for state treasurer. The county voted for Casey Jr. again in 2006 when he campaigned on a pro-life plank in his successful bid for the U.S. Senate. By the same token, Westmoreland County voters have given light support to pro-choice Republicans, such as Tom Ridge when he ran for his second term as governor in 1998.

The problem with the culture-war thesis, however, is partly one of timing and partly one of voting trends. Much of the Rust Belt continued to support Democrats at the presidential level from 1968 to 1996. Yet the Democratic Party developed a reputation as a culturally liberal party starting in the 1970s and accelerating in the 1980s and 1990s. The culture-war school fails to account for this time lag.

In the case of Westmoreland County, I believe that the delay is attributable to a shift in institutional weight. As unions have fallen by the wayside, their place as the county's dominant civic and political institution has been taken over by Christian churches in general and the Catholic Church in particular. I was reminded of this fact again on Saturday afternoon as I pulled into the BP gas station on East Pittsburgh Avenue in Greensburg, the county seat. Blaring for several blocks downtown was the sound of a public announcer calling a football game featuring Seton Hill University, a small Catholic liberal arts university in town. "Fumble, recovered by Seton Hill!" the announcer yelled, which elicited a loud "yeah!" from the spectators huddled on the wet aluminum benches at Offutt Field. "Sack by number 55, Rob Ellis! First and ten Seton Hill from the Seton Hill 49-yard-line." In other areas, the local Catholic college probably could not hold a football game in the middle of downtown with its PA system blaring. In Westmoreland County, this tradition reflects the esteem in which the Church is held.

A few blocks from Offutt Field is the headquarters of the Diocese of Greensburg, sitting on a ridge amidst a rolling expanse of green law. Half a mile away is North Main Street, which Kevin Phillips might have called the "Catholic sidewalks" of Greensburg.

At the northern tip is a Knights of Columbus hall, a split-level tan brick building where fifty men from Council 1480 gather on the first Thursday night of every month. One-third of a mile away, at the crest of a hill, is the Aquinas Academy, where 442 students in preschool through the eighth grade will be taught by the Sisters of Charity this school year. Next door to the school is Blessed Sacrament Cathedral, a Gothic-style church built in 1852. At the most recent Sunday Mass I attended, the church was packed elbow to elbow; there were young married couples with small children, as well as seniors. After Mass, four nuns from the Sisters of Charity, wearing black and white habits, sold $3 raffle tickets for the Clelian Heights Holly Berry Craft Fair. Three blocks away, on South Main Street, is a St. Vincent de Paul store, with used sweaters and pants on display in an airy two-floor building that occupies two storefronts.

There are many other churches on North Main Street—Episcopal, Lutheran, Presbyterian, United Methodist, Church of God—as well as a Jewish synagogue; and the Christian Coalition has an active branch in the county. But the Catholic Church plays the most prominent role in civic and political life. In 2003, local Catholic officials including Tom Balya, a Democrat on the Greensburg City Council, met with Bishop Anthony Bosco. "The bishop put out a pastoral letter saying that abortion is the main issue, rather than all of these other issues, like the death penalty and the war in Iraq," said Balya. "We met with him. We thought it was bullshit." In August 2004, only months after being installed in the Greensburg diocese, Bishop Lawrence Brandt implicitly attacked John Kerry's stated position that he is worthy to receive Holy Communion despite his pro-choice view on abortion. "Any public official who says, 'I can vote for abortion and still be a Catholic in good standing,' is being intellectually condescending to every Catholic by making himself or herself the sole judge of what 'Catholic' means," Brandt wrote. Although Balya and others resented the bishops' efforts, regular Catholic voters appreciated or were persuaded by them. "We've got a lot of very vocal Catholics who think well of their church," remarked Rosemary Trump, "and in the parishes they'll hear priests telling them to protect the life of fetuses."

In addition to churches, the National Rifle Association and sportsmen's hunting clubs remain vibrant. In the county's exurbs and rural towns, voters tend to be wary of politicians whom they suspect of wanting to restrict, let alone take away, their guns or rifles. "Guns are a big issue," said Debbie Irwin, a former GOP county chairwoman. "I had a woman on the committee who's 82 and has killed three deer already. That's how she eats." Rosemary Trump said that the Catholic Church in alliance with the GOP and the NRA is "a powerful combination" against Democrats.

—␣␣—

UNIONS ARE NOT the only institutions in Westmoreland County that have changed. So has the Democratic Party. As the stories of Irmo Antonacci and Betty Nemchik show, the national party up through 1968 basically represented their Christian humanist values. That year, the Democratic presidential nominee was Hubert Humphrey, who eloquently defined the party's political philosophy as being to help "those in the dawn of life, those in the shadows of life, and those in the twilight of life."

Humphrey's maxim was endorsed by Robert P. Casey, who kicked off his 1986 gubernatorial bid in Westmoreland County. As the Democratic candidate for state auditor general in 1968, Casey had attended the party's national convention in Chicago and came to admire Humphrey as they campaigned together:

> His words summed up for me what it meant to call myself a Democrat. Whatever its faults, at the end of the day, to be a Democrat was to have a mission. To be a Democrat was to identify with the afflicted, the vulnerable, the powerless. Let the other party look after those at the plateaus and summits of life. Democrats would look to those still struggling down below. That was the Democratic Party of my father, and Humphrey spoke for it.

Casey learned that most state party leaders shared those populist and Christian values as well. When he ran for governor again in 1970, he stopped by the office of the mayor of Philadelphia, hoping for an endorsement. According to Casey, Mayor James H. J. Tate, an Irish Catholic of the old school, asked him the following questions: "What county in Ireland did your people come from? How do you stand with your bishop?" Casey was amazed: "I felt like I was in the confessional rather than sitting there with the state's most powerful political leader."

Despite a reputation as being aloof and hotheaded, Casey adhered to the values of Christian humanism as governor. He supported the interests of working-class voters on economic *and* cultural issues. He signed into law the children's health-care initiative, proposed by the former state senator Allen Kukovich of Westmoreland County, which dramatically expanded health coverage for poor children; he funded domestic-violence and rape-crisis programs at record levels; and he championed nutrition and economic programs for women and children. He also signed into law the 1989 Abortion Control Act, which required parental consent for minors, informed consent for women considering abortion, a twenty-four-hour waiting period, and spousal notification.

As a result of these stands, Casey was an exceedingly popular governor. In his 1986 race, he knocked off the scion of a politically prominent family, the Scrantons. In his 1990 re-election bid, he carried 66 of the state's 67 counties, including parts of the state that had never voted Democratic, and won with 68 percent of the vote.

Less than two years later, the Democrats opened their national convention at Madison Square Garden in New York City, with Casey attending as head of the Pennsylvania delegation. But despite his impressive record on social justice and his overwhelming popularity, Casey's stance on cultural issues made him a pariah among national party leaders. When he asked to address the delegates about why the party should change its plank in support of abortion rights, he was not only rejected but also humiliated. He received a standard-form letter of rejection from DNC officials. It was, Casey remarked, "the kind of letter they might have sent Lyndon LaRouche, had he asked to address the convention." To party leaders, cultural libertarianism trumped economic issues and public sentiment.

Casey had suspected as much for years, but found out firsthand on the second night of the convention. One of the guests on the platform July 14 was Kathy Taylor, a *Republican* pro-choice activist who had campaigned for Casey's opponent in 1990. On the convention floor was Karen Ritter, a state Democratic legislator, selling large buttons with pictures of Casey dressed up as the pope. At that point, Casey recognized that the Democratic Party, or at least the national or presidential wing of the party, had been transformed. "What was going on here?" he wondered. "What had become of the Democratic Party I once knew?"

TWO

The New Deal Democratic Party: Of the People and For the People

In September 1947, a famous memo called "The Politics of 1948" argued that big-city and state bosses no longer ran the Democratic Party. The thirty-three-page memo outlined a political strategy for President Truman in the election less than fourteen months away. It acknowledged that a few of the bosses' political machines, such as Frank Hague's in Jersey City and Ed Kelly's in Chicago, were still important; but it went on to assert that the party bosses "everywhere ... are in profound collapse" and that "the old 'party organization' control is gone forever." The memo explained:

> Hague and Kelley [*sic*] admit publicly they are through as political bosses of the first magnitude. They have left no one in their places; their organizations are shot through with incompetence. There are a few signs of revival in New York under Mayor O'Dwyer, but hardly enough to justify any optimism.... Curley, still Boston's great vote getter, fills his cell with threats of smashing the party in Massachusetts—and no one doubts for a minute that he can do it. Pennsylvania is torn between Lawrence and Joe Guffey and every time Lawrence gets some federal patronage to dispense, Guffey sings the praises of Henry Wallace as publicly as possible.

The chief author of "The Politics of 1948" was James H. Rowe Jr., a thirty-eight-year-old aviation consultant to the Bureau of the Budget. After growing up in Montana and attending prep school in California, Rowe graduated from Harvard and later served as a Supreme Court clerk and as an adviser to the International Military Tribunal at the Nuremberg trials. Like most of the bosses, Rowe was a Roman Catholic. But like many young men of his education and region, Rowe assumed that the forces of modernization had all but destroyed the bosses. "Better education, the rise of the mass pressure group, the economic depression of the 1930s, the growth of government functions—all these have contributed to the downfall of 'the organization,'" he said.

For decades, Rowe's modernization thesis was echoed in the media. For instance, in his 1952 classic, *The Future of American Politics*, Samuel Lubell wrote, "Today, the plight of the Irish Democratic bosses, who managed most of the big-city machines, is not unlike that of the wearied rulers of the British Empire, who are everywhere on the defensive before the rising 'nationality' elements they once ruled." In 1955 and 1956, *The Last Hurrah,* a thinly veiled account of the final campaign of Boston's Mayor James Michael Curley, was a hit novel and movie.

"The Politics of 1948" became influential; Truman kept a copy in his desk in the Oval Office and followed many of its recommendations. But as an analysis of the bosses and a prophecy for their future, Rowe's modernization thesis overshot the mark.

Even in 1947, the memo's claims about the bosses' fecklessness were overstated. The only reason that Senator Harry Truman of Missouri became president was that the big-city and state bosses in 1944 orchestrated a virtual conspiracy in his behalf. A leader of the group was DNC chairman Robert E. Hannegan, who as boss of the Twenty-first Ward in St. Louis put Truman over the top in his tight 1940 Senate primary race. Concerned about President Roosevelt's failing health, Hannegan and a handful of other bosses decided to remove the sitting vice president of the United States, Henry A. Wallace, whom they viewed not only as a bit of a kook but also as too close to radical union leaders and socialists. Rowe himself admitted decades later that Roosevelt had told him in late 1944 or early 1945 that the bosses "said they just couldn't take Wallace; he [Roosevelt] would just have to, in effect, get rid of him."

To be sure, the postwar Catholic bosses were not political celebrities. Few appeared on *Meet the Press* or *Issues and Answers.*

Their faces rarely graced the pages of *Time, Newsweek, Look,* or *Life.* They were not colorful figures with funny accents and homespun backgrounds. Few statues or paintings were done of them even in their hometowns. Today, the Catholic bosses are all but forgotten. Even prominent political historians confuse their names, fail to identify them, or call the best of them "political hacks."

Nonetheless, the Northern Catholic bosses were the conductors of the national Democratic train. A good example is the Democratic National Convention of 1964. Indeed, the first night of the convention in Atlantic City was a refutation of Rowe's the-end-is-nigh-for-the-bosses prediction.

—⚮—

Monday, August 24, 1964. David L. Lawrence—the "Lawrence" named in Rowe's memo, a former mayor of Pittsburgh and governor of Pennsylvania—was chairman of the Credentials Committee. A husky, broad-shouldered man of seventy-five years, Lawrence projected an air of venerable authority. He wore a dark Beau Brummel suit with a pair of wireless oval glasses, and his gray hair was combed straight back. Although mostly unknown to the public, Lawrence had achieved almost legendary status to the political class and to faithful newsreaders. The latest *New York Times* featured a profile of him titled "A Convention Pro: David Leo Lawrence." The cover story of *Harper's* for August was the magazine's second profile of Lawrence in eight years, this one titled "The Man to Watch at the Democratic Convention." His opponents called him "King David" or "David the King," while his supporters referred to him as "Mr. Democrat" or "the Old Pro." Lawrence was also the only mayor in Pittsburgh's history to have been elected four times—in 1945, 1949, 1953, and 1957—and one of four Democrats to have won a gubernatorial race since the Civil War. President Lyndon B. Johnson recognized Dave Lawrence's clout. One day in February 1960, Lawrence was sitting outside a meeting room in the Capitol awaiting the arrival of Johnson, then the Democrats' Senate majority leader. After Johnson accidentally brushed past him while talking to a delegation representing big-city commuters, Lawrence remarked, with a wink, "All right, if he's mad at me, I don't have to support him at Los Angeles." Hearing this and seeing the face, a Johnson aide tracked down the senator, who pulled a fast 180. "Quicker than you could say eighty-one Pennsylvania votes," a reporter for the *New York Times* observed, "the senator was pumping the governor's hand."

The man who introduced Lawrence at the convention was John Moran Bailey. In addition to being the boss of the Connecticut Democrats, Bailey was chairman of the Democratic National Committee. On television, Bailey did not come across as a power broker; besides being nearly bald, he wore nothing flashier than a black suit, dark tie, and white shirt. ("His image on TV ain't worth a damn," President Johnson once told Mayor Richard Daley of Chicago.) But to those who had seen him work a back room, Bailey was practically an icon. A pair of wayfarer glasses was forever propped on his forehead, an unlit cigar was stuck in his mouth, and he talked incessantly and wittily in a voice once described as a whiskey tenor. His opponents called him "King John." Although Bailey had never held elective office, his long reign as state chairman, from 1946 to 1975, would lead Connecticut Democrats out of the political wilderness. They won the governorship in 1954, captured both houses of the state legislature and the state's seats in Congress in 1958, and held their majority status until 1970. Bailey was appointed to the DNC post in January 1961 because of the key role he played in the presidential campaign of Senator John F. Kennedy. As Theodore H. White described it in *The Making of the President, 1960,* "None of the young men in [the Kennedy campaign], so youthful and so fresh, could win the confidence of the aging power-brokers who wield such influence in the Democratic Party; Bailey, then a ripe fifty-four years old but still youthful, was the man for such a job."

Among the 5,200 delegates and alternates on the main floor below Bailey and Lawrence was a successor to Ed Kelly of Chicago. His name was Richard Joseph Daley, and no one doubted for a minute that he was a political boss of the first magnitude. A short, pudgy man with jowls for cheeks, he looked like the autocrat that he was. Mayor Daley was also popular. He had already been elected three times—in 1955, 1959, and 1963 (and he would win election three more times). As Theodore H. White showed, Daley had played a role in Kennedy's nomination, not so much in making him the nominee as in preventing the candidacy of a rival. As head of the Illinois delegation in 1960, Daley had almost single-handedly stopped the convention boomlet for Adlai Stevenson, the state's former governor and two-time presidential nominee. Daley informed Stevenson on the Wednesday of the convention that Kennedy would get 59½ of Illinois's delegates, while Stevenson would get only two. "With that, the hope of a real Stevenson candidacy had ended," White wrote, "and the demonstration in the Sports Arena four hours later was meaningless." Daley's power was not lost on Lyndon Johnson. On becoming president in November 1963, Johnson wooed him immediately. Three days after Kennedy's assassination, the new president invited Daley, along with four other top Democrats including Lawrence, to sit in the executive gallery at the joint session of Congress.

Lawrence, Bailey, and Daley were not the only powerful Democratic bosses in 1964. A few were Jewish and Protestant, but most were Irish Catholic. (Johnson in his post-presidential memoir *The Vantage Point* referred to them simply as "the Catholic bosses.") Although lacking the national staying power of Lawrence, Bailey, and Daley, they had either once helped determine a Democratic presidential nominee's fortunes or would do so in the future. There was Colonel Jacob Arvey, former boss of Chicago's Twenty-fourth Ward and a member of the Democratic National Committee. Arvey had helped Truman carry Illinois in 1948 and helped nominate Adlai Stevenson in 1952. There was Robert F. Wagner Jr., mayor of New York City. Wagner was influential in Kennedy's decision to put Johnson on the national ticket at the 1960 convention. There was Jesse M. Unruh, speaker of the California State Assembly. Unruh would serve as Senator Robert F. Kennedy's liaison to the bosses and would help Kennedy carry the crucial primary in California in 1968. There was Stanley Steingut, the boss of Brooklyn. Steingut would help Vice President Hubert Humphrey carry New York State's delegation in 1968. There was James H. Tate, the mayor of Philadelphia, who would help deliver Pennsylvania to Humphrey in 1968. And there was Representative William J. Green III of Philadelphia, who at twenty-six was an unusually young boss. His late father, William J. Green Jr., had been an early and influential supporter of John Kennedy in 1960. Representative Green would also help deliver Pennsylvania to Humphrey in 1968.

To be sure, the bosses' power had eroded by 1964. In fact, the first serious effort to reform the national Democratic Party began at the 1964 convention, when the citizen-intellectual wing of the party loosened the bosses' grip over the presidential nominating process.

So how was it that the Catholic bosses, nearly a generation after the forces of modernization had supposedly wiped them out, continued to steer the Democratic train down the boss nomination track in 1964? The answer owes nothing to the Whig theory of history or Max Weber's modernization thesis. Rather, it has everything to do with politics. The postwar Catholic bosses produced good and equitable Democratic results, which reflected the values of the party's working-class and Judeo-Christian constituents.

—⁓—

IT WAS NEARLY MIDNIGHT after the second day of the 1948 Democratic convention when David L. Lawrence stood up inside the steamy caucus room. Seated around the fifty-nine-year-old mayor of Pittsburgh were more than a hundred Pennsylvania delegates, alternates, spectators, and minor officials. Lawrence was about to prepare them for a historic vote the next day, July 14. It was not on whether to support the national ticket of Harry Truman and Senator Alben Barkley of Kentucky; the state party chairman, John S. Rice, had already taken care of that—at least 70 of the delegation's 74 votes would go for Truman. This concerned a likely vote on whether the party should extend full legal protection to an unprotected class of human beings—black Americans.

Lawrence had already thrown his support behind the goal. In early July, his name was among the fifty prominent Democrats who had signed a declaration in favor of a strong civil rights platform at the convention. The Democratic Party, the state-ment declared, must endorse the four main recommendations of the President's Commission on Civil Rights: outlaw lynching, outlaw the poll tax, create a permanent commission to eliminate discrimination in hiring, and abolish segregation in the military. The declaration hailed the report of the Civil Rights Commis-sion, *We Hold These Truths,* released in October 1947, as "one of the most important measures of moral strategy devised by the United States of America in modern times. Although its recom-mendations do credit to all sections of American life represented on the non-partisan committee, its sponsorship will remain a landmark in the history of this Democratic Administration."

Lawrence could not be certain, however, that his delegates would even get the chance to vote for a strong civil rights plat-form. Earlier on this Tuesday evening, the 108-member Platform and Resolutions Committee had rejected the following proposal:

> We call upon the Congress to support our president in guarantee-ing these basic and fundamental rights: (1) the right of full and equal political participation, (2) the right of equal opportunity of employment, (3) the right of security of person, and (4) the right of equal treatment in the service and defense of our nation.

The proposal was the work of Platform Committee members Hubert Humphrey, the mayor of Minneapolis, and Andrew Biemiller, former U.S. representative from Wisconsin. After the strong civil rights resolution was defeated, Humphrey and Biemiller considered filing a minority report for the full convention.

Humphrey feared that a minority report might "tear the party apart." National party leaders, including President Tru-man, had argued against a strong civil rights plank on the grounds of party unity. If the plank were approved, they argued, the South would leave the Democratic coalition. Indeed, Gov-ernors Strom Thurmond of South Carolina and Ben Laney of Arkansas were threatening to bolt the party and form a third political party. National party leaders supported the more mod-erate civil rights plank of 1944, with its vague language. They believed that Americans for Democratic Action—a new interest group whose members, such as Humphrey, came from the citizen-intellectual wing of the party—were simply stirring up trouble. (It was ADA members who had drafted the civil rights declaration that Lawrence, as well as several Northern bosses, had endorsed.)

Despite his uncertainty about whether the strong civil rights plank would come up for a vote, Lawrence prepared his delegates to support it—but without offending those who opposed it. He recognized that his delegation was, as two Pittsburgh newspapers wrote, "divided" on the issue.

Francis Myers of Philadelphia was the chairman of the Platform and Resolutions Committee, which had rejected the Humphrey-Biemiller proposal. Myers, who was up for re-election in two years, favored the moderate plank. Lawrence had supported Myers in his successful Senate bid four years earlier and did not want to antagonize him now. Myers was sensitive to perceived slights to his authority. His reputation for having an overlarge ego was such that George Elsey, a Truman aide who was assigned the task of hand-delivering twenty copies of the platform draft to Myers, heard that the chairman would not accept an important document from a young White House nobody and decided to pass the copies on to the secretary of the Senate.

Lawrence, having attended every Democratic convention since 1912, also empathized with the delegates. They had sat through two sessions of the convention, one in the afternoon and one in the evening. Everyone expected Truman to lose in November. And many of the delegates had felt cramped on the convention floor. Don Gingery of Clearfield complained, "I wish somebody would do something about the people who tramp on the feet of us who sit in the front row. We're pinched in there like a lot of chickens." According to the *Pittsburgh Press,* the delegates responded to Gingery's complaint with "applause, applause, applause."

Faced with a divided and grumpy delegation, Lawrence played it safe. Rather than ask for a roll call or a head count, he discussed the importance of showing up at Philadelphia's Convention Hall at 11 A.M. Many planks would be important to them in Pennsylvania, Lawrence told the delegates. "Such as what the platform says about civil rights, the Taft-Hartley Labor law, and Palestine. The Palestine question will be particularly important in our large centers where there is a big Jewish vote." Alluding to the strong civil rights plank, he added, "And some Southerner might want to poll the delegation, so you'd better be there to answer." The delegates applauded.

For all his careful maneuvering in behalf of the liberals' civil rights plank, Lawrence was a consistent and pivotal supporter of Harry Truman. In 1944, Lawrence had joined a handful of party leaders in their quest to dump Henry Wallace on the national ticket in favor of the junior senator from Missouri. It was Lawrence who, at the height of the Wallace stampede at the Chicago convention, had called for the convention to recess until the next morning. In 1948, Lawrence was one of the few party leaders who consistently supported Truman instead of Dwight Eisenhower, whom numerous bosses and liberals had tried to draft to replace the sitting president. In late May, at the peak of the draft-Eisenhower frenzy, an Associated Press headline declared, "Pennsylvania Group Indorses Truman over Vigorous Protests."

Besides considering him a competent politician who could help the state ticket in November, Lawrence supported Truman for moral reasons. He admired his honesty and loyalty, two prime virtues in the postwar bosses' moral code. In April 1944, on a long drive from Pittsburgh to York, Pennsylvania, for a Young Democrats dinner, Lawrence heard Truman stick up for his friend Tom Pendergast, the former boss of the Kansas City Democratic Party who was in prison for income tax evasion. "I always had a very high regard for his innate honesty," Lawrence recalled. "He didn't run away from Pendergast when he got into difficulty, he stood by his friend regardless of the situation and that rates very high in my appraisal of people."

Truman rewarded Lawrence for his support. It was no coincidence that Lawrence was the co-chairman of the 1948 Democratic convention and delivered the opening speech. After Truman won the nomination and the general election, he reportedly told Lawrence of the key role he had played in putting and keeping him on the national ticket. According to Joseph Barr, a

Lawrence ally and longtime mayor of Pittsburgh, Truman at the dedication of his presidential library in the mid-1950s said to Lawrence, "You got me in all this trouble. You made me the vice president and then president."

Despite his high regard for Truman and party unity, however, Lawrence considered civil rights for blacks a more important value. Not that he had always supported blacks; in the 1930s, he had opposed a black man for a top state position on the grounds that white voters would resent the appointment. Lawrence likely changed his mind for moral and political reasons.

Morally, Lawrence recognized that blacks were a vulnerable class of citizens, lacking legal protection in employment, housing, and many other areas. "In civil rights, the government of this country has an immediate duty, one which will affect not only our material might but our moral right as well," he told an annual conference of the National Urban League. "No nation as committed to freedom, democracy, and liberty as we are, can long fight its enemies without first living what it is protecting."

Politically, Lawrence recognized that Democrats needed to appeal to black voters. If they didn't, a significant number of blacks could defect either to Henry Wallace, who campaigned in black urban neighborhoods, or to Thomas Dewey, the Republican presidential nominee, whose party had passed a strong civil rights plank at its convention. Lawrence was not the only Pennsylvania Democrat who took the threat seriously. In May, the Philadelphia lawyer Raymond P. Alexander urged Francis Myers to reach out to this racial minority. "In Philadelphia alone, according to the latest registration, there are 156 thousand Negro registered voters. This sum is growing yearly," Alexander wrote. "There are about 300 hundred thousand [sic] registered Negroes voting in Pennsylvania, an astounding figure. We controlled (the democrats) and have the support of 75% of the Negroes in '32 and '36, and perhaps as much as 70% in 1940, and perhaps a little less in 1944. Today it is going down rapidly."

1948 was not the first time that Lawrence had supported the party's black voters instead of white Southerners. In 1944, he and several other bosses had blocked the vice-presidential bid of Jimmy Byrnes—a former segregationist senator from South

Carolina, Supreme Court justice, and Franklin Roosevelt's "assistant president." According to Andrew M. Bradley, a black Democratic official from Pennsylvania, Lawrence did so partly because he had talked with Bradley about Byrnes' record. "I said, 'The main thing among black voters is that he, when he first came to Washington, as a member of the House of Representatives from South Carolina, he just took an unholy delight in snipping at appropriations for Howard University or anything having to do with colored people," Bradley recalled. The other Catholic bosses acted from similar motives. As Roosevelt told Byrnes days before the opening of the convention, "All of us agree you were the best qualified man and all of us would rather have you than anyone else, but they said they were afraid you would cost the ticket two or three hundred thousand black votes."

David Lawrence's decision to support the strong civil rights plank instead of the moderate one might not sound important, but it was. Lawrence ensured that the Democratic train would travel toward a new destination: racial equality. And he encouraged blacks, not bigoted Southern whites, to climb aboard. In doing so, Lawrence underscored the moral power of postwar Catholic bosses. Although often portrayed as corrupt and provincial, many bosses in the forties, fifties, and sixties were anything but. They helped extend legal protection to an unprotected class of human beings and acted primarily out of public, not private, concern.

—ᴡ—

THE SHOWDOWN OVER the Democratic Party's position on civil rights began the next day on the convention floor. In the course of the four-hour debate, a funny thing happened. James M. Curley, the mayor of Boston and former governor of Massachusetts, presented his own plank—urging the president to make Ireland an independent republic. After acknowledging the leaders of the convention, Curley announced to the twenty thousand delegates and spectators in attendance that Irish-Americans were a marginalized group. "Provision has been made to consider the needs of about every element of the population of the United States with the exception of that of Irish extraction," he declared, noting that 90 percent of Irish Americans "have always voted the Democratic ticket and will continue to vote the Democratic ticket."

Perhaps nothing illustrates the differences between the prewar and postwar Catholic bosses more starkly than Curley and Lawrence at the 1948 Democratic convention. Both were Irish Catholic, came from humble beginnings, were ward bosses, wanted to help others, lost children under tragic circumstances, and held office as mayors and governors. But the similarities between the two men end there.

Curley's public morality was often sectarian and provincial. He famously was the "tribal chieftain" of Boston's Irish Catholics. In 1909, while serving as a city alderman, Curley implied that dogs, not children, were the "natural product" of a Yankee Protestant neighborhood. By contrast, Lawrence's public morality was often nondenominational and universal. Besides supporting civil rights, Lawrence served as a character witness in court for several Protestant and Jewish Democrats accused of being Communists in the 1950s.

Curley was convicted on corruption charges and incarcerated twice. In 1904, he spent two months in the state prison for helping friends pass a civil service exam. In 1946, he was convicted of improper official conduct, including mail fraud, and spent five months in a federal prison in mid-1947. By contrast, Lawrence in 1940 and 1941 was cleared by all-Republican juries on corruption charges. He had been accused of buying cheap, substandard gravel for Pittsburgh and charging the city for regular gravel; but the evidence showed that the case against him was trumped up. It so happened that the state prosecutor in the case, Charles J. Margiotti, had been passed over by Lawrence in his bid for the governorship in 1938.

After winning election as mayor, Curley lived the life of a rajah. He owned a mansion on a hill and a summer home. During the Depression, he took long vacations to Europe. Given his steady but not too flashy government salary, the source of Curley's income was open to speculation. By contrast, Lawrence lived in a modest home in a middle-class section of Pittsburgh.

As governor, he canceled the previous administration's order for a $10,000 limousine in favor of an old Ford with 90,000 miles on the odometer. He died with $110,000 to his name. Lawrence made most of his money from an insurance business he owned on the side. He never drank because his mother had warned him that alcohol was a source of fighting and trouble for the Irish.

Unlike Curley, Lawrence had been groomed as a political leader. The son of a Pittsburgh ward chairman, he was apprenticed as a young teenager to William Brennan, a labor attorney who represented the steelworkers at the Homestead Strike of 1892. His training paid off. After receiving an appointment as chairman of the Allegheny County Democratic Party in 1920, he helped make the Democrats into the majority party in western Pennsylvania. He formed a political partnership with Joseph Guffey in the 1930s, and after Guffey ran successfully for the U.S. Senate, he received Guffey's seat on the Democratic National Committee in 1940. By 1948, Lawrence was named as a candidate for DNC executive director.

The contrast between Curley and Lawrence points to a larger truth. By changing their ways, the postwar Catholic bosses acquired an unaccustomed but deserved moral legitimacy. Careful political observers began distinguishing them from their predecessors. A boss was now called a "new-style boss," "political pro," or "modern political boss." As Arthur Schlesinger Jr. wrote in *The Politics of Upheaval* in 1960, "a new type of boss was emerging—the one who could make the adaptation to the forces whose significance [DNC chairman James] Farley declined to recognize." In 1963 and 1964, a young Yale undergraduate by the name of Joseph Lieberman accompanied and studied John M. Bailey. Two years later, the Houghton Mifflin Company published Lieberman's *The Power Broker: A Biography of John M. Bailey, Modern Political Boss.*

At the Philadelphia convention, Lawrence was, in the words of the *Philadelphia Inquirer,* the "dominant factor" in the Pennsylvania delegation. He certainly played some role in winning approval for the strong civil rights plank. According to Andrew Biemiller, Lawrence ordered his delegation to vote for the plank at the urging of Edward J. Flynn, boss of the New York

Democratic Party. But Biemiller's account is incomplete at best. Lawrence had signed his name to the Humphrey declaration at least ten days before the convention began. Also, according to Frank N. Matthews, a longtime political reporter for the *Pittsburgh Post-Gazette,* Lawrence and other state party leaders convinced Senator Francis Myers to drop his opposition to the strong civil rights plank.

Pennsylvania's support for the plank was crucial to its passage. Delegations from the Plains, rural New England, mid-Atlantic, Mountain West, and Southern state parties opposed the plank almost unanimously. When it came time for Pennsylvania to vote, the resolution was trailing. "Pennsylvania casts 74 votes aye!" shouted John Rice. The plank was ahead, and it never trailed again. The final vote for the resolution was 651½ to 581½. Had Myers succeeded in pealing off only 36 of the delegation's 74 votes, the plank would have failed.

Lawrence was not the only boss who whacked his delegation into line. John Bailey convinced all 20 of his Connecticut delegates to back the plank. Jacob Arvey prevailed upon all 60 of his Illinois delegates. Frank Hague, mayor of Jersey City, successfully lobbied all 36 of his New Jersey delegates. Flynn's New York delegation cast all 98 of its votes for the plank.

Indeed, Hubert Humphrey credited the bosses for passing his plank. In his 1976 autobiography, *The Education of a Public Man,* Humphrey wrote that the bosses supported the minority report for political and moral reasons:

> One can explain the victory at that convention in part by conscience, in part by political realism. Ed Flynn and David Lawrence and Jack Arvey and John Bailey of Connecticut probably supported us because they wanted something to attract the votes of liberals, Negroes, minorities, and labor. Maybe they wanted to protect us from the appeal on the left of Henry Wallace's Progressive Party. Perhaps there were those in the Northern urban wing who hadn't forgotten that the South deserted Al Smith in 1928 and didn't mind offending them in a kind of get-even gesture twenty years later.
>
> As I came to know the party bosses better, I found that they agreed with the spirit, the principle, the rightness of our plank.

They reflected, and our victory reflected, a deep current running in the party and in the country that would make the next quarter century one filled with turmoil and triumph.

The passage of the strong civil rights plank at the 1948 convention certainly affected the Democratic Party profoundly. First, the "Solid South" began to dissolve. In the four elections before 1948, roughly three-quarters of white Southerners voted for the Democratic presidential candidate; in the five elections from 1948 to 1964, about half voted for the party's nominee. Southern white Democrats began to lose their grip on the national party machinery. Indeed, the Northern bosses generally and Catholics specifically were the undisputed conductors of the Democratic train. A headline in the next day's *Philadelphia Inquirer* declared: "Big-City Groups Win Party Rule from Deep South."

The national Democratic Party was committed not only to battling economic inequality but also to fighting for racial equality. Democrats would support legislation aimed at securing civil rights for blacks and increasing government intervention in behalf of blue-collar workers.

And David Lawrence had shown that in this new Democratic Party, he was a leader.

—⚋—

UNLIKE HARRY TRUMAN, the high school graduate who attended law school at night while a senator, Adlai Stevenson came from an entirely different background than most of the party bosses. Stevenson was the grandson and namesake of Grover Cleveland's vice president in his second term. The son of a newspaper owner, he graduated from Princeton University in 1922. He worked as an official in the U.S. Department of Agriculture when Henry Wallace was secretary and served overseas planning the postwar reconstruction of Europe.

Stevenson also came from a different wing of the Democratic Party. He was a hero to the citizen-intellectual activists. After winning election as governor of Illinois in 1948, Stevenson had stood for good government and vetoed state legislation that would have cracked down on alleged subversives and Communists in government. Since early 1952, he had been the subject of a draft movement by a group called the Independent Voters of Illinois, whose leaders were university professors and public school teachers. Bald and scholarly looking, he was the prototypical egghead politician.

Stevenson's personal history was unsavory to many of the bosses' Catholic constituents. He had been divorced from his wife for three years. He had also given a character deposition on behalf of Alger Hiss, a spy for the Soviet Union, convicted of perjury in 1950.

Yet on the eve of the 1952 Democratic convention in Chicago, Stevenson was the odds-on favorite to win the party's presidential nomination. His good fortune did not owe to his vote-getting prowess in the presidential race; he had not entered a single primary or convention in 1952. As late as mid-June, he was far behind in the delegate count. According to the Associated Press, Senator Estes Kefauver of Tennessee had 117 of the 651½ delegates needed to win the nomination, while Stevenson had 32. Stevenson's bid, complained the syndicated columnist Drew Pearson, "makes a mockery of the American system of primaries."

Nor did Stevenson use any elaborate back-channel maneuvers to ingratiate himself with party leaders. He told anyone who would listen that he had no interest in running for president in November. On July 20, at the Illinois delegation's caucus meeting at the Morrison Hotel in Chicago, he reiterated his desire not to run for president. "I have no ambition for the presidential nomination," he told his fellow delegates. "I ask you therefore in the spirit of our cause to abide by my views and do not nominate me for the presidency. I urgently want to be a candidate for the governorship and nothing else."

To be fair, Stevenson did hold natural advantages over the rest of the Democratic field. Unlike Averell Harriman of New York, he had won an election. Unlike Kefauver, he maintained cordial relations with Southern leaders. Unlike Senator Richard Russell of Georgia, he favored civil rights. Unlike Vice President Alben Barkley, he was not old (he was fifty-two). And unlike

Harry Truman, he would not tear the party apart by winning the party's nomination.

Even so, Stevenson was the favorite to win the party's presidential nomination mainly for one reason. The big-city and state bosses had organized in his behalf.

The chief organizer was Jacob Arvey, a former newsboy and shipping clerk who was bald and stood no more than five feet tall. After serving as an Army colonel in the South Pacific in World War II, Arvey was elected head of the Cook County (Chicago) Democratic organization. He got behind Stevenson early in his 1948 campaign, and after Stevenson won handily he promoted the governor's candidacy along with his friends and fellow DNC committee members David Lawrence and John Bailey. At the Illinois caucus meeting on July 20, Arvey listened to the governor's plea that the delegates not vote for him, considered his words, and decided not to heed them. "The Democratic Party and the country," he announced, "are more important than the personal wishes of Arvey or Stevenson or anybody else."

Lawrence reached a similar conclusion. The Pennsylvania delegation was caucusing at the Morrison around the same time. When the state chairman ordered a roll call for the delegates' presidential preferences, he first called on Lawrence, the state's national committeeman. "Stevenson," Lawrence replied. According to the *Pittsburgh Post-Gazette,* many in the delegation followed his lead: 31 of the state's 70 votes went for Stevenson. The runner-up, Kefauver, received 14.

The *New York Times* cited the support of Lawrence and his delegation as evidence that Stevenson's candidacy had picked up steam. In reality, Lawrence had done more for Stevenson than vote for him in the caucus. He had handpicked James Finnegan, a Philadelphia Democratic leader, as the chairman of Stevenson's campaign in exile. He had chosen Francis Myers, who had lost his Senate re-election bid in 1950, as the leader of Stevenson's forces on the convention floor. And he had asked Governor Henry Schricker of Indiana to place Stevenson's name in nomination.

Although unusual, the bosses' support for Adlai Stevenson in 1952 highlighted an essential ingredient in their rule: The postwar bosses organized for their political base and beyond it. Not only did they deliver legislation and set national policy for those seated at the front of the Democratic train—blue-collar workers and Catholics; they also supported presidential candidates whose main constituency sat toward the back—citizen-intellectuals.

When Lawrence was asked later about his work in support of Stevenson, he implied that he had been scandalized by the efforts of the citizen-intellectual activists. In his view, they had committed the most mortal of political sins: They were disorganized.

> If you ever saw a shenanigan organization, there it was. The first thing the group wanted to do was to elect me as a floor leader for Stevenson. I explained why that was the last thing they should do. The opposition would tag me as a city boss and say the bosses were trying to dominate the convention. Finally, I was able to talk them out of it and talk them into Senator Frank Myers, on the basis that he was the whip of the Senate with wide acquaintance over the country, and therefore able to do Stevenson tremendous good among the congressmen and senators who were delegates. It worked out beautifully, and I was very happy to be in on it.

Eight years later, as governor of Pennsylvania, Lawrence was viewed as having a consummate political organization. As Lawrence O'Brien tells the story in his memoir, *No Final Victories,* the Kennedy campaign in 1960 decided to skip Pennsylvania's primary for fear of alienating Lawrence, who considered running as a favorite son:

> In California, we had pushed Pat Brown, warning him that if he ran in his state's primary as a favorite son and didn't support Kennedy, Kennedy would run against him in that primary. You didn't treat Dave Lawrence that way. The difference was that Brown, although the governor, had no real organizational base and thus had little control. Lawrence, along with Congressman Bill Green, the Democratic leader in Philadelphia, did have a political organization, one that exercised considerable control. We had to respect their power, just as we respected Mayor Daley's in Chicago. If Lawrence wished

to run in his state's primary, we accepted that. We wanted to do nothing to offend Lawrence or Green and, in particular, we wanted no pro-Kennedy write-in movement that could be interpreted as an effort by us to put pressure on Lawrence and Green. All of Kennedy's political operatives were given strict orders not to set foot in Pennsylvania.

There was a reason that the postwar bosses had real organizations or machines. They controlled massive amounts of patronage. As governor of Pennsylvania, Lawrence presided over an estimated 50,000 to 60,000 patronage jobs. As mayor of Chicago, Richard J. Daley controlled more than 40,000 jobs. John Bailey presided over thousands of patronage positions.

Although the New Deal is often thought to have eliminated mass political patronage, actually it helped perpetuate it. Lawrence's organization in Pennsylvania is a classic example. Before the New Deal, the state Democratic Party controlled little patronage and was in the minority. After the New Deal, Lawrence and his political associate, Joseph Guffey, used the Roosevelt administration's federal relief programs to build a formidable state party. As the political scientist Michael Weber detailed in his biography of Lawrence, *Don't Call Me Boss,* from 1935 to 1937 the Works Progress Administration spent $70 million in Allegheny County. In 1940, half of the state Democratic committeemen and most of the ward chairmen in Allegheny County were on the government payroll.

There were downsides to mass patronage. For one, patronage was parceled out on political, ethnic, racial, and other group considerations, rather than individual competence or ability. Job applicants were hired and employees fired on the basis of their political affiliation.

Also, patronage begot corruption. In Daley's Chicago, patronage workers fixed the traffic tickets of politically connected individuals. In Lawrence's Pittsburgh, police officers were hired on patronage considerations and consequently the city's police force was by all accounts terrible. A longtime reporter for the *Pittsburgh Post-Gazette,* Frank Hawkins, wrote that "Pittsburgh may be the only city in the country where a criminal can hold up a person in broad daylight and the cops won't respond." Lawrence himself acknowledged that the city's police were incompetent and corrupt. He once told Andrew Bradley, a black Pittsburgh official, "Now I know this is wrong. There is no question that it is, but [the newspapers] don't have a political organization to run; I do. I am building something to take the place of that, and I'll do away with that...."

But there were also virtues in mass patronage. First, it personalized government, bringing it closer to ordinary people. Mayor James Tate of Philadelphia once explained, "Too often the liberal fallacy overlooks the compelling fact that the Democratic Party needs the sustained daily effort of thousands of committeemen to service the legitimate needs of the little people, whose identities are often distorted and ignored by the increasing complexities of life." Young Democrats agreed with Tate's line of argument. Rosemary Trump, the Democratic chairwoman in Westmoreland County, met Lawrence in 1964 as a student at American University in Washington, D.C.: "I remember people saying, 'How do you start in politics, how do you get involved?' He was kind of agitated. He said, 'Start at the local level. Go out and meet and greet [voters], build from the committee on up, and if you're interested in a career, start at the committee and precinct level." Joseph Lieberman followed his mentor around the state to various meetings. "Party workers were impressed with Bailey's credentials as a political strategist and wanted to take their concerns to him for advice," Lieberman wrote. "He was completely accessible to them—as no other chairman before him had been—and they appreciated it."

Patronage also gave the bosses a broad, working-class political base instead of a narrow, upper-class one. Accordingly, many of the postwar bosses took a populist stance. They favored government regulation over the workings of the free market. "Government should help those who need it most," Lawrence said, in a fine epigram that could be equally applied to the political philosophies of many other bosses.

To a large extent, the postwar Catholic bosses delivered for their working-class and Catholic base. They won government benefits for workers, defeated and enacted laws that threatened their constituents' moral and religious values, and extended legal protection to an unprotected class of human beings.

Mayor Daley, the best known of the postwar bosses, is also the most ambiguous figure. His record in representing the interests of his working-class, Catholic, and black constituents was mixed at best. Unlike Lawrence and Bailey, who negotiated with their opponents, Daley usually disregarded them. As Adam Cohen and Elizabeth Taylor detail in *An American Pharaoh,* Daley almost single-handedly destroyed a vibrant working-class, Italian American neighborhood, and one that was integrated to boot. In its place he built the main campus for the University of Illinois at Chicago. Of course, the school enabled working-class Chicagoans to attend a state university without having to travel downstate to Champaign. Yet the university's construction in the late 1950s and early 1960s displaced 14,000 residents and 630 businesses on the Near West Side. What's more, Daley did little to challenge racial segregation in the city's schools, workplaces, and housing.

On the positive side, Daley built tangible monuments for ordinary people—O'Hare Airport, expressways, a convention center, schools, streetlights, bridges, hospitals. As Lawrence did in Pittsburgh, Daley was able to stem the flow of middle-class residents out of the city, thus providing a tax base that could help the poor and working classes. In Daley's reign, according to Nicholas Lemann, "no matter how bad things got in Chicago, and they got pretty bad, the city never died in the way that Detroit and Cleveland and St. Louis did."

Daley's mixed legacy has obscured that of other postwar bosses. Scholars have devoted too little attention to the records of David Lawrence and John Bailey. Studying these records would reveal that both bosses genuinely and effectively represented the range of interests of their working-class, Catholic, and black constituents.

As for cultural and religious issues, Bailey's Democrats in Connecticut could have taken the side of the affluent and mainline Protestant congregations; by 1962, Connecticut was about 51 to 55 percent Protestant and ranked first in the nation in household income and share of skilled workers. Instead, they took the side of the working classes and Catholics.

In 1957, Democrats helped pass legislation in Connecticut that enabled towns, with the consent of a referendum, to provide free bus transportation to students in private and Catholic parochial schools. In Lieberman's description of the campaign, "Public commentary became surprisingly bitter. Catholics charged that some of the state's newspapers, especially in Hartford, were not reporting the facts accurately. Non-Catholics protested a statement by Connecticut's bishops in which they urged parishioners to 'watch the vote' of their local representatives on the bill. While Republicans were split over the measure, Democrats—led by Bailey—stood solidly behind it." Indeed, Bailey moved his quarters to the Republican House Speaker's office in order to work on strategy with GOP supporters of the bill. On the final ballot, all thirty Democrats in the state house of representatives backed the measure. The legislation passed by a single vote, 134 to 133.

Up until the mid-1960s, when the Supreme Court struck them down, Connecticut's laws on birth control were the nation's strictest. Even married women were forbidden to get information about a prescription. Measures to undo this state of affairs had come up repeatedly since the early 1920s. When the state senate voted on a version of the bill in 1957, all five Democrats opposed the bill, while only twelve of the twenty-six Republicans did so. The same scenario played out on an abortion bill more than a decade later. In May 1972, the state house of representatives considered legislation to ban abortion except when necessary to save the life of the mother. The measure passed overwhelmingly. Of the 63 Democrats who voted on it, 48 approved and 15 opposed. By contrast, of the 47 Republicans who voted, 29 approved and 18 opposed.

The record of Lawrence and Daley on social issues is unclear. Apparently, votes on matters relating to contraception, abortion, and church-state relations never arose. Lawrence presided as governor of Pennsylvania in 1960 when the Food and Drug Administration approved the sale of contraceptives, but the legislature seems never to have made a public resolution or a vote on it. Daley was near the end of his long run as mayor when in 1971 a three-judge panel of the U.S. District Court in Illinois invalidated the state's law against abortion. Daley made no public comments on the decision.

Nonetheless, Lawrence and Daley might well have supported keeping legal protection for unborn infants. Lawrence's son, Gerald, believes that his father would have done so. "It wasn't something that was discussed. Abortion is wrong. That would be it. End of discussion," he said, adding that he doubts his father would have taken a stance of personally-opposed-but-publicly-in-favor on the issue of abortion. "I don't know that he'd take that position. That's sort of the easy way out. He just thought, what's wrong is wrong and what's right is right." As for Daley, pro-life advocates in Illinois considered him to be an ally of their cause.

On economic issues, the record of Lawrence and Bailey is clear. They supported the interests of working-class, Catholic, and black voters. Critics of the bosses argue that their efforts largely failed. According to the urban historian Clarence Stone, "Big-city machines undercut broad attention to the collective problems of the urban working classes and permitted policy issues to be displaced by personal and neighborhood-based conditions, thus weakening the potential for the emergence of politics organized around the shared concerns of the poor and less affluent."

Lawrence represented his black constituents by working to extend legal protection to them. He recognized that blacks were a rising political constituency in his city. Pittsburgh's black population doubled between 1910 and 1940, rising from 25,623 to 54,983. Running for mayor in 1945, Lawrence agreed to establish an organization that would investigate instances of racial or religious discrimination and recommend corrective measures. In 1952, he shepherded to passage a citywide measure to outlaw discrimination in hiring, promotion, tenure, firing, and salary decisions. Six years later, he helped enact a fair housing bill in Pittsburgh, only the second such law in the country.

Bailey represented the party's working-class, Catholic, and black constituents in a more traditional way. He did not pioneer any policies, but he did support those that served his constituency. His major stumbling block was that before 1965, representation in the Connecticut legislature was not based on the principle of one-man-one-vote, but rather on the state's counties—a system that gave disproportionate power to small towns, which tended to oppose liberal legislation. This political structure hamstrung Bailey, who since 1948 had written the party's platform every year. He and his Democrats in the early and mid-1950s did pass a few major bills: state aid for all patients in state institutions, a bonus bill for Korean War veterans, and the state's first adult probation system. Even so, the structure did not prevent Bailey from enacting liberal legislation. After Democrats won a majority in both houses of the state legislature in 1958, they passed a state ban on discrimination in housing. And after the state switched to the one-man-one-vote principle of redistricting in 1965, Bailey's Democrats, aided by extra clout from the big cities in particular, passed a raft of legislation. That year alone, the state legislature created for the first time a commissioner on higher education, passed interest-free loans to college students, and enacted a special $10 million program of education aid for disadvantaged children.

—⁓—

ON THE FIRST DAY of the 1952 Democratic National Convention in Chicago, Lawrence lieutenants Jim Finnegan and Francis Myers went to the law office of Marshall Holleb and his brother-in-law, Representative Sidney Yates of Illinois. Finnegan and Myers were there for a key organizational meeting with Holleb and Yates, two leaders of the Independent Voters of Illinois, and a handful of top party officials. Finnegan and Myers suggested that the draft-Stevenson movement take the following actions: announce that Myers would be Stevenson's floor leader; operate out of the IVI's headquarters on the fifteenth floor of the Hilton Hotel; keep contact with Jacob Arvey and other bosses; and have Governor Schricker of Indiana place Stevenson's name in nomination. The IVI and party leaders agreed.

The next day, Tuesday, July 22, the IVI's headquarters at the Hilton expanded from three rooms to fourteen. Lawrence moved in. As Al Weisman, an IVI official, recalled, the draft-Stevenson movement was transformed: "The first thing I noticed was the presence of a switchboard on Tuesday and everybody ordered room service. That was when I realized we'd made it. Their publicity man from Pennsylvania came in and told me, 'Let's get some food up here,' and picked up the phone and by God there was food for everybody. And a switchboard. And we were pro. We were first class." That night, Senate candidate John Kennedy of Massachusetts, future governor Mike DiSalle of Ohio, Sargent Shriver, and other rising stars of the Democratic Party arrived. The men were enlisted to ask party leaders to sign a draft-Stevenson statement.

Lawrence needed to collaborate with the activists. The Pennsylvania delegation, which he influenced but could not control, was bitterly divided among the various presidential candidates. When the first ballot for the nomination was called Thursday afternoon, Lawrence delivered only 36 of the delegation's 70 votes for Stevenson. So by working with the IVI and other party bosses, he and Arvey kept Stevenson's hopes alive. New Jersey gave 28 of its 32 votes. Indiana awarded 25 of its 26 votes. Illinois gave 53 of its 60 votes.

Although Stevenson trailed Kefauver on the first ballot, he did not stay there. On the evening of Thursday, July 24, the New York State chairman Paul Fitzpatrick arrived at the private dining room of Arvey at the Stockyards Inn. Fitzpatrick announced that Averell Harriman was withdrawing from the race and throwing his delegates to Stevenson. Harriman's move pushed Stevenson nearly over the top, giving him a commanding lead after the second ballot.

Despite not winning a single primary in 1952, Adlai Stevenson was nominated on the third ballot, on Friday, July 25. After walking up onto the convention platform early Saturday morning to deliver his nomination speech, he immediately headed toward Lawrence. Sticking out his hand, Stevenson thanked Lawrence for the confidence he had shown in him.

Lawrence was similarly pleased. He later recalled, "I have been in politics all my life. My father and grandfather before me were also in politics. I have heard of many so-called drafts, but the drafting of Stevenson was the only completely genuine draft of which I have ever known."

—⟋⟋—

MOST EVERY SUNDAY afternoon in the later 1940s and the 1950s, the mayor of Pittsburgh took up the collection during the noon Mass at Saint Mary of Mercy, the downtown church where he had been baptized. David Lawrence's weekly ritual was symbolic of his lifelong Catholic faith. He always revered his mother, Catherine, a daily communicant and charter member of the Rosalia Foundling Home and Maternity Hospital. Growing up, Lawrence went to Saint Mary's High School, a two-year commercial school. On the night his son, Jerry, was born, he went to the chapel in Mercy Hospital and asked God for His aid: "I prayed that God would let me live to see my youngest child through college." After two of his young sons died in a car accident in 1942, he took his family members every year after Christmas dinner to the local cemeteries, where he placed wreaths on the graves of his relatives and close colleagues.

But in 1960, when John Kennedy ran for president, Lawrence was caught in the horns of a dilemma concerning his Catholicism. On the one hand, he secretly admired Kennedy's boldness and wanted to support him. On the other hand, he was now governor of the Commonwealth and wanted the Democratic Party to win in the fall. Should he throw his delegation behind his coreligionist or the Democratic candidate most likely to get elected?

John Bailey did not need to answer that question. In Connecticut, as in the fictional city of *The Last Hurrah,* the Democratic Party was the political agent of the Catholic Church. For years in the 1940s and 1950s, the state party held its annual convention in Hartford at a Knights of Columbus hall. Bailey, a Catholic politician who gave up cigars for Lent, faced no conflict in supporting Kennedy or in working for him.

But Lawrence did need to answer the question

To be sure, the Catholic Church in Pennsylvania exerted a fair amount of pull. In 1956, Lawrence and Kennedy were the headliners at the Columbus Day banquet for the Knights of Columbus. But anti-Catholic prejudice in the state was strong. It wasn't just the memory of Al Smith, a Catholic Democrat who lost in a landslide in 1928; Smith lost Pennsylvania by 987,000 votes, a nearly 2-to-1 margin. It was Lawrence's own political history. He believed that anti-Catholic prejudice defeated him in his first race for elective office, in 1931.

Lawrence's fear was not without foundation. Popular anti-Catholic feeling endured into the 1950s, as evidenced by Paul Blanshard's best-selling book, *American Freedom and Catholic Power.* ("In spite of the high civic standards of many individual Catholics," Blanshard wrote, "several of the most publicized political machines in American cities have essentially been Catholic machines in the sense that their leaders and their most important followers have been Roman Catholics.") Also, Lawrence was the first Catholic mayor of Pittsburgh as well as the first Catholic governor of Pennsylvania. "I was always fearful of the religious situation in the Pennsylvania Dutch area," he recalled, referring to Lancaster, Berks, York, and Lebanon counties in the southeastern part of the state, each of which was populated heavily by German Protestants. "They were very religious people and they are very, very wonderful people—good citizens, clean, decent, honest." Even so, Lawrence believed, they would not vote for Catholic candidates. In the heavily Democratic year of 1958, Lawrence won the governor's race by only 76,000 votes.

In addition to anti-Catholic prejudice, the Kennedy clan weighed on Lawrence. Before Lawrence O'Brien realized that the Kennedy campaign should not set foot in Pennsylvania, members of the Kennedy family had lobbied Lawrence for his support. In the fall of 1959, Bobby Kennedy chastised Lawrence for not endorsing his brother in 1956. "Certainly, my brother is not assured of obtaining the nomination," Kennedy wrote to Lawrence on December 4, "but I think it would be most unfortunate if he was turned down on the grounds that he is a Catholic—by non-Catholics who are bigots or by Catholics who have a fear of 'rocking the boat.'" (Lawrence responded indignantly to Kennedy's public statement that he had given his word to Kefauver. "The fact is I was not *against* your brother," he wrote to Kennedy. "I was *for* Senator Estes Kefauver.") In the winter of 1960, the family patriarch, Joe Kennedy, traveled to Harrisburg to meet with Lawrence and pointed out that Governor Mike

DiSalle of Ohio, Mayor Richard Daley, and John Bailey, all fellow Catholics, supported Kennedy. So why didn't Lawrence?

Lawrence's unbending stance throughout the next several months filled the Kennedys with dismay. Three weeks before the 1960 convention in Los Angeles, Rose Kennedy wrote in her diary, "We are all furious at Governor Brown of California and Governor Lawrence of Pennsylvania because they will not come out for Jack now. Their support would clinch the nomination for him. Joe has worked hard on Lawrence all winter, but he still can't believe a Catholic can be elected. He has been one of the most exasperating and tantalizing forces. . . ."

Lawrence had no interest in perpetuating anti-Catholicism. In fact, he believed that eliminating anti-Catholic prejudice was a noble goal. "It would be a fine thing to elect a splendid Democratic president, and slay the dragon of bigotry in the process," he said at a dinner in behalf of the state's Democrats in Springfield, Missouri, on January 29, 1960. He added that it would be "morally and politically inexcusable to bar the candidacy of any man because of his religion."

Lawrence's opposition to Kennedy was political: He didn't think Kennedy could help the local ticket back home. Like many postwar bosses, he aimed to win elections, not to support an ideological soul mate. Years later he explained, "I was firmly of the conviction that a Catholic couldn't be elected president. I had run in Pennsylvania and I was the first Catholic to be elected there. I just skimped through with a 76,000 majority. I was fearful that we would lose Pennsylvania and that any chance I would have as governor of getting a majority in both houses of the General Assembly would go skimmering if Kennedy was head of the ticket."

What changed Lawrence's view of Kennedy was not the lobbying of his family members. It was that Kennedy began to show real political strength.

In April, Kennedy won the West Virginia primary handily. Coming back from a trip to Israel, Lawrence heard about Kennedy's victory from an Associated Press reporter at the airport in Rome. Publicly, Lawrence said, "It certainly has enhanced his chances." Privately, Lawrence was shocked at

Kennedy's unexpectedly strong showing in a heavily Protestant state. "When I heard that he won by 100,000, I just couldn't believe it. I did know West Virginia very intimately—knowing the religious complexion there, which was worse from a Catholic standpoint than in Pennsylvania, that shook my thinking a bit about whether or not he might win."

In May, Kennedy did surprisingly well in the nonbinding Pennsylvania primary. Even though his name was not on the ballot and his aides had mounted no statewide campaign on his behalf, Kennedy received 183,000 votes.

In July, Daley announced at the convention that Stevenson would get only a handful of Illinois's delegates. "I kept picking it up as I went along," Lawrence reflected two years later. "Then of course the real climax was in Chicago when the Illinois delegation met on Sunday and they declared in their convention for Kennedy. When Stevenson couldn't get his own state, it was hopeless. I so told Stevenson."

On the Saturday afternoon before the 1960 Democratic convention opened, Lawrence met with Jack and Bobby Kennedy at a hotel in Pasadena. He recalled saying to them, "I'm going to tell my delegation on Monday morning that I'm going to support Kennedy."

Lawrence's support was an important ingredient in Kennedy's eventual nomination. Although Kennedy would have won without receiving 64 of Pennsylvania's 81 delegates, he would not have won on the first ballot.

—m—

WHETHER IT WAS A coincidence or not, both John Kennedy and David Lawrence stayed at the Biltmore Hotel in Los Angeles. On the morning after he won the nomination, Kennedy asked Lawrence to meet him in his room. After Lawrence and his friend arrived, Kennedy pulled them into his bathroom. "Now look, Dave, I don't want to go down there and ask that guy," Kennedy told Lawrence. "Are you sure now?"

John Kennedy had intense doubts about whether Senator Lyndon Johnson of Texas should be his running mate. His

younger brother, Bobby, opposed Johnson and favored Senator
Henry "Scoop" Jackson of Washington. Robert Kennedy
believed that Johnson would hurt the ticket with Northern liberals and labor leaders. His view was influenced by recent lobbying against Johnson by Walter Reuther, head of the United
Auto Workers; Governor Mennen "Soapy" Williams of Michigan; and Joseph Rauh, vice president of Americans for Democratic Action and party chairman of Washington, D.C.

Two weeks before the convention, ADA circulated a five-
page letter to Democratic delegates that opposed putting Johnson on the national ticket. Johnson, the letter declared, was a
"conservative, anti–civil rights, gas-and-oil senator":

> In Los Angeles you are going to be faced with the greatest razzle-
> dazzle campaign that gas, oil, and Dixiecrat money can buy. This
> gaudy effort will be in the interest of conservatism, not in the inter-
> est of the Democratic Party or the liberal principles on the basis of
> which the Democratic Party wins elections. The Democrats have
> never won and cannot win now as the party of conservatism. . . .
> We are confident that the Democratic convention in Los Angeles
> will write a liberal platform. For it to do this and then nominate
> Senator Johnson would be political hypocrisy of the worst sort.

At the convention, labor and intellectual leaders tried again
to block Johnson from the ticket. In late August, ADA leaders
nearly succeeded in passing a resolution that failed to endorse
Johnson.

In contrast to the Kennedys and the Northern liberals,
Lawrence entertained few doubts about Johnson.

Lawrence knew that Johnson would accept the vice-presidential bid. In June 1960, Johnson and House Speaker Sam Rayburn invited Lawrence and his friend Matt McCloskey, the
DNC's treasurer, to lunch at the Mayflower Hotel in downtown
Washington. After telling Johnson that "it just isn't in the
works" for him to win the party's nomination, Lawrence said
that the Texan shouldn't take himself out of the running. "If
Kennedy does get it," Lawrence said, "I think it would make a
great team if you would take the second spot." Though Rayburn
opposed the idea, Johnson expressed his willingness to serve.

Lawrence knew that Johnson had shown an ability to win votes. In the 1960 nomination race, Johnson received more support from delegates than any other candidate except for Kennedy.

Lawrence also knew that Johnson would bolster the national ticket. In the months leading up to the convention, he considered supporting Johnson as president or vice president. It wasn't just that Johnson was a masterful legislator. It was that he could appeal to white Southerners without incurring automatic opposition from black leaders. Considering that a Roman Catholic was the presidential nominee, the Democrats needed a Southern Protestant to balance the ticket.

Lawrence's support for Johnson hardly represented a radical break with tradition. Of the nine elections held between 1932 and 1964, a white Southerner took the second spot seven times. Instead, Lawrence's support typified the bosses' ability to assemble a successful national ticket. Even after the death of Franklin Roosevelt, Democrats won three of the five presidential contests between 1948 and 1964.

Winning the White House is more than a matter of choosing the best candidates, of course. If the Democrats had a minority coalition, the bosses' acumen in picking nominees would not have mattered. Their candidates would have lost regularly, as the party did in the pre–New Deal era of 1896 to 1928.

Of the nine presidential elections during that time, Democratic candidates lost seven times. The party's representative figure was William Jennings Bryan, the eloquent prairie populist from Nebraska who ran as the party's presidential nominee three times (in 1896, 1900, and 1908) and lost each race. Bryan the candidate, however, wasn't the problem; he won a larger share of the popular vote than four of the other five Democratic nominees during this era. The Democrats' problem was a lack of constituents. A majority of voters did not even support Woodrow Wilson, the party's lone winner during this period. A mere 29 to 41 percent of Americans backed the other four candidates—Alton Parker, James Cox, John Davis, and Al Smith. So no matter whom the bosses selected in the smoke-filled rooms, the Democratic nominee was unlikely to win. He simply had too few natural followers. His appeal was limited to the three groups of the Bryan coalition: white Southerners, Midwestern farmers, and urban Catholics.

By 1932, the Democrats had a majority coalition. Millions of Americans rallied behind the Democratic banner. In the 1920 and 1924 elections, 9.14 million and 8.38 million voters respectively had pulled the Democratic lever. By contrast, 22.8 million and 27.7 million did so in the 1932 and 1936 elections. The Democratic vote had more than doubled in eight years and more than tripled in sixteen years. The party's representative figure was Franklin D. Roosevelt, the former secretary of the Navy, the party's vice-presidential nominee of 1920, and governor of New York. Although fewer Americans cast their ballots for Roosevelt in 1940 and 1944, he received 54.7 percent and 53.4 percent of the vote. Only once before, from 1860 to 1880, had Americans voted for a presidential candidate from the same political party four consecutive times.

The Roosevelt coalition was larger primarily for two reasons.

First, it was larger demographically. Tens of millions of Americans joined the electorate. Most of these were Catholic, and as a rule they belonged to one of three categories. Some were eligible to vote but had not done so (or had not registered). For example, voter turnout in the 1920 and 1924 presidential elections was around 44 percent; in the 1936 presidential election, turnout was almost 57 percent. In total numbers, 27 million Americans voted in 1920, and 45 million did so in 1936. Many of the new voters were recently naturalized immigrants. Twice as many Americans were naturalized during the 1920s as in the previous decade. (It has been estimated that the process of naturalization and voter registration of immigrants took an average of ten to twelve years.) The third group of new voters consisted of young people who were just reaching voting age, including many children of immigrants. The proportion of immigrants and children of immigrants in the population grew by more than 25 percent from 1920 to 1930. Also, the birth rate of foreign-born women was significantly higher than the rate for native women.

All these demographic trends showed up in the presidential election of 1928. The Democrats' nominee that year was Al Smith, the Catholic governor of New York. Smith received over seven million more votes than had John W. Davis four years earlier. His greatest area of strength was in the nation's twelve biggest cities, which he carried by 38,000 votes. By contrast, Davis and Cox had lost those urban areas by roughly 1.5 million votes. As Kevin Phillips remarked in *The Emerging Republican Majority,* "Even before the Great Depression, Smith sparked a revolt of the urban ethnic groups which foreshadowed the makeup of the New Deal coalition."

The Roosevelt coalition was larger also because of the times and the party's general philosophy. In *The Real Majority,* Scammon and Wattenberg noted, "While the Republican issue had been somewhat a combination of social and economic factors, the new issue that put Democrats over the top was a straight economic issue." Because of the Depression, much of the American middle class had become poor overnight, and "those who didn't become poor became frightened."

After 1944, the Roosevelt coalition lost steam. The economic issue waned, while race relations and foreign policy concerns waxed. Democrats therefore had little margin for error, as Samuel Lubell pointed out. "The political crisis which wracks the United States today is largely a reflection of the fact that the nation no longer has an effective majority," Lubell wrote in *The Future of American Politics.* "By 1952, the Democratic coalition had become so furiously divided that it had lost all capacity for decisive political action."

So how did Democratic presidential nominees regularly win after Roosevelt's death? The answer did not lie with any of the coalition's five main members. Strong support from white Southerners wasn't the reason. While 70 to 80 percent of Southerners backed Roosevelt during his four terms, an average of 50 percent supported Democratic nominees thereafter. Strong support from blacks wasn't the reason. Although blacks were a key constituency in a few Northern states, they represented a small slice of the electorate. For example, in 1952 only 5.2 percent of voters were black. Strong support from Jews or intellectuals wasn't the reason, either. Although both groups were an important constituency in the state of New York, they were a marginal one elsewhere. Strong support from Catholics and labor groups was an important factor, but it was not enough to get Democratic candidates over the hump. By 1956, Catholics represented one-fifth of the U.S. population, up from 16 percent when Al Smith ran. While the number of Catholic voters surged, their growing ranks were sure to alienate Protestants.

Democrats won mostly for the same reasons that kept the bosses in power. Patronage gave them good organization to get out the vote. They supported and delivered for their working-class constituents. They transcended their base to reach out to other wings of the party. And in assembling the national ticket, the bosses operated according to one litmus test: whether the presidential and vice-presidential nominees would help the local party back home. In other words, the Catholic bosses chose nominees for reasons having little to do with their vision of the common good or personal ideology. They wanted to win—and did. Carmine DeSapio explained,

> We weren't just dealing with a group of college historians and summa cum laudes and forget about the rank and file of the people. Our objective—you hear all this philosophical talking sometimes that it is better to lose an election than sacrifice a principle—nobody wants to lose an election—the name of the game is to win. We start off by trying to win it by the selection of the candidates who reflect that democratic philosophy that we represent. To win it with good candidates, good issues, good organization; now if you want to call that bossism then that's bossism. But if you want to call it from a practical standpoint those things that are necessary in order to achieve your objective, then that's what it is.

If anything, DeSapio sold the Catholic bosses short. They did more than elect Democratic presidential nominees with regularity. They made it possible for the New Deal Democratic Party to enact its policy goals—the legislation and regulation of the New Deal, Fair Deal, New Frontier, and Great Society. If not for the Catholic bosses, Lyndon Johnson likely would not have signed on to civil rights and voting rights for blacks; health insurance for the elderly, poor, and infirm; federal aid to local schools; and food stamps for the poor.

In the spirit of winning the game, Lawrence assured Kennedy, in the bathroom of his suite at the Biltmore, that Lyndon Johnson would accept the vice-presidential nomination. Kennedy then contacted Johnson. Although many Kennedy and Johnson aides tried to undo the alliance, they failed. In a press release on July 14, Kennedy wrote, "After discussions with all elements of the Democratic Party leadership, I have reached the conclusion that it would be the best judgment of the convention to nominate Senator Lyndon B. Johnson of Texas for the office of Vice President."

On the convention floor, Lawrence placed Johnson's name in nomination and delivered an address in his behalf. Then he shook hands with Johnson, who told him, "Dave, I'll remember what you did for me to my dying day."

By 1964, the Democratic Party seemed to be in great shape. Lyndon Johnson had signed into law the most far-reaching civil rights legislation since the passage of the Thirteenth and Fourteenth Amendments. The Republicans had nominated the arch-conservative Barry Goldwater. The party's presidential nominee was poised to win the White House once again. And James Rowe Jr. was working for President Johnson, the man who may never have been on the party's national ticket were it not for David Lawrence.

THREE

The Democratic Bosses: Not By the People

In the spring of 1963, a black sharecropper was thrown into jail after attending a voter registration drive in Winona, Mississippi. This was not the first time that Fannie Lou Hamer had been punished for taking part in the state's democratic process. A year earlier, Hamer had been forced to leave the plantation on which she worked because she had tried to register to vote. But the episode in 1963 was revealing of the lengths to which some whites would go in order to prevent her from voting in the future. Hamer recounted the abuse she suffered in jail:

> And it wasn't too long before three white men came to my cell. One of these men was a State Highway Patrolman and he asked me where I was from, and I told him Ruleville, he said, "We are going to check this."
>
> And they left my cell and it wasn't too long before they came back. He said, "You are from Ruleville all right," and he used a curse word, and he said, "We are going to make you wish you was dead."
>
> I was carried out of that cell into another cell where they had two Negro prisoners. The State Highway Patrolman ordered the first Negro to take the blackjack.

Though not terrorized, well-off black Mississippi Democrats were discouraged from participating in the state's democratic process. Aaron Henry, a forty-two-year-old college graduate, owned and operated the Fourth Street Drugstore in Clarksdale. When Henry and other blacks tried to vote in the state

67

Democratic Party's primary in the spring of 1964, they were prevented from doing so. "We went to the precinct conventions," Henry recalled.

> In Clarksdale, there we arrived before the hour of 10 A.M., the time scheduled for the convention. After the arrival of several blacks that were clearly in the majority from the standpoint of the number of whites present, the hours of the convention were deliberately set back to give the white delegation president an opportunity to inform their mothers, their fathers, their cousins, and their friends in order to swell their delegation with whites so as to negate the presence of blacks. In other cases, blacks were even denied the right to enter the buildings where the conventions were held.

Seeking to organize blacks in all eighty-two of the state's counties, Hamer and Henry founded an alternative to the all-white state party. But their Mississippi Freedom Democratic Party met fierce resistance. Local black leaders received death threats. In one county, an MFDP building was burned down.

Undeterred, the MFDP sought to represent Mississippi at the 1964 Democratic National Convention. After it held its first convention in early August, the MFDP petitioned the Democratic National Committee: Would its sixty-eight delegates be recognized on the convention floor in Atlantic City? In its brief, the MFDP made a strong case that its delegates should be seated, showing that the all-white state party had systematically discriminated against black Democrats.

The arbitrating board in the dispute was the Credentials Committee, which held a hearing on August 22 in a large room at Atlantic City's Convention Hall. Aaron Henry, the first witness for the MFDP, charged that discrimination against registered black Democrats began at county conventions, where white party leaders not only engaged in dirty tricks against blacks but also prevented them from voting. Henry's charge was not disputed.

Joseph Rauh, counsel for the MFDP, contended that black Democrats had been rebuffed throughout the state, as not one delegate was black. "They did not have a black at their entire state convention," Rauh exclaimed. "Not only is there no black on their delegation; there wasn't a black at the whole state convention. They excluded them all!" This allegation also was not disputed. E. K. Collins, a state senator in Mississippi, admitted that there were no black delegates, "because they weren't elected by the county convention, but they were there as spectators."

Rauh argued that the all-white regular state party was determined to exclude black Democrats in the future. As he noted, the state party had recently passed a resolution committing itself to a segregated society and had called for the repeal of the Civil Rights Act. If the practices of the regular party prevailed, black citizens might never be able to vote, to attend meetings, to serve as officers, or to run for positions in the state party. This charge, too, was undisputed.

From the perspective of most reporters, the story of the MFDP had opened a window into Mississippi's closed society. But the reporters got only part of the story. The struggle over the MFDP exposed the greatest weakness of the decentralized boss system: it was undemocratic as a procedure. In Mississippi, this weakness took on a sinister quality. Black Democratic voters did not choose the party's presidential nominee; racist white state party leaders did.

The Credentials Committee hearing on August 22, 1964, was a watershed moment in the history of the Democratic Party. In the South, as a live national television broadcast revealed, the people did not control the party of the people.

—ɷ—

WHAT SHOULD NATIONAL PARTY leaders do? The traditional solution in the Democratic Party would be a classic compromise. Members from both delegations should be seated.

Joseph Rauh liked the idea. At a meeting with national party officials in Washington on August 13, he proposed that both the white and the black Mississippi delegations be recognized on the convention floor.

David Lawrence and John Bailey also liked the idea. Upon hearing Rauh's proposal, they had nodded their heads and smiled in agreement. "Seat them both, that's great stuff," Rauh recalled hearing them say. Elaborating, Lawrence told Rauh, "Well, in Pennsylvania, I'd do that. Why, anytime when two guys are in a fight, I say, well just calm down, fellas, we'll seat you both."

But President Johnson did not like the idea. His strong preference was for the regular Mississippi delegation to be seated. Johnson's position came not from sympathy with his fellow Southerners, as some MFDP members suspected, but from simple pragmatism. If the Democratic Party were unified for the election, he would get the majorities in Congress needed to pass his civil rights and Great Society legislation. If the party were split, civil rights bills would be defeated. On the morning of August 25, Johnson told Bailey by telephone that if the MFDP were seated, 15 to 20 percent of Democrats would bolt the party.

> I think it's going to hurt like hell in the North. And we haven't gotten anything implemented yet. I haven't got a dime to carry out this bill [the War on Poverty]. I haven't got any lawyers. I haven't got any money to pay for this commission. And with the way [members of Congress are] performing, they won't give it to me. I'll have to keep this Congress here till January to even get anything through there, and I don't think I can get it through. I had to have cloture to get the other bill [the Civil Rights Act].

Johnson's opposition was significant. If he had agreed to the compromise, the boss system would have endured for at least four more years. The dream of party reformers for an un-bossed nomination process would have been deferred.

But Johnson could not prevent the MFDP from having its day in the sun. In mid-August, Rauh sought to seat both Mississippi delegations by passing what was called a minority report. If eleven of the committee's 110 members approved the minority report, all fifty state delegations would vote on it, possibly on primetime television. Although Johnson had convinced some committee members to switch sides and oppose the minority report, he had failed to persuade a sufficient number of them. On the Thursday before the convention opened, Rauh boasted that the minority report would be approved in committee that weekend and put up for a vote on the convention floor. "Eleven and eight, we got 'em" Rauh asserted. "It's a cinch."

After the old-style compromise failed, national party leaders attempted to solve the dispute by a more recent method. State parties, as a condition of being seated at the convention, would pledge support for the national ticket. In 1956, the Mississippi and South Carolina delegations had been required to put the party's presidential nominees on the state's ballot as the regular Democratic nominees.

On August 20, Johnson told Hubert Humphrey to make the MFDP the following offer: In exchange for calling off their protest, the national party would promise that black Democrats would not face discrimination at future conventions. Rauh stood his ground: the MFDP must be seated.

On August 21, Representative Edith Green of Oregon suggested that members of both the white regular party and the MFDP take a loyalty oath: Only those delegates who pledged to support the Democratic presidential ticket in November would be seated on the convention floor. Johnson opposed Green's proposal on the grounds that the South would walk out.

At Johnson's request, Walter Reuther flew in to Atlantic City early on August 25 to attempt to broker the impasse. As the president of the United Auto Workers, Reuther threatened Rauh, the UAW's general counsel, with the loss of his job if he did not withdraw the minority report. Rauh refused.

The same day, Humphrey, Reuther, and Walter Mondale made a proposal that consisted of three parts: the no-discrimination pledge, designating two members of the Freedom Party as at-large delegates, and seating the regular party. Rauh declined the offer.

As late as noon on August 25, Johnson predicted to aides that the minority report would be put up for a vote on the convention floor. Johnson was wrong.

That morning, David Lawrence had left his room at the Claridge Hotel, strolled along the boardwalk, and entered the Shelburne Hotel, an eleven-story brick building in Colonial Revival style. Taking the elevator up to the ninth floor, Lawrence walked to the suite of Hubert Humphrey, where the Minnesota senator, Reuther, Mondale, and other leading Democrats were working on the settlement. Over breakfast, one of the men made a suggestion: create a national commission to ensure that state parties do not discriminate against blacks in the future.

The likely author of the second proposal was David L. Lawrence. He was the head of the federal Commission on Equal Opportunity in Housing. He believed that the national party needed to take a stronger stand against unfaithful state parties. And when Humphrey and Reuther called Johnson that afternoon, Johnson asked for Lawrence's view of the proposal. "He's 100 percent!" Humphrey told him. Added Reuther, "He's *enthusiastic* about it. We had breakfast this morning where we worked out this proposition, and he's enthusiastic for it." Lawrence never revealed who came up with the idea. A month after the settlement, he wrote to a friend, "I had great help from both Senator Humphrey and Walter Reuther in working out the solution."

Lawrence played a key role in settling the Mississippi dispute. According to Godfrey Sperling of the *Christian Science Monitor,* the commission proposal was decisive in bridging the settlement. It was "a 'sweetening' that satisfied enough liberals on both the credentials committee and among the delegates to make it impossible for the Freedom Party to get the numerical support needed to put forward a minority report on the floor."

Lawrence called the settlement a "turning point in the history of the Democratic Party," and he exaggerated only a bit. The national party had committed itself to a new goal: Henceforth, the party's presidential nominating system in the South would be democratized. Lawrence supported this goal. He believed that white Southern opposition to civil rights was hurting the national party politically. "We certainly do not want the South to leave the party, but we have got to stop kowtowing to them," he said in early 1957. "We did not kowtow in 1948 and we won. We did kowtow in 1952 and 1956 and we lost. Nobody worked harder than I did to placate the South in 1952 and 1956, but it didn't work out."

Lawrence also possessed the credentials and skills to lead such a reform commission. He had thrown crucial support behind the Northern liberals in their bid to pass the strong civil rights plank in 1948. He had not alienated Southern party leaders. And he was a renowned negotiator; in 1946 alone, he had successfully mediated a 115-day Westinghouse strike, a 53-day hotel strike, a 27-day lights-out power strike, a 26-day steel strike, and a jurisdictional dispute over local breweries between the Teamsters and the local CIO. From Johnson's perspective, Lawrence was the perfect man for the job. As Johnson told the assistant attorney general, Burke Marshall (who considered appointing Lawrence to head a commission that would look into the deaths of three slain civil rights workers in Mississippi), "The South *likes* David Lawrence. They *respect* him. *Every one of them:* the Dick Russells, the Lyndon Johnsons—everybody that he was against. He's never been for us. I mean he was strong for Jack Kennedy against Lyndon Johnson. But he does it in such a way that you *respect* him, you *like* him."

Naturally, Lawrence was named chairman of the eighteen-member commission, which became known as the Lawrence Commission. It's worth noting that most of its members were committed to integrating black Southern voters. John Bailey had championed civil rights legislation in Connecticut in the 1950s. William Dawson was still a powerful black ward boss in Chicago. Mayor Robert F. Wagner Jr. of New York had barred housing discrimination in the city and hired tens of thousands of black civil service employees.

At the winter DNC meeting in January 1965, Bailey created the Committee Against Discrimination. "I cannot think of anything more important than this problem," he said at the Sheraton Park Hotel in Washington. "We profess to believe in the Democratic process and I believe that we do want a truly Democratic society with truly Democratic elections."

Significantly, the charter of the commission made no mention of the South. The majority report of the Credentials Committee, which the delegates approved Tuesday night, stated:

> It is the understanding that a State Democratic Party, in selecting and certifying delegates to the Democratic National Convention, thereby undertakes to assure that voters in the State, regardless of race, color, creed, or national origin, will have the opportunity to participate fully in Party affairs and to cast their election ballots for the President and Vice President nominees selected by said delegates.

The South had not been mentioned for a reason. The Lawrence Commission was meant to keep moderate white Southerners in the Roosevelt coalition. Although Johnson had lost the white Southern vote in 1964, he had carried the majority of Southern states. Berl Bernhard, a young civil rights attorney at the time, recalls that Johnson and Bailey held pragmatic but moral views of the commission's job. "Johnson was very clear about this," Bernhard said. "We had to enforce equal opportunity … but he kept saying, 'We've got to find a way not to alienate more people than we help.' … Bailey said, 'We've got to do this, but let's minimize our losses.'" Indeed, Bernhard had been hired as the commission's executive director partly because he had not repelled white Southerners. When Bernhard, a native of New York City, was offered the post in the fall of 1965, top White House aide Harry C. McPherson Jr. wrote a memo to Johnson introducing him this way: "Berl was associate director of the Civil Rights Commission during the Eisenhower Administration, and director from 1961 to 1963. In that capacity, so far as I can learn, he performed with great distinction and made no violent enemies even in the South."

In one respect, the Lawrence Commission did aid Southern state parties. If state parties were accused of racial discrimination, the national party had to show that the state party was guilty. The burden of proof rested with the national party.

Nonetheless, the Lawrence Commission focused on undemocratic delegate selection procedures in Southern state parties. In September 1966, Bernhard wrote a confidential seventeen-page memo highlighting the failure of the Mississippi state party to end discrimination against black voters. "For obvious reasons," he wrote, "any actions taken by the Lawrence Committee should be done through correspondence directed to *all* executive committees of the 50 states rather than correspondence directed specifically to the executive committee of any particular state."

The Lawrence Commission did more than identify undemocratic procedures in Southern state parties, however. It took four steps to make them more democratic.

First, the Lawrence Commission eased the rules on unseating racist delegations. If a (Southern) state party had discriminated against black voters, the national party could replace it with a more representative (i.e. partly or mostly black) delegation. On June 22, 1966, Rauh had written to Lawrence complaining about the intransigence of white Southern state parties: "The leaders of the 'regular' Democratic Parties of Mississippi and Alabama could not care less whether their representatives sit in the convention. If this is the view of the committee or its chairman, I respectfully suggest that its basic job can never be accomplished. It is only the threat to seat others—backed up by a clear intention to carry out that threat if necessary—that will open the Democratic parties in these areas." Within a year, the commission had adopted Rauh's proposal.

Second, the Lawrence Commission promulgated national rules that forbade state parties from discriminating against black Democrats. After Lawrence died in November 1966, his replacement as commission chairman was Richard J. Hughes, governor of New Jersey and formerly a county and superior court judge. On July 26, 1967, Hughes wrote to all fifty state Democratic chairmen about six "minimal prerequisites" they must adhere to:

1. All public meetings at all levels of the Democratic Party in each State should be open to all members of the Democratic Party regardless of race, color, creed, or national origin.
2. No test for membership in, nor any oaths of loyalty to, the Democratic Party in any State should be required or used which has the effect of requiring prospective or current members of the Democratic Party to acquiesce in, condone or support discrimination on the grounds of race, color, creed, or national origin.
3. The time and place for all public meetings of the Democratic Party on all levels should be publicized fully and in such a manner as to assure timely notice to all interested persons. Such meetings must be held in places accessible to all Party members and large enough to accommodate all interested persons.
4. The Democratic Party, on all levels, should support the broadest possible registration without discrimination on grounds of race, color, creed, or national origin.
5. The Democratic Party in each State should publicize fully and in such a manner as to assure notice to all interested

parties a full description of the legal and practical procedures for selection of Democratic Party officers and representatives on all levels. Publication of these procedures should be done in such fashion that all prospective and current members of each State Democratic Party will be fully and adequately informed of the pertinent procedures in time to participate in each selection procedure at all levels of the Democratic Party organization.

6. The Democratic Party in each State should publicize fully and in such a manner as to assure notice to all interested parties a complete description of the legal and practical qualification for all officers and representatives of the State Democratic Party. Such publication should be done in timely fashion so that all prospective candidates or applicants for any elected or appointed position within each State Democratic Party will have full and adequate opportunity to compete for office.

Third, the Lawrence Commission investigated whether the Southern state parties were complying with the six national standards. At the meeting in Washington on October 9, 1967, Bailey made a suggestion: After the Southern state parties chose their presidential delegates in the spring and summer, the commission should meet again to ensure that the electors were not chosen in a discriminatory fashion. Bailey authorized two DNC staff aides to travel to Mississippi in order to determine whether the state party was complying with the committee's six guidelines.

In late July 1968, the aides went to Mississippi and investigated the state party's practices. Not surprisingly, they found that the state party had prevented blacks from participating in the selection of delegates. In two majority-black counties, Holmes and Coahoma, the white-controlled parties were up to their old tricks. Precinct meetings began long after the statutory time of 10 A.M. The local newspapers published incomplete and erroneous information about party meetings. Some local parties gave no public notice at all. "Many of the patterns of discrimination against black voters which characterized Mississippi politics in the past are being perpetuated today," the aides concluded in their confidential memo. "At best the Hughes guidelines were completely ignored and there is evidence that they were held in contempt by some party officials."

Fourth, the Lawrence Commission enforced the national rules against discrimination. On August 20, 1968, less than a week before the Democratic National Convention began, the Credentials Committee met in Chicago. By a vote of 84 to 10, the committee unseated the intransigent Mississippi delegation. (Fannie Lou Hamer became an official delegate, while Aaron Henry was named co-chairman of the state party.) Later, the Credentials Committee split the Georgia delegation in two, giving half the seats to an insurgent delegation and half to the regular white party.

The Lawrence Commission was virtually ignored during its four-year existence (1965–1968). Stories about its work tended to land deep inside the newspaper. Yet the commission had done more than any other national body to make the nomination system in the South more democratic. As the aspiring reformer Ken Bode wrote, the Lawrence Commission had taken "significant steps . . . in the area of civil rights."

But for all that the Lawrence Commission had achieved, it could never democratize the party's nominating process completely.

The task was impossible for a simple reason. The boss system was undemocratic internally. Whether in the North or in the South, voters did not choose the presidential delegates; state and local party leaders chose them. These bosses—who usually were governors, mayors, and state party chairmen—held the balance of power. In both 1952 and 1968, the voters chose a different presidential candidate than the bosses. Nonetheless, the bosses' candidate prevailed.

The bosses' authority flowed from the decentralized nature of the system. Every state made its own rules and laws about when, why, how, and which delegates would be selected. In *The Making of the President, 1964,* Theodore White remarked, "it is important to grasp that 1,300 to 3,000 delegates who appear at the two great national conventions . . . are chosen not by national but by state laws. There are fifty such independent systems of law on delegate choice, and as they change from year to year, only a political technician with staff can keep in mind all their intricacies, dates, sharp and pointed legal distinctions, and dominant personalities."

Testifying before the Credentials Committee in 1964, the Mississippi state senator E. K. Collins noted, "The laws have been on the books since the days of Reconstruction as to how our parties will operate, how the people will be selected for not only your county and state offices, but will be selected for delegates to precincts, to county and to district caucuses, and to state conventions." In fact, the boss system was created in the 1820s and early 1830s, when followers of Andrew Jackson overthrew the congressional-based nominating system, better known as King Caucus. For more than a century, party leaders viewed the boss system as a great way to deliver for their supporters. Though not democratic for voters, the system was democratic for constituents.

As late as 1958, few intellectuals expressed concern about the undemocratic nature of the party's nominating system. In an exchange with the liberal economist Leon Keyserling in the *New Republic*, Arthur Schlesinger Jr. gave a qualified endorsement to the boss system:

> I quite agree with Mr. Keyserling when he says he would "rather trust a good part of our political programs to the seasoned politicians than to the eggheads" (if by "seasoned politicians" he means, as I assume he does mean, the Wilsons, Roosevelts, Trumans, and Stevensons as well as the Kellys, Hagues, and DeSapios). I have never suggested otherwise.... The question which I sought to discuss is not professionals vs. intellectuals. The question which I have sought to discuss is professionals-who-seek-out-ideas-and-work-with-intellectuals vs. party hacks.

In the 1950s and early 1960s, only fringe organizations such as Manhattan reform clubs and Students for a Democratic Society had complained about undemocratic state parties.

But in 1968 the issue was no longer abstract. For millions of young people, the fact that voters did not select the Democratic Party's presidential nominee became extremely relevant. Men were being drafted to fight a war in Vietnam. Senator Eugene McCarthy of Minnesota was running for president in opposition to the war. If young people could not nominate a presidential candidate who would prevent them from being shipped off to a jungle and brought home in a pine box, what good was the system?

One antiwar activist appalled at his Northern state party's undemocratic methods was Geoffrey Cowan. A third-year student at Yale Law School, Cowan had taken a class on American political reform taught by the eminent legal scholar Alexander Bickel. The course, along with his opposition to the war, prompted him to read Connecticut's election laws in the fall of 1967. Unsurprisingly, Cowan concluded that the state's procedures were undemocratic. "I decided that the rules were rigged and that we needed to find a way to open up the Democratic convention," he said.

Cowan discovered, for example, that challenging the regular party was absurdly difficult. In towns with more than five thousand people, the town committee named delegates to the state convention. Challenging the committee required choosing a rival slate, paying a filing fee, getting a petition in its favor circulated by a resident of the town, and obtaining 5 percent of the registered Democrats to sign it.

Cowan's biggest obstacle in the state was none other than John Bailey. For years, Bailey's undemocratic methods of choosing candidates had been alternately ignored, winked at, and celebrated. As late as 1966, another Yale student, Joseph Lieberman, portrayed Bailey as a political maestro. "He never seemed to be going anywhere in particular except in and out of that back room off-stage at the Bushnell Auditorium—but just kept moving from group to group," Lieberman wrote of Bailey's skill at working a back room. "He would grab an arm, look straight into the eye of its owner and, regardless of how far he was standing from the other, manage to sound as if he was whispering a very important and confidential piece of information into his ear." At the 1962 state convention, Lieberman said, Bailey had nominated an obscure municipal court judge for Congress. The judge was Polish, and Polish voters needed their own candidate. "All over the hall," wrote the reporter David Broder, "the weary impatient delegates suddenly heard this conversation.

It's Grabowski. Who's Grabowski? Bailey's man." A former congressman challenged Grabowski, but Bailey's man prevailed.

But in 1968, Bailey was no longer regarded by college-educated Democrats as an accomplished political broker. He was King John presiding over his Round Table. His fall from grace came at a DNC meeting in Chicago on January 8, barely more than a month after McCarthy had announced his candidacy. "We will return next August to nominate our President, Lyndon Johnson, and our Vice President, Hubert Humphrey," Bailey declared. "We know who our nominees will be."

After his supporters decided to mount their challenge in Connecticut, McCarthy fared well in the April 10 primary. In the thirty-one towns that held primaries, he won 44 percent of the vote. How many delegates McCarthy deserved to receive is difficult to say, because Connecticut had hundreds of towns. But the fact that Bailey determined the number underlined the undemocratic nature of the state's presidential nominating system. After Bailey declined to give McCarthy ten of the state's forty-four presidential delegates, McCarthy's supporters on June 22 walked out of the state convention in protest. "We leave with the understanding not to leave this party but to change it," Joseph Duffey told the three thousand people assembled at the Bushnell Auditorium in Hartford. "We have come to a point where we can go no further. This system will not yield fair representation."

That night, Cowan gathered his fellow aides in Westport, Connecticut, for a meeting of the McCarthy Steering Committee. They agreed to undertake an ambitious task: to study the election laws in all fifty states. Their research would show that the boss system had cheated McCarthy out of his rightful number of delegates.

Using this research as a foundation, Cowan created an alternative reform commission in the summer of 1968. It was called the Commission on the Democratic Selection of Presidential Nominees. Although the commission possessed zero legal status, the six-member panel had not only a credible name, but also a credible chairman, Governor Harold Hughes of Iowa. Moreover, its attacks against the boss system were credible. The panel released a ninety-one-page report, *The Democratic Choice,* detailing the less-than-democratic processes by which boss-dominated states chose presidential delegates. "All state delegate selection systems which rely in whole or in part on direct appointment of delegates by state party executives," the report declared, "should be prohibited outright and replaced with systems which permit meaningful popular participation in the selection process."

McCarthy's aides were not done attacking the Northern state parties. Around the time that the Harold Hughes Commission had its first and only meeting, on August 13 in Winnetka, Illinois, a group called Lawyers for McCarthy was assembling a case against the party's boss nomination system. The organization filed twelve challenges against state parties. Half of these challenges accused parties in Northern and border states of having marginalized pro-peace voters. Like the MFDP, the organization contended that county and state party leaders had excluded McCarthy supporters from participating in party affairs.

In the week leading up to the Chicago convention, Lawyers for McCarthy appeared before the Credentials Committee, which held its hearings at the Conrad Hilton Hotel downtown. The organization made a compelling case against boss rule in several of the states at issue.

McCarthy lawyers charged that party leaders in the Seventh, Eighth, and Ninth congressional districts had acted like old-style exclusionary bosses. McCarthy supporters had been denied the most basic rights of political participation: the right to be recognized at meetings; the right to place names in nomination; the right to make motions to begin, delay, or end meetings; and the right to secure a proper vote and vote count. To illustrate the overall problem, Lawyers for McCarthy said that two meetings in the Seventh and Eighth districts had lasted two or three minutes.

The Indiana state party's counsel, Thurmond DeMoss, did not deny the charges, but admitted that antiwar activists had been excluded. "There may have been some negative votes at the district caucuses," he said. DeMoss's comments about the state party bolstered the McCarthyites' cause. He said that McCarthy supporters had represented a small fraction of the delegates overall and that the party leaders were ignorant of parliamentary niceties.

In their other five challenges, Lawyers for McCarthy made a different argument against the Northern bosses: Instead of excluding McCarthy supporters, party bosses had marginalized them.

Pennsylvania was a good example. In April, McCarthy won 78.5 percent of the state primary. In June, he received less than 20 percent of the state's presidential delegates (24 of the 130). What happened? McCarthy was awarded none of the state's 52 at-large delegates, which were controlled by the bosses. "The at-large delegates do not represent what the Democrats of Pennsylvania voted for," McCarthy lawyer Henry W. Sawyer III argued on August 20. Sawyer also noted that the members of the central committee that appointed the at-large delegates were chosen in 1966, two years before they could be opposed.

Lawyers for McCarthy had shown that the Indiana and Pennsylvania parties had acted undemocratically. But the group failed to show that either party had violated the rules of the new boss system. It won the moral argument but not the legal one. Richard Hughes, the chairman of the Lawrence Commission who also chaired the Credentials Committee, said that the rules were "far from perfect" but the delegations were "chosen according to existing state law or party rule." Accordingly, the Credentials Committee rejected the challenges to the Indiana and Pennsylvania parties, as well as four other state parties.

Lawyers for McCarthy also attacked another undemocratic procedure used predominantly in the North. Their target was the unit rule, in which a state's delegates vote as a group. The Lawyers for McCarthy pressed their cause in the Rules Committee, whose hundred-plus members squeezed into a small room at the Conrad Hilton Hotel. On Thursday, August 22, former DNC chairman Steven A. Mitchell contended that the unit rule was used "to control minorities and to stifle dissenters" and urged that the procedure be outlawed.

Earlier in the same meeting, Harold Hughes had presented the recommendations of his unofficial reform commission. Hughes advocated six steps to ensure that the party's nomination system be made more democratic in 1968 and in the future: The public should have meaningful access to the delegate selection process; the purpose of meetings at all levels of the nominating process should be clear; delegates should be chosen no more than six months before the national convention begins; each state delegation should operate by the principle of one-man, one-vote; and the use of the unit rule should be outlawed.

On the Friday before the convention opened, the McCarthyites' attempt to demolish the boss system failed. The Rules Committee rejected a motion to democratize the party's nominating process in 1972. But aides to the Harold Hughes Commission, including Geoff Cowan, were not done. They pursued another strategy to destroy the boss system: passing a minority report in the Rules Committee. The language of the report read:

> BE IT RESOLVED, THAT THE CALL TO THE 1972 DEMOCRATIC NATIONAL CONVENTION SHALL CONTAIN THE FOLLOWING LANGUAGE:
>
> It is understood that a state Democratic Party, in selecting and certifying delegates to the National Convention, thereby undertakes to assure that such delegates have been selected through a process in which all Democratic voters have had full and timely opportunity to participate. In determining whether a state party has complied with this mandate, the convention shall require that:
>
> *a.* The unit rule not be used in any stages of the delegate selection process; and
>
> *b.* All feasible efforts have been made to assure that delegates are selected through party primary, convention, or committee procedures open to public participation within the calendar year of the National Convention.

After the minority report circulated on the weekend before the convention, more than 10 percent of the Rules Committee members voted for it. The approval of the minority report meant that all delegates at the 1968 Democratic National Convention would vote on a historic reform.

The passage of the minority report in the Rules Committee was a major victory for the young activists. Few Democrats had wanted to challenge the Northern delegations in the Credentials Committee. George McGovern had not backed the efforts of the McCarthyites. Most of Bobby Kennedy's aides had not backed them. As three British reporters noted in *An American Melodrama: The Presidential Campaign of 1968,* the credentials battle was "the reverse of the peace-plank operation," in which McGovern, McCarthy, and a few stray Kennedy aides tried to win support for a dovish position on Vietnam. Even within the McCarthy campaign, the credentials fight garnered little support. Joseph Rauh did not support the activists' efforts. The boss-dominated Northern state parties, he said, "aren't worth the gunpowder that's needed to blow them up." Nor was there support from Tom Finney, who hunted for uncommitted delegates for McCarthy after defecting from Johnson's camp. "You've got to stop the kids," he told McCarthy's chief delegate hunter. "They're tearing the party up by the grass roots."

John Bailey recognized that the Rules minority report could destroy the boss system. When it was put up for a vote late Tuesday night, Bailey walked down from the platform to the convention floor to urge his state delegation to oppose it. "Everybody votes with the chairman on this one," one Democratic aide recalled him saying. Richard Daley and Pennsylvania's two bosses (Joseph Barr and James Tate) did the same. But Bailey and other bosses failed to alert Humphrey's lieutenants, who announced on the convention floor that they took no position on the minority report. Indeed, Joseph Crangle of Buffalo and Representative Don Fraser of Minnesota gave speeches in favor of the minority report.

Few delegates grasped the implications of the vote. By Cowan's own account, "Nobody understood what the voting was about. Nobody. Hughes spoke for it. Don Fraser spoke for it. A Humphrey delegate spoke for it. A second Humphrey delegate seconded it." When Harold Hughes spoke in favor of the minority report, he did not exactly dispel the confusion. He described the vote as essentially a matter of eliminating the unit rule, a way to "build the selection process for 1972."

Late on the evening of Tuesday, August 27, the Rules minority report squeaked by. The roll call was 1,350 to 1,206.

—⁓—

THE LESSON OF the 1960s Democratic Party was that the boss system could not be restructured. Simply put, the process was undemocratic. Because the system was decentralized and relied on local and state party leaders, it could never fully accommodate all voters. The death of the boss system was inevitable.

After 1968, the Democratic Party needed a new structure. It needed to replace the old nominating system with something else.

The nominating system that seemed destined to prevail was a democratic one. After all, the Rules minority report declared that "all voters" would have a "full and timely" opportunity to choose the party's presidential nominee. The report even specified that "all delegates" would be chosen in the calendar year of the nominating convention; no longer could state parties pick delegates two or three years before voters were even paying attention to the presidential race. If these changes were enacted, voters rather than bosses would select the party's presidential nominee. The people would, at last, control the party of the people.

So the triumph of the activist system was not inevitable. But owing to an internal coup d'état, the national Democratic Party chose an activist system over a democratic one.

FOUR

A Small Group of Men

Walking back from the convention to his hotel room after midnight, Eli Segal felt exhilarated and "excited as hell," so exultant that he had to restrain himself. Segal's response that night in Chicago was unusual for someone who worked for the McCarthy presidential campaign. Earlier on that hot and steamy August evening, during the second session of the 1968 Democratic National Convention, McCarthy had in effect conceded defeat in his bid for the party's nomination. "It marked the climax, and the death, of that insurrection against the war and the leadership of the Democratic Party which had begun so many months before, and which had been sustained with such passion and ferocity," wrote three British reporters in *An American Melodrama*. Unbeknownst to the reporters, Segal had been working on another insurrection against the war and the leadership of the Democratic Party. He had been working in behalf of the minority report of the Rules Committee. Scurrying around on the floor of the International Amphitheatre, the short, prematurely balding young man had lobbied delegates to support the minority report. After it passed at 11:38 P.M., Segal felt transformed, though he dared not share his feelings with his colleagues. "I went from being anti-Vietnam," he said, "to being a reform Democrat, that night."

Segal had a big stake in the outcome of the vote: It was his memo that served as the intellectual template for the entire reform movement in the Democratic Party.

Segal's main job in the McCarthy campaign had been direct-
ing his operation in the states without primaries—Oklahoma,
Georgia, Iowa, and North Dakota. Except for Iowa, the party
leadership in those states had never needed to accommodate the
citizen-intellectual wing of the party and consequently lacked
new-style bosses such as John Bailey and David Lawrence to broker among the party's competing factions. When the state party
leaders gave McCarthy few or no delegates, his young aides came
away feeling, with some justification, that they had been disre-
spected. "I had found in one state after another that the delegates in these had been picked two or *three* years earlier," Segal
recalled. "Effectively, McCarthy couldn't even get those delegates if he *tried.*" Another young McCarthy aide who found the
work embittering was David Mixner, a student activist from
New Jersey. "Do you know what it's like to work sixteen to
eighteen hours a day and sleep on couches and win the election
and get no delegates?" Mixner said. "These were people [the
bosses] who were subverting everything I was raised to believe.
They were corrupting democracy."

Following the advice of Geoff Cowan, Segal examined the
party's nominating process. Had he studied the recent history
of the boss system, his memo might have shown that the 1968
Democratic contest was an anomaly. First, President Johnson
had suddenly announced on March 31 that he was not seeking
re-election, giving Vice President Humphrey only weeks to enter
state primaries. Then, Robert Kennedy, who had won every primary he entered but one, was shot to death on June 5. As
Richard C. Wade, a historian and McGovern adviser, acknowledged in a 1970 article, in 1968 "the system was actually working until the assassination in California. An incumbent President
had been dumped. Kennedy had bested McCarthy in the primaries, and surely Humphrey would have been destroyed in
New York where his delegates had been entered. In this perspective, it was the violence in Los Angeles not in Chicago which
defeated the Democratic Party."

Segal lacked the perspective to see the election in this light.
He was twenty-five years old and had never worked in a presidential campaign before. As a recent graduate of the University

of Michigan Law School, he analyzed the boss system in the best and only way he knew how: He examined the methods by which state Democratic parties had chosen their delegates in 1968. His research found, not surprisingly, that the most undemocratic procedures were those in boss-dominated states such as Pennsylvania, Michigan, and Louisiana. Echoing McCarthy, Segal argued that "a small group of men" rather than voters chose the nominee. In a seven-page memo titled "Unfair Methods of Delegate Selection for the 1968 Democratic National Convention," he observed:

> Although the selection process varies from state to state, a common pattern has emerged here—a small group of men has the legal authority to name the delegation without any regard to the wishes of the Democratic voter.... There will be 2,622 votes cast at the national convention. When we add the 100 votes cast by the 50 national committeemen and 50 committeewomen to the votes cast by the delegates chosen by the above processes, we find that over 600 votes (1/4 of the total) will be cast by delegates whose selection is an affront to democracy.

Like "The Politics of 1948," Segal's memo was influential. It served as the blueprint for the Harold Hughes Commission, the ad hoc panel whose recommendations informed the minority report of the Rules Committee. That report, *The Democratic Choice,* also attacked the power of a small group of men: "As delegates assemble for the 1968 Democratic National Convention, the demand for more direct democracy and the call for an end to 'boss control' of the nominating machinery can be heard, with an intensity not matched since the Progressive Era."

Considering that a boss-controlled convention approved a measure to eliminate boss control at future conventions, Segal's elation at Chicago was understandable. He had wanted to get rid of the small group of men—the cigar-chomping politicians making their deals in smoke-filled rooms. In their place, he had wanted to give power to Democratic voters in primaries and caucuses. He had wanted to base the party's nominating process on the ideal of "participatory democracy." To men of Segal's generation, this was a big deal; the Port Huron Statement, the founding document of Students for a Democratic Society, had as one of its central aims the "establishment of a democracy of individual participation." Now the Democratic Party, the world's oldest political party, was on record seeking a similar goal. State Democratic parties would be required to choose delegates by a process in which "all Democratic voters have had full and timely opportunity to participate."

For a while, Segal was hopeful that party leaders would fulfill their promises. On January 14, 1969, DNC chairman Fred Harris created a successor to the David Lawrence Commission (1965–68). He called it the Commission on Party Structure and Delegate Selection (1969–72).

But in Segal's eyes, things went downhill from there.

On February 7, Harris named Senator George McGovern of South Dakota as chairman of the commission, which became known as the McGovern Commission. To Segal, McGovern was no reformer. Although he had made a few noises at Chicago in support of reform, his proposal was a far cry from that of McCarthy, who had called for the "full-scale structural and institutional reform of the Democratic Party." Segal admitted, "[I]t was months before I thought McGovern himself was okay."

On February 8, Harris named the other twenty-seven members of the commission. Most of them weren't reformers, either. Instead, most had supported Humphrey in 1968—including George Mitchell, a national committeeman from Maine; Warren Christopher, a deputy attorney general in the Johnson administration; and Austin Ranney, a political scientist from the University of Wisconsin. Segal distrusted them all. "We felt at the time that most of these people were part of the 'good old boy network,' that guys like John Bailey and [Governor Richard] Hughes of New Jersey and [Pittsburgh mayor] Joe Barr would at some point call them up and get them to go a certain way," he told Byron Shafer, author of *Quiet Revolution.*

Segal was hired as chief counsel to the commission in mid-February; but even so, his worries were not allayed. It wasn't that the commission members would see him as a student radical; he was married with a young son at home. It was that he was Jewish. People treated him differently. While traveling to a

Southern state in the 1968 campaign, Segal told David Mixner, "There's a large Klan there and a history of segregation. With a last name like Segal, how do you think I'm going to be greeted by the locals?"

Segal felt surrounded by opponents, faint hearts, and strangers. He couldn't let this commission end up like the Kerner Commission, whose provocative recommendations in 1968 for solving the underlying causes of urban riots had been ignored by federal officials. He needed to come up with some idea to keep the reformers in power. If he didn't, all of his hard work—the memo, the Harold Hughes Commission, the Rules minority report—would have been in vain. And a small group of men would continue to control the Democratic Party.

So Segal contrived a plan. He would set up an executive committee to control the agenda of the McGovern Commission. He borrowed the notion from Fred Dutton, a member of the Harold Hughes Commission who was also named as a member of McGovern's commission. Dutton had suggested in a memo to McGovern that the commission set up a "small executive committee ... in order to give Harold Hughes some special status." Although a great admirer of Hughes, Segal wanted to create a small executive committee for a more consequential reason: it would be able to recommend changes to the party's nominating system and evaluate the findings of staff about the state's procedures.

Segal had no interest in making the membership of the executive committee representative of the commission or the Democratic Party. Nor did he simply want commissioners who belonged to the party's citizen-intellectual wing, the tradition his father had raised him in. He wanted commissioners who belonged to the citizen-intellectual wing *and* were sympathetic to the New Politics. His own political sympathies had moved toward the New Left and New Politics movements while he was at Brandeis University. He helped found a group affiliated with the Student Nonviolent Coordinating Committee and helped start an organization that brought famous speakers to campus, among them Dick Gregory, the radical attorney Mark Lane, and Malcolm X. He had little interest in working for Bobby

Kennedy's presidential campaign because, like many young McCarthyites, he regarded Kennedy's pledge to restore "law and order" as code for racism.

There was nothing illegal about Segal's plan. It did not violate the letter of the commission's mandate. But it did violate the spirit of the mandate.

Taking a page from Mayor Daley's playbook, Segal stacked the executive committee with likeminded Democrats. "The executive committee was important," Segal said later. "If you took that commission and looked at the executive committee, then you could really see the slant toward reform. With two or three exceptions, you had the hard-core there. Seven of the ten were hard-line reformers, and two of the others never came." Indeed, three had been members of the Harold Hughes Commission: Hughes, Dutton, and Representative Don Fraser of Minnesota. David Mixner was Segal's friend from the McCarthy campaign. Aaron Henry had been a member of the original Mississippi Freedom Democratic Party in 1964. Three others—Bill Dodds of the United Auto Workers, McGovern, and Adlai Stevenson III—could be persuaded to support reform.

Doing his bit for the party reform effort, McGovern added to the group's political homogeneity. First, weeks after accepting the chairmanship, he hired three consultants for the commission. Richard Wade, who taught history at the University of Chicago, had advised McGovern during his brief presidential bid in 1968. Alexander Bickel had supported McCarthy; a prominent legal theorist who taught at Yale, Bickel was the author of a recent book on party reform (and the teacher of Geoff Cowan). Anne Wexler had worked for McCarthy and had spearheaded the creation of the Harold Hughes Commission. Second, McGovern later agreed to hire a director of research. Ken Bode had recently earned a Ph.D. in political science and had worked for the campaigns of all three antiwar candidates in 1968.

The differences between the leaders of the McGovern Commission and those in charge of the Chicago convention were stark. In 1968, the chairman of the Democratic National Committee (John Bailey), the chairman of the Platform Committee (Representative Hale Boggs), the chairman of the Credentials

Committee (Governor Richard Hughes of New Jersey), and the kingmaker at the convention (Mayor Daley of Chicago) were all Roman Catholic; were professional politicians; were based either in the big cities or in state houses; and had a cross-racial, Catholic, and working-class constituency. In 1969, the chairman of the commission (McGovern), the general counsel to the commission (Segal), the chief of commission consultants (Wexler), the director of research (Bode), and the most active commissioner (Dutton) were all either mainline Protestants or non-Orthodox Jews; were predominantly activists or political aides; were based in the universities; and had a largely suburban, upper-class, white constituency. The leadership of the Democratic Party was about to change.

Anticipating party regulars' suspicion that the activists might use the executive committee to hijack the party, Segal fortified his position. On February 25, four days before the first meeting of the full commission, he wrote a confidential memo to McGovern, warning him that "your talk on the organization structure, priorities, and timetable of the Special Committee must be approached with great care if we are to avoid discord." Segal's fear did not materialize. The commission unanimously approved the creation of an executive committee.

Segal's plan was approved democratically. Yet the executive committee eerily resembled the group that "Unfair Methods of Delegate Selection for the 1968 Democratic National Convention" had railed against. Nine of the ten members were men. And when the executive committee held a second meeting, McGovern announced that in order to evaluate its preliminary recommendations, they needed "a small group." This one would be composed of three consultants: Anne Wexler, Alexander Bickel, and Richard Wade. So Eli Segal was poised to substitute one small group of men for another.

While the big-city and state bosses were back home, their hands off the party machinery, this small group of people would recommend that a new set of conductors drive the Democratic train and take it down another track.

—✖—

WHEN AL BARKAN got wind of the executive committee, he thought that organized labor should ditch the McGovern Commission. A large, barrel-chested man with crooked teeth, Barkan was the political director for the AFL-CIO. He had kept close tabs on the commission. After finding out that organized labor had only one representative on the commission, he had demanded and received a private meeting with the DNC chairman, Fred Harris. Barkan complained, to no avail. Then he found out that the commissioners, at their first meeting on March 1, had passed a resolution banning the use of proxies or substitutes at meetings. Considering that organized labor's representative, I. W. Abel, had not attended the inaugural meeting, labor needed to devise a plan of attack. So Barkan invited four other labor leaders to lunch at the Hay-Adams, an elegant 1920s-style hotel two blocks from the White House. How should organized labor respond?

Barkan argued for pulling out. He had never liked the Rules minority report. He thought it was a scheme by party radicals to take power away from the bosses, whom he liked. After all, the bosses were smart enough to pick candidates who won—Roosevelt, Truman, Kennedy, Johnson. Barkan didn't think much of the commission's membership either. I. W. Abel, president of the United Steelworkers, was the only voice for organized labor. Worse, the executive committee was filled with New Politics radicals. "There were twenty-eight members," Barkan told Byron Shafer. "Then they went to a ten-member executive group. If we thought the first group was unrepresentative, this executive group was worse. These ten people held periodic meetings in 1969, with the staff doing everything. If ever there was a staff running away with things, that was it."

Labor leaders felt proud and indignant. They would not grovel to the antiwar radicals for more clout on the commission. Labor had done more than any other Democratic constituency to try to elect Hubert Humphrey in 1968. As former DNC chairman Lawrence O'Brien recounted in his autobiography, *No Final Victories,* "In the end, the fact that there was any Democratic campaign at all was largely due to organized labor." O'Brien's assessment was shared by more neutral observers, such as the three British reporters who wrote *An American Melodrama.* "Con-fronted with the very serious crisis of the [George] Wallace chal-lenge on their own ground," they concluded, "the unions entirely outperformed the middle-class liberals who had been criticizing them so severely for their lack of sensitivity to the moral issues raised by the war in Vietnam."

Organized labor's reaction to the McGovern Commission was typical; the other wings of the Democratic Party responded to the activists ineffectually or not at all. The New Politics crowd dominated the commission agenda not only because of their bold efforts, but also because the traditional party leadership failed to fight back. It was as if the train conductor's control pan-els were open and only the activists were trying to grab hold of them.

The big-city and state bosses never counterattacked against the New Politics activists. They were either too old, too young, too inexperienced, or too busy. Mayor Daley was playing defense for the conduct of his police the previous summer and feuding with Humphrey over his loss of the election. John Bailey was back in Connecticut dealing with the state legislature and anti-war insurgents in the Democratic caucus. David Lawrence had died in November 1966 and his de facto successor, Mayor Joe Barr of Pittsburgh, lacked experience in national party affairs. Mayor James Tate and Representative Bill Green, both of Philadelphia, were similarly inexperienced in operating the national party machinery. Colonel Jacob Arvey, a DNC com-mitteeman from Illinois, was seventy-three years old. Jesse Unruh was mounting a run for governor of California.

Also, most bosses probably failed to grasp the significance of the McGovern Commission. The year 1969 was a tumultuous one: student radicals continued to occupy university buildings, the United States sent men to the moon, the Woodstock music festival took place, and the antiwar movement staged the largest protest marches in the nation's history. The proposals of a com-mission looking at internal party structure in Washington, D.C., didn't seem to matter much. "I don't think that anyone could have foreseen in 1970 . . . the results of the guidelines two years later," O'Brien wrote in *No Final Victories.* "We were feeling our way, taking steps no major political parties had ever taken. We knew that the old rules had brought deep divisions in 1968 and we were groping toward something better."

The bosses' general incomprehension was echoed in the mainstream press. As a rule, the media ignored the McGovern Commission. When reporters did write about it, few understood the stakes involved. After the commission's first hearing, on March 1, only David Broder of the *Washington Post* noted that the "strong reform elements appear to hold a commanding majority on the executive committee." By contrast, the *New York Times'* story, running on page 41, made no mention of the executive committee at all. Even the most thoughtful press accounts of the commission expressed uncertainty about its significance. Paul Hope, a reporter for the *Washington Star,* wrote in mid-February, "Some see [the commission] as an opportunity to revolutionize the party—to make it more truly reflect the voices from the grass roots. Others see it as amounting to very little."

As late as 1972, many political observers assumed that the bosses still controlled the party machinery. On the left, reporter Jack Newfield complained in the *Village Voice* that the "New Democratic Coalition reformers [had failed] to renew or reform the Democratic Party." In the center, Richard Scammon and Ben Wattenberg in *The Real Majority* dismissed the idea that George Wallace, former governor of Alabama, could win the party's presidential nomination in 1972 on the grounds that the bosses would prevent him from doing so: "Any such attempt would be blocked by the bosses—in this instance, 'liberal' bosses who would certainly be able to find some intellectual rationale for not listening to the voice of the people as expressed in a few state primaries."

Worried about a New Politics takeover, Barkan pressed his case against the commission during the lunch at the Hay-Adams Hotel. His pitch was enough to convince AFL-CIO official Lane Kirkland. Together they cast the deciding votes: Organized labor would pull its lone member from the McGovern Commission. Although technically still a member, I. W. Abel never attended any of its hearings or meetings. "We are not against reform per se," the AFL-CIO wrote in a statement in September 1969. "But we do fear that the zeal of the reformers may throw out proven systems." Labor leaders hoped that without their input, the McGovern Commission would collapse of its own weight.

McGovern was incredulous. "I always thought that was strange that they turned their back on the commission like that," he said, adding that Abel "could've made a difference." Eli Segal was grateful. "The so-called regulars more or less turned the commission over to us," he said. "A lot of people that could have just showed up, like I. W. Abel, never came. Meanwhile, David Mixner suddenly sits at the table and said, 'I'm here, I'm going to do what I think is right.'"

By late winter and early spring of 1969, the New Politics activists had the party machinery in their grasp. Segal had already moved into the headquarters of the Democratic National Committee, located on the sixth floor of the Watergate office-apartment-hotel in northwest Washington. Now they just needed to ensure that they stayed in the conductor's car with their hands on the party levers.

—⁓—

THE NEW POLITICS activists could not acknowledge publicly that they dominated the McGovern Commission, that their proposals to reform the party represented the wish list of a single ideological faction, or that many of their so-called reforms in reality were rules changes. That would never do. The commission would lack legitimacy. The Democratic National Committee and the 1972 Democratic convention might reject its recommendations.

The activists needed to create an impression of unity and consensus. While they could not say so, because it would undermine their worldview and their self-conception, they needed to act like old-style bosses. So they came up with a story line: that all members of the Democratic train—Catholics, union members, blacks, citizen activists and intellectuals—had participated in creating a new nominating system. The activists sought to manufacture an impression of unity in three ways.

The first way was by claiming that the membership of the commission was representative of the party as a whole. The commission's first public report, titled *Mandate for Reform* and released in April 1970, asserted that the commissioners "represent all ideological and geographical elements of the Party." The report echoed the founding resolution of the McGovern Commission approved in January 1969: that the panel would be composed of "representative Democrats."

But the reality was another story. Besides having only one representative from organized labor, the McGovern Commission had few Catholics. Of the panel's twenty-eight members, the only Catholics were Albert A. Pena, a member of the liberal Texas delegation that had not been seated at the Chicago convention, and Jack English, chairman of the party in Nassau County, New York. Catholics had made up about one in four Humphrey voters in 1968, yet they received only one in fourteen slots on the commission in 1969.

One reason for the underrepresentation of Catholics was a change in the DNC's leadership ranks. When Lawrence O'Brien, who had taken over from John Bailey in August 1968, had been the DNC chairman, Catholic names had dotted the list of hypothetical appointments to the party reform commission. One list drawn up days before the November election, "Suggested Names for Committee on Selection of Delegates," mentioned thirty members. Of those, seven were Catholic: Senator Edmund Muskie of Maine; Vic Bussie, AFL-CIO leader in Louisiana; Mayor Joseph Alioto of San Francisco; Representative Henry Gonzalez of Texas; Senator Hale Boggs of Louisiana; Mayor James Tate of Philadelphia; and Eugene "Pete" O'Grady, state party chairman in Ohio. Under this roster, Catholics would have represented more than one in four of the commissioners. A second list drawn up three weeks after the election, also titled "Suggested Names for Committee on Selection of Delegates," named seventy-eight Democrats. Of these, fifteen were Catholic: the above names plus John Bailey; James Rowe; former Representative Tom Carroll of Kentucky; Representative Hugh Carey of New York; Boston politico Al Cella; Representative James O'Hara of Michigan; Maxine Morrison, a defeated candidate for Congress from Nebraska in 1968; and Patricia Sheehan, mayor of New Brunswick, New Jersey. Under this roster, Catholics would have represented slightly less than one in five commissioners.

The prevalence of Catholic names on the list was unsurprising given O'Brien's attachment to the Catholic wing of the party. The son of Irish immigrants, O'Brien had idolized James Michael Curley growing up in Springfield, Massachusetts, and had worked for the Kennedys most of his adult life. As late as November 26, 1968, Democratic leaders named a representative number of Catholics or white ethnics on a reform commission. But in early December, O'Brien, wanting financial security for his family, accepted a six-figure salary with a Wall Street brokerage firm. Humphrey needed to pick a new chairman, so he asked Senator Fred Harris of Oklahoma, who four months earlier had been his second choice as a vice-presidential running mate. On January 11, Harris accepted the offer.

The son of poor migrant farm workers in rural Oklahoma, the thirty-eight-year-old senator had no ties to the urban, Catholic base of the Democratic Party. Harris was not exactly a traditional or regular Democrat, either. In 1965, he had voted against Medicare, a cherished goal of economic liberals since Roosevelt's last term. In 1967 and 1968, he had served on the Kerner Commission, which singled out "white racism" for the riots in the big cities, and had written much of its famous introduction. Harris saw himself less as a New Deal Democrat than as a champion of unpopular causes. In January 1969, he viewed the peace movement, whose poll numbers had dropped below even those of Johnson and Nixon, as an unpopular cause worth fighting for. "I took the job primarily to reform the party and speak out on the issues, particularly the Vietnam War," Harris recalled. Therefore, when he came up with a list of hypothetical appointments to the reform commission in 1969, he chose party officials he knew—a group that did not include Catholics.

Another reason that Catholics were underrepresented was the assumptions of the New Politics activists. According to the activists, Catholics should have organized in their own interest. "Who spoke for the Italian construction worker or the Polish gas station attendant?" Segal said to Lanny Davis. "They should have had someone pushing for them. It's the American way—

get organized or get overlooked." In fact, the activists played a key role in blocking the de facto leaders of Catholics, the bosses and their supporters.

On January 14, Harris enacted, with the DNC's unanimous support, a resolution that created what came to be known as the McGovern Commission. To the activists, Harris's resolution was an outrage. It had merged two reports of the 1968 convention—the Credentials majority report and the Rules minority report. As Thomas Alder, staff director of the Hughes Commission, explained to Byron Shafer, "The DNC had run a resolution through the convention to set up a commission to continue the work of the *Richard* Hughes Commission," referring to the reform panel dominated by supporters of the bosses and organized labor (the Lawrence Commission).

Irate leaders of the New Democratic Coalition demanded a meeting with Harris. On January 18, Harris met with the NDC and promised that he would not appoint any opponents of reform. According to an NDC press release, "Chairman Harris, although evidently uncomfortable at being forced to define his position, promised the New Democratic Coalition delegates that no persons opposed to party reform would be appointed to either commission." In effect, Harris agreed to appoint no allies of the bosses. He denied feeling undue pressure from the NDC, but he also admitted that in making appointments to the reform commission, he did not consult with any state or big-city bosses. "I didn't talk to any of them," Harris said. "It just didn't seem necessary." His decision not to appoint any bosses was understandable. After all, the bosses had little interest in overhauling the party's nomination system. But the decision to appoint only two Catholics was not representative of the Democratic constituency.

Another way that the New Politics activists set out to create an impression of unity was by claiming that the commission's field hearings had represented every segment of the party. According to a commission press release, the main goal of the hearings was to "elicit grass roots sentiment on what the Democratic Party does and what it should do." And it is true that the McGovern Commission did travel to seventeen cities and hear from five hundred witnesses.

But few party bosses and labor leaders testified—a fact that the New Politics activists complained about, always privately of course. The activists wanted the bosses and labor leaders to testify for appearances' sake; it would lend credibility to the McGovern Commission in the eyes of the rest of the party. At a meeting of the executive committee on May 26, after the commission had held hearings in seven cities, Eli Segal asked, "How can we can get the regulars to testify?" A discussion ensued among the eight commissioners and four staff members present. Their answer: "Regulars do not feel [the] necessity, obligation, or even justification to testify."

Four months later, regulars continued to shun the hearings. On September 21, two commission aides wrote a confidential memo to McGovern about labor's participation at the hearings. They discovered that only twelve witnesses had identified themselves as labor representatives. Of the five hundred Democrats who testified before the commission, less than 3 percent belonged to organized labor.

Also, Eli Segal coached a major Democratic figure about his testimony before the commission. On Tuesday, April 29, he called Allard Lowenstein to talk to him about his appearance at a hearing in Manhattan the following Saturday. Lowenstein, a congressman from New York, was best known as the cofounder of the Dump Johnson movement in 1967, the first organized effort to replace President Johnson with an antiwar Democratic nominee. Segal wanted to make sure that Lowenstein imparted his wisdom to the commissioners. "Despite all the rhetoric to which the McGovern Commission has been subjected," Segal complained in a letter to Lowenstein, "there has been little concrete analysis of the barriers—legal or illegal—to participation."

Segal identified what he perceived to be four abuses of the boss nomination system, and suggested that Lowenstein cite them in his testimony. "One word of warning," he advised. "Many commission members would prefer to forget Chicago— and the months that preceded it." Not leaving things to chance, Segal recommended that Lowenstein elaborate on the obstacles facing an insurgent campaign: "[W]hile we were running around the primary states, in fact, while you were running around in

1967, delegates were being locked up for the convention. Set in this context of the loss of confidence in our political institutions, I think this material would provide dramatic illustration of the controversy we're looking for."

In addition, leaders of the McGovern Commission prevented a number of state Democratic leaders from testifying at the hearings. In mid-May, Fred Dutton, the treasurer of the commission, sent a confidential memo to McGovern, Harold Hughes, Bill Dodds, Robert Nelson, and Segal, in which he urged that they embarrass the heads of state Democratic parties. Dutton wrote, "1. Let's fine a State leader or organization resisting any reform hearings in his State and lambast [sic] him, or it. 2. Let's have the staff put together two horrendous case examples and publish those, as perhaps the seating of the present national committeemen and women from Georgia and Mississippi."

Within days of Dutton's memo, the commission instigated a feud with state party leaders. The problem began when the staff failed to tell Louisiana Democrats about a hearing scheduled for New Orleans. Somehow J. Marshall Brown, a Democratic national committeeman from Louisiana, heard about the hearing, and he responded by "ordering" the commission out of the Bayou State. "I find it very hard to understand Sen. McGovern's motives, and even harder to justify his actions," Brown wrote. He forwarded the letter to Harry Truman, Lyndon Johnson, all three Democratic presidential candidates in 1968, every Democratic member of Congress, and every member of the DNC.

The ensuing spat raised Fred Harris's ire. On May 21, he wrote privately to McGovern to register his disapproval over his handling of the matter. "This kind of complaint continues to plague us and cause us all sorts of problems. I just see no reason why notice can't be given." Harris then added, in a handwritten note at the end of the letter, that Louisiana Democrats were not alone in their complaint about the commission. "George—since writing this, George Bristol on my staff got a complaint similar to Marshall Brown's from, of all people, Blaine Whipple, national committeeman from Oregon and a former McCarthy ally."

The third way that New Politics activists worked to create an impression of unity was by claiming that the commission drew up the guidelines after seeking the advice of state party leaders. *Mandate for Reform* stated, "After integrating the testimony, consulting with experts in universities, studying news accounts and seeking the advice of state party leaders, the staff gradually evolved a tentative set of standards which could achieve the objectives of a National Convention."

In reality, the leaders of the McGovern Commission consulted with the other wings of the party as much as Mayor Daley consulted with the young antiwar activists at Chicago.

To take the most relevant example, Segal sought out his fellow activists in the New Politics. On June 30, he wrote separately to John Schmidt and Wayne Whalen, two of his close friends in the McCarthy campaign. What would happen, he asked them, if state parties resisted the commission's guidelines? On which grounds could the commission claim authority over state parties? Five weeks later, Segal turned to an old friend from law school to interpret the mandate of the McGovern Commission. "Dear Dick," Segal wrote on August 8 to Richard Herzog, a lawyer for the prestigious Washington firm of Covington and Burling. "We need some brilliant interpretation of two overlapping resolutions passed at the 1968 Democratic National Convention."

There was a reason Segal sought a "brilliant interpretation" of the two resolutions: He and Ken Bode wanted the commission to require state parties to adopt proportional representation, which ensured that delegates could vote according to the dictates of their own conscience or ideology rather than the state party boss. On June 19, Segal had written a confidential memo to the panel's consultants in which he argued that the commission had "much clearer instructions" to enforce the timeliness standard (picking delegates in the calendar year of the convention) than the standard on full participation (ensuring that Democratic voters aren't prevented from voting at the county level of the delegate selection process). "I don't want to see these questions on which reasonable men can disagree confused with questions on which they cannot," he wrote at the time. Indeed,

Segal did not even refer to the fact that Democratic voters must have a "meaningful" chance to participate. But by August, Segal had reversed his position. "Our problem is short," Segal wrote to Herzog. "We feel it is important that the word 'meaningful' be included in the Call to the Convention."

Even in financing the commission, the New Politics activists turned to their own network of supporters. Fred Harris had agreed in May to let the reformers seek their own financing. With the DNC still in the red, mainly as a result of the Humphrey campaign, the leaders of the McGovern Commission tapped "the ideological money"—contributions from Holly- wood, media executives, and radical-chic causes. At the executive committee meeting of May 28, McGovern announced that he and Harris had hired Sid Green, a fundraiser for McCarthy's campaign in New York. According to a summary of the meet- ing, Green said he would "contact people in all segments of the party; he would not concentrate on McCarthy supporters." His efforts failed. According to an August 28 financial statement, the commission had received only $26,707.50 in contributions— not nearly enough to cover the heavy expenses associated with the field hearings. As a result, the commission was $26,382.97 in debt. By early fall, the antiwar insurgents stopped trying to raise money from the other four wings of the party. On October 2, Bob Nelson asked for donor mailing lists from Don Green, Paul Schrade, Donald Peterson, and Blair Clark, respectively the executive director, the two co-chairmen, and the treasurer of the New Democratic Coalition, most of whose members had sup- ported McCarthy in 1968.

In summer, the national press did write about the McGovern Commission's attempts to provoke and alienate fellow Democrats. On June 15, the *Washington Post* carried a syndicated column by Rowland Evans and Robert Novak with the headline "McGovern- Daley Clash Spotlights Civil War Raging among Democrats." On June 27, *Time* ran a largely negative story about the commission with the tagline "Almost as divisive as the convention itself."

By the fall, however, the press forgot about the commission's factionalism. Many political observers portrayed *Mandate for Reform* as largely a party-wide effort. For example, the *Washington*

Post editorialized, "The document is the more significant because it was adopted by a group—officially known as the Commission on Party Structure and Delegate Selection—which represents every segment of the party."

—⚏—

THE LEADERS OF the McGovern Commission claimed that the hearings affirmed their vision for the party. "From the statements of rank-and-file Democrats and party leaders at the hearings," *Mandate for Reform* said, "the commission has concluded that there is a genuine, broadly based commitment to reform within the Party."

It is difficult to square this claim, however, with the Daleyesque tactics to which leaders of the McGovern Commission resorted. One top commission aide acknowledged that he flew in ideologically compatible commissioners for key votes. Ken Bode, the director of research, sought out members who supported proportional representation, whereby a candidate receives delegates equal to his voting percentage in the primary, caucus, or convention. Bode acknowledged that he did this for the commission's meetings on September 23 and 24. "Pena was flown in for this," he said, referring to Albert Pena of Texas. "We knew where our votes were. And we tried to bring them in. We knew that Pena was with us on [proportional representation] so we brought him in. We found the wherewithal to get him there.... We wanted [Earl] Graves, and he would be with us on everything. We did our best, and we got him for one day."

There *was* a genuine, broadly based commitment to reform within the Democratic Party, though it differed from the proposals adopted by the McGovern Commission. According to the testimony at the field hearings and letters to the commission from political scientists, most Democrats argued that the nomination system should be rooted in small *d* democracy. But there was no consensus in the party about reform. At the hearings there were three main groups—democrats, bosses, and activists—each suggesting that the Democratic train roll down its own preferred nomination track.

The first group, the democrats, consisted mainly of statewide elected officials of a younger generation than the bosses. They argued that by reforming the party machinery to include antiwar and young Democrats, the party could preserve the Roosevelt coalition. They sought to replace the boss system with a democratic system in which states would choose delegates in the calendar year of the convention, hold binding presidential primaries instead of caucuses, ban ex-officio delegates as well as the unit rule, and publicize meetings at which delegates are selected.

The best-known democrat who spoke at the commission hearings was Senator Edward Kennedy of Massachusetts. In 1969, he was the favorite to win the party's presidential nomination, and he did not intend to alienate his Catholic and working-class constituency. In mid-1970, Kennedy would tell party reformers, "We simply cannot allow a love affair with campus youth on the issue of war to weaken or obscure the close tie the party has always had with the labor movement and the working man. The class gap is opening under us and threatens us far more seriously."

Appearing at the ornate Senate Caucus Room on April 25, Kennedy gave his blessing to the commission's democratic mandate. "In the field of delegate selection," he said, "you are blessed with a forceful and unequivocal mandate—'full and timely opportunity to participate,' 'the unit rule not be used in any state,' 'procedures open to public participation within the calendar year.' These principles express our needs, our hopes, and our demands." In the rest of his speech, Kennedy nodded in the direction of the activists without endorsing their agenda. For example, he raised a question about imposing delegate quotas: "Should we continue to make an effort to insure automatic representation of such groups as unions, political clubs, racial minorities, and youth on delegations, and if so, how can this be done in the context of popularly elected delegations?" He also supported several popular and uncontroversial proposals: for instance, that states modernize their voter registration laws and relax their voting residency requirements.

The second well-known democrat who appeared before the commission was Senator Edmund Muskie of Maine, the party's nominee for vice president the previous year. Muskie was also a top presidential contender for 1972. Having come out recently against the war, he sought to appeal to the young baby-boomers without alienating his blue-collar and Catholic constituency. So he endorsed small *d* democratic reform but not so much as to become a captive of the activists. "It is not enough," he told the commissioners, "to suggest that our problems can be solved by changing the guard from one establishment to another. The challenge and the involvement which brought the issue of party reform to the surface must have a continuous avenue for expression."

Like Kennedy, Muskie affirmed the commission's mandate. But unlike Kennedy, he endorsed several specific democratic reforms: the one-man, one-vote proposal for convention delegates; allowing young people of less than voting age to "work side by side within the Party structure with Democratic voters"; and banning discrimination against any qualified voter.

Another democrat who spoke at the field hearings was Robert Casey, the auditor general of Pennsylvania. The same age as Kennedy, he belonged to a younger generation of Catholic leaders. Casey criticized the nomination process as "archaic, and in many cases unfair and unresponsive to the will of the vast majority of members of our party." He also urged the commissioners to reform the boss system: "It is equally clear that unless the committee, with the active aid and cooperation of interested and concerned Democrats throughout the nation, pursues a course of immediate and meaningful reform, the Democratic Party cannot possibly fulfill our destiny as the party which claims to speak for all of the people of the country." To remedy those ailments, Casey proposed two reforms. First, state parties should be required to pick their presidential delegates in the calendar year of the convention; and second, the number of state delegates should be reduced, so as to decrease the chances that delegations are boss-run.

Though Casey criticized the boss system, he knew from first-hand experience the flaws of an unbossed system. In the 1966 Democratic primary in Pennsylvania, Casey's opponent, Milton Shapp, a self-financed cable TV magnate, owed his victory largely to an expensive feature-length movie he aired called *The Man Against the Machine*. From this experience, Casey concluded that the boss system ought to be retained. "Don't kill the machine," he told the six commissioners in attendance. "The candidate of modest means must rely on the regular party structure if he is ever going to aspire to high public office. He cannot mount an independent campaign in any meaningful way. So we have to preserve what is good and what is worth preserving about the regular party organization, and there is considerable that is worth preserving."

In the question-and-answer session with the commissioners, Casey was asked about ways to boost the number of black delegates. "I think you can get into discrimination in reverse," he said to commissioner Louis Martin, one of only three blacks on the commission and former head of the minorities division at the DNC. "Frankly, aspects of the quota system are to me philosophically offensive, because that just reverses the process and guarantees and welds in people who may not for a number of reasons be qualified to be there."

Many political scientists also favored small *d* reform. In their correspondence with the McGovern Commission staff, several scholars argued that caucus elections were inferior. They pointed out that in a caucus a mobilized minority of voters could easily prevail over a diffuse, numerically superior number of voters. William Boyd, assistant director of the National Municipal League, criticized caucuses as "inferior" because "the average citizen has little or no interest in or knowledge of [the caucus]. Conversely, however, it does lend itself to blitz tactics by a well-established minority within the party as witness the Goldwater movement in 1964."

Several scholars criticized the New Politics activists. Clarence A. Berdahl, a political science professor at the University of Illinois, wrote in an April 10 letter, "Although I have long been a critic of the National Convention system, I consider that some of the charges against the 1968 Democratic convention are greatly exaggerated and that the convention performed about as well as previous conventions and probably carried out the general rank-and-file preferences."

The second camp at the hearings, the bosses, argued that because the Democratic Party had succeeded in enacting social welfare legislation and serving the little guys in society, they needed only to accommodate the new groups in the party. They never referred to the mandate of the McGovern Commission and rarely mentioned the war, but they were not above attacking the Democrats they called "party wreckers." The bosses, not surprisingly, wanted to make only minor reforms to the boss system.

One boss who provided testimony was Mayor Tate of Philadelphia. Though *Mandate for Reform* mentioned that Tate had given remarks, the report omitted one key fact: When the commission held its field hearing in Philadelphia on May 25, at the campus of St. Joseph's College, Tate never showed up. He claimed to be out of town, but his record suggested he had no intention of going anyway. In *The Democratic Choice,* he was quoted as saying, "I don't care who does the electing as long as I do the nominating." In May 1968, along with a handful of other state party leaders, Tate had awarded McCarthy only 21 of the state's 104 delegates, despite McCarthy's winning 71.6 percent of the Democratic vote in a nonbinding primary in April. (McCarthy was the only Democratic candidate who had spent time in the Keystone State.)

In his statement at the hearings, the fifty-nine-year-old Tate did make some concessions to antiwar and young Democrats, such as support for lowering the voting age. But Tate, whose whole life had been spent in working-class and Catholic Philadelphia, had little use for the longhaired, upper-middle-class youth of the McCarthy campaign. So instead of suggesting reform of the state's nomination process, he blasted liberal reformers and defended patronage politics:

> If someone thinks he can better function as a committeeman than the incumbent, the obvious answer is to resort to the democratic process and run against the incumbent. Yet many, instead of putting their egos and their concern on the line, resort to empty rhetoric and conveniently criticize the system. Be not mistaken, elections are not won alone by any one segment of our party. A victorious Democratic Party needs the daily contributions of the

committeeman, as well as the campaign year enthusiasm of the college student and the housewife volunteer.

Mayor Daley also gave testimony at the hearings. He appeared on June 7 at the Sherman House downtown, appropriately enough in the Louis XVI Room. Daley, like Tate, showed disdain for the New Politics activists. He failed to tell the commission staff whether he would attend, and when he did arrive, at 9:25 A.M., he was almost half an hour late. When he sat down in front of the microphone, the sixty-seven-year-old mayor made one noteworthy proposal: that presidential candidates enter at least one-third of the primaries. In practice, Daley's proposal would have prevented candidacies such as that of Hubert Humphrey, who had entered no primaries in 1968.

After wrapping up his testimony, Daley revealed his true feelings about party reform. In his question-and-answer session with commissioners, he jousted with McGovern, who at one point condemned the boss system for failing to "bridge that gap to the individual citizen who may feel that those leaders that you and other people are talking about do not necessarily reflect their will." Daley shot back, "I feel that about you. You speak for the Senate; you do not speak for the people of your state." Before leaving, Daley defended the boss system, repeating twice his "very strong" support of "party responsibility."

The third camp at the hearings, the New Politics activists, was made up mostly of antiwar campaign aides with few elected officials. The activists' vision was a party resembling less a big tent than an ideological club. Citing the horror of the Vietnam War and recent Democratic electoral defeats, the activists pronounced the Roosevelt coalition to be morally and politically bankrupt. They wanted to destroy the boss system and establish a system based not only on small d democracy but also on participatory democracy. In so doing, they argued, the party could create a new Democratic coalition without Southerners and party bosses.

One activist who testified at the hearings was Donald O. Peterson, the forty-four-year-old co-chairman of the New Democratic Coalition. Peterson had personal ties with the antiwar insurgents on the McGovern Commission. In 1962 he had managed McGovern's senatorial campaign, and in 1968 he had headed the Wisconsin delegation for McCarthy. Accordingly, Peterson's testimony was familiar to his audience. "Your job is not simply to make a few reforms, some structures, to a structure which is basically sound," he told the commissioners. "Your mandate is not simply to make delegate selection more timely. Your task is to eliminate all that machinery which stands between the people of the Democratic Party and the effective control of the party." To that end, Peterson spoke in favor of seven rules changes. Among them was an affirmative action plan for underrepresented groups in the party. "We will not get more delegates of average income, or more young delegates, or more black or Mexican-American delegates, unless this commission impresses on every Democratic organization the need to open its doors to full participation by all Democrats."

Another activist who appeared before the commission was Paul Schrade, the other co-chairman of the New Democratic Coalition and the western region director for the United Auto Workers. (Schrade, who was forty-three, was regarded as something of a heroic figure among the commissioners; he had been in the kitchen pantry on the night of Bobby Kennedy's assassination and was shot in the head by one of Sirhan Sirhan's .22 caliber bullets.) At the Los Angeles hearing, held on June 21, Schrade made a series of proposals inspired by the New Politics. Among the most notable was a call for demographic quotas. "We ought to set minimum quotas to guarantee representation to the blacks, browns, the students, women, labor unions, from all of the major constituencies of the Democratic Party," Schrade told the commissioners. He also proposed purging members of what he called the "Reactionary Southern Democratic-Republican Coalition." "This is one of the basic problems of the Democratic Party. We are not doing anything to get rid of the people who do the most damage to the Democratic Party program," Schrade said. "There are certain Southern Democrats who ought to leave the party.... Big-city bosses must go, because the party cannot afford their failure to support the national campaigns as they play their political game. Typical of that was Chicago." Schrade went on to opine that the "Old Coalition has collapsed."

To be sure, some traditional Democrats did endorse parts of the activist system. Governor Richard Hughes of New Jersey, responding to a question by McGovern about whether he supported caucus elections, said that he did support them. But it's extremely misleading to claim, as *Mandate for Reform* did, that there was "genuine, broadly based commitment to reform" among Democrats. The activists failed to mention that their version of reform differed dramatically from that of most Democrats.

—⚊—

Austin Ranney arrived at Room 318 in the Old Senate Office Building a little before 9 A.M. on November 19, 1969. He had flown in from the Midwest, where he was a professor of political science at the University of Wisconsin, Madison. A balding man with glasses, he wore his standard-blue academic suit. Since hearing Hubert Humphrey's thrilling speech in support of civil rights at the 1948 convention, Ranney had become a charter member of the intellectual wing of the Democratic Party. Besides editing the *American Political Science Review,* he had served on the advisory group for the Lawrence Commission, the panel of eight academics who advised and counseled the commission on its recommendations. Earlier in the year, Ranney had received a call from Fred Harris asking if he would serve on another commission, and he readily agreed. Now he was standing in the Old Senate Caucus Room, one of the grandest and most historic rooms in the nation's capital, the site of countless Senate investigations, such as those into the sinking of the *Titanic,* Pearl Harbor, Army vs. McCarthy, and Vietnam.

Walking into the room, Ranney felt anxious. These were the last two days of meetings before the McGovern Commission issued its final recommendations. Plus, he had missed the previous two meetings, in September. And Ranney was a bit naïve. As late as 1967, when most university academics had come out against the war, he had served on a panel of professors who supported it, convened by the Johnson administration. Walking past the fifteen-foot walnut-oak doors of the Caucus Room, looking down at the Italianate black-veined marble floors and up at the French-style windows, he was nervous and tense; none of the nineteen other commissioners greeted him with a smile and a handshake, as would be the case at a faculty meeting. Ranney sat down at one of the several long walnut-oak tables in the vast, airy room.

Austin Ranney was about to make history. For years, the young members of the citizen-intellectual wing of the Democratic Party had sought to break into the conductor's car, take control of the party levers from the bosses, and steer the Democratic train down another track. This day, a middle-aged member of the citizen-intellectual wing, inadvertently, was about to help them finish the job.

Despite his nerves, Ranney remained an idealist. In his hands was a draft of a new rule for the commission, one that he believed would help blacks in the party. He got the idea partly from his teaching days at the University of Illinois, when he and his friend Jack Peltason had appointed two black students as teaching assistants. Lucius and Twiley Barker became the first two blacks in school history to earn Ph.D.s in political science and went on to distinguished academic careers. Also, Ranney had attended the 1968 convention and thought the delegations included too few blacks.

After sitting down in his chair, Ranney listened to McGovern, Segal, and Bode speak, and heard the responses from a few other commissioners. Then, after McGovern read requirement A-1, that state parties may not discriminate against state voters, Ranney addressed the commissioners and reporters present:

> This may or may not be the appropriate time to bring this up, but let me mention it very briefly. As you know from my reaction to the report, not having the benefit of the decision of the September meeting, my very strong impression from the hearings I attended is that when we got to the proportionality issue … we could take care of it by adding something to A-1. We're going to run into, I think, a very real problem and the real problem of not having enough representation of minority groups…. I have a very strong feeling in many of the testimonies that our black fellow Democrats

feel that something more is needed than a no-discrimination rule, that at least for the time being. They would like some assurance that there would be blacks on the delegation in some reasonable proportion to blacks in the Democratic Party. Now I personally react very sympathetically to that suggestion. I think that it would be good both on moral grounds and political grounds and that others should do it. . . . I want to suggest as possible for A-1, that we add yet another clause and I have drafted this because I want to try the idea out for size on you, that the Committee at the very least urge that leaders of the state delegations, that the state party leaders, make every effort to see that they would be included as members of the delegation in adequate, fair, or whatever the word may be, representation of minority groups in the population.

McGovern informed Ranney that at the September meetings the commissioners said "it was not feasible to go on record for a quota system." Ranney backed down from his proposal. "I think that we would like to at least urge—I don't think we could require because that would mean quotas—but I would like to urge that members of minority groups be adequately, fairly, or whatever word we want to use, in the presence of the delegation," he said. Then McGovern, discarding his previous comment that the commissioners went on record opposing a quota system, responded, "Professor Ranney, one of the staff here suggests this language: We urge that the state parties make every effort to secure adequate representation of minority groups. Would that suit your purposes?" Ranney agreed to it and beamed with pride.

But a minute later Ranney's mood changed. "To my surprise, and this showed how naive I was," he recalled, "people said, 'Well, what about women? What about young people?' I was appalled. Young people and women weren't being discriminated against, and we didn't need any quotas for them." The first person who spoke out for adding a quota for women and youth was Fred Dutton, the bespectacled and balding former adviser to the Kennedys:

Mr. Chairman, I would say that . . . we ought to consider whether or not we should also represent and write some sort of adequate or fair representation for young people and for women and for ethnic groups. I just don't see how we separate one from two. I realize that the party has long been on record championing the right of the whole minority issues, but I think one of the important problems of the next decade will be that we try to bring in the young people. It's an important political base. It's a means substantively to bring about social change and frankly strengthening the reform elements within the party.

After a few commissioners commented on the proposals, Senator Birch Bayh of Indiana changed the terms of the debate. A tall, handsome man with a shock of dark hair, Bayh decided that Ranney's proposal was too timid. About to leave the meeting before a buzzer went off alerting him to a vote on the Senate floor, he proposed new language for guideline A-1:

To keep our party moving forward in this matter of racial equality, racial opportunity to participate with all due respect to Professor Ranney's proposal, I'm all for a moral statement; it's better than nothing. But if we leave it at there then I'm not sure we've moved much further than we are right now, if indeed we've moved at all. I don't think we can or we should, regard to the decision we had earlier, getting involved with requiring a group of Mexicans or blacks, but that certainly we could take the professor's motion as verbalized by the staff and add two or three words to sort of give a guideline that says that to meet this requirement that there could be some reasonable relationship between the representation of delegates and the representation of the minority group in the population of the state in question. This doesn't require. It doesn't make it absolute and I don't think it should, but it sort of gives a guideline that those who are in the process of setting up states can realize well, that we have to shoot for this target and think that if we don't do that we're not being very moral because we're not really putting the emphasis on behavior, how we make that morality a reality.

Several commissioners agreed with Bayh that "reasonable" is a better word than "adequate.' But commissioner Will Davis added that the language might be construed as a quota. Hearing Davis's remark, Fred Dutton jumped in once again:

Implicit in this discussion has appeared the word quota. I think we would strengthen our party, I think we would move ahead if we have some reasonable relationship for racial minorities, for ethnic groups, for women and for young people. There's no reason why our National Convention shouldn't have 50 percent women; it shouldn't have 10 or 15 percent young people. Well, you just have to face up to it and decide that we are going to change it, we are going to change the male domination and turn what people are afraid of in this quotas as it is applied to the racial groups, turn it around and make it an advantage, build in an appeal to women and to young people and the ethnic groups, where let's say much of the racial friction exists, assure them adequate representation, they're underrepresented in the national convention. I'm not for a specific quota but why shouldn't they have some reasonable relationship between their share of the population and their participation in our party at our national convention?

A few minutes later, Dutton explained one reason why bringing young people into the Democratic Party was vital:

[T]he 21 to 30 group is grossly underrepresented. It will be a very large group during the 1970s. They don't vote proportionately to the rest of the population but if the politicians in the next few years do with them what FDR did with the poor people, we've got millions of more voters in our political base and our society brings them into its regular processes and this is what we should be trying to accomplish here.

From Ranney's initial proposal, the debate among the commissioners had changed fundamentally. It was no longer just about urging state parties to include racial minorities. It was about requiring—mandating—that all state Democratic parties have a "reasonable" number of minorities, women, and young people. In other words, the commissioners were considering adopting an undemocratic measure. They were talking not about processes but about results.

After a few more members talked, commissioner Samuel Beer sought to address the room. Like Ranney, Beer was a leading light in the intellectual wing of the Democratic Party. He had written speeches for Roosevelt in the mid-1930s and now taught government at Harvard. As president of Americans for Democratic Action, Beer had written to delegates at the 1960 convention urging them to vote against the nomination of Lyndon Johnson for vice president. Now Beer came across, improbably, as the conservative:

> Mr. Chairman, I'd like to speak out against Fred Dutton's proposal most emphatically on the grounds that I think what we're doing here is usurping the function of the voters themselves. If the voters want more men than women, let them have them. If they want more old than young or vice versa, then they should have them. Now our charge is to eliminate discrimination, that's quite right so that we do eliminate it and give them a free chance to present themselves to the Democratic voters in a choice of delegates. It's not for us to say to the voters of a state, you've got to elect 50 percent women. If voters want 75 percent women or 75 percent men, it's up to them. It's not for us or the Democratic Party to change, to constrain, the choice of the voters with regard to age or sex or any of the like. Now I think that the best case can be made for black people, but we've passed over that. In the case of youth, young people, and women, I think it would be a great mistake and would make us look really ridiculous and would never work if we tried to say that you must have proportionate representation of young people and women in your convention.

Ranney endorsed Beer's position, as did commissioner George Mitchell. After two more members spoke, Dutton replied to Beer. He defended his women-and-young-people proposal not on the grounds that it would advance direct democracy, but rather that it would achieve good political results:

> The argument is bogus. He says the voters should have a choice. What we're trying to handle here is slate making in primary states and the county and state conventions. It is basically the situation where voters don't have a chance now and the reason we can keep the heavy domination by men is because the voters don't get involved in the act.... As far as the idea being ridiculous, I can't think of anything more attractive or a better way to get votes with

media politics than to have half of that convention floor in 1972 made up of women.... I think in the politics of 1970s the women's liberation movement is going to be almost, not quite as strong, as the black movement and I think politicians should recognize this before, not after the fact. The other thing is there are a lot more votes if we're talking about building a practical party group, we're talking about winning elections, we've got to provide the symbols, we've got to have the redistribution of power which will active women, which will appeal to women, which will active young people, which will appeal to them and this is a tangible device for doing just that.

After another half-hour of debate, McGovern called for a vote on guideline A-1, which Ranney sought to amend. It required state parties to choose minority delegates in "reasonable relationship to their presence in the state." The measure passed, 10 to 9. Voting in the guideline's favor were nearly all the members of the executive committee—David Mixner, Katherine Peden, Bill Dodds, Aaron Henry, and Dutton. (The votes of Don Fraser, LeRoy Collins, and Adlai Stevenson III went unrecorded.) McGovern declined to vote, while Harold Hughes opposed the measure on the grounds that it was too weak.

Before lunch, the commission got around to voting on A-2, the guideline proposed by Dutton. It required state parties to choose women and young people, defined as those between 18 and 30 years of age, in "reasonable relationship to their presence in the state." The measure passed, 13 to 7. McGovern and Fraser joined the five executive committee members who backed guideline A-1.

The executive committee was not the only part of the McGovern Commission leadership that played a pivotal role. So did Richard Wade, one of three consultants to the commission and an ally with McGovern. Wade later acknowledged, "I gave Bayh the 'reasonable relationship' language. I was worried about the blacks. There had been an earlier argument pushing percentage in the national Democratic vote instead. I was for that. The argument in the executive committee had broken this out on the basis of opposing quotas. 'Reasonable' was my word to get around quotas."

The New Politics activists had barged into the conductor's room, ordered the small group of men to release their hands from the party levers, and talked about driving the Democratic train down another track. Yet they had unintended help from other Democrats. The absence of I. W. Abel, president of the United Steelworkers of America, contributed to the passage of guideline A-1. In one interview Ranney said, "My opinion was that I believed then, as I do to this day, is that it was a tactical mistake. If he had been there, it would have made a difference."

In addition, chairman Fred Harris had allowed Mixner, who was supposed to have been a member of another party commission, to remain on the McGovern Commission. Due to a clerical error, Mixner received a telegram informing him that he was to join the commission; the telegram was supposed to have gone to Peter O'Toole, a youth activist rather than a former McCarthy campaign aide. "I talked to Eli, Anne, and Sam Brown, and we decided to take advantage of the slip-up," Mixner says today, chuckling at the thought. Ranney also played a vital role. Although he voted against guideline A-2, his vote for A-1 made the difference in its favor.

Even those who worked closely with Segal and Bode considered the informal quotas to be essentially alien to the cause of party reform. Joseph Gebhardt—now a civil rights lawyer in the Washington, D.C., area—admitted, "At the end, I felt there might be a conflict or a tension, a tension between mandatory quotas and getting an open process."

Actually, Gebhardt underestimated the significance of the changes. The soft quotas represented more than a conflict or tension. They confirmed that the New Politics activists had become old-style bosses.

FIVE

Power to the People—the Right Kind of People

Over the weekend of May 10–11, 1969, Fred Dutton concluded that the reformers were blowing their one shot to
bring real change to the Democratic Party.

Dutton was at his big house at 5316 Blackstone Road in
Westmoreland Hills, Maryland. Back in the early 1960s when
he was assistant secretary of state for congressional relations,
Dutton had used the house to lobby members of Congress. Invit-
ing key members of the House and the Senate for escabeche and
sweet-and-sour bean sprouts, which his wife had learned about
from a Peruvian maid, Dutton used an insider strategy to
advance the administration's agenda. "I like to keep things on a
social level," he once told a reporter. This strategy had worked
before. In 1963, Dutton played a key role in the passage of the
nuclear test ban treaty. But when applied to the McGovern Commission, an insider strategy did not work. Wooing Washington
insiders was one thing, but how do you lobby commissioners in
person when they are spread out around the country? Worse, the
reformers' outside strategy—using the media, activists, and
elected officials to lobby the non-reformers on the commission—
was not succeeding, either. In the past two weeks, the commission had held national hearings in Washington, in New York,
and in Detroit, and none had gotten major coverage in the *New
York Times*, the *Washington Post*, or the big magazines, much less
on the three TV networks. Eugene McCarthy, Teddy Kennedy,
and Edmund Muskie each had testified at the Washington

hearing without endorsing the principle that one-man, one-vote should govern the party's internal affairs, which reformers at the time thought was the key to the whole thing. The reformers lacked a live controversy with state party leaders or organizations resisting reform. Yes, the reformers could still lambaste the regulars over Chicago, but Humphrey's people were now telling other Democrats that they needed to stop beating that horse.

Dutton knew better than to start too late. Three years ago, he had taken over the campaign of his old boss, Governor Pat Brown of California, in the last five months of his race for re--election. Although even Rowland Evans and Robert Novak had praised him for turning things around, Brown had gone down the drain, to Ronald Reagan no less. Dutton didn't want a repeat of that fiasco. Flustered, he walked over to his typewriter and pounded out a 1,500-word memo to five members of the executive committee—McGovern, Harold Hughes, Bill Dodds, Bob Nelson, and Segal. Under the subject line "McGovern Commission 'Soup-Up,'" Dutton wrote:

> I believe the overall party reform effort is going to die aborning if it does not quickly show acceleration, flair, excitement [sic], personality, magic, etc. So far we are running like a dry creek. There is a great ground swell among the American people for a greater voice, a larger piece of the action, more participation and involvement in public affairs. That is true all the way from the far right and George Wallace's followers to the upward-mobile McCarthy middle class, the black community and most young people. But we are not getting on that wave and riding it with grace and effect, much less being wave-makers ourselves. We need controversy, a target, some appealing rhetoric—and quickly.

Despite the failure of the outsider strategy, Dutton rejected the idea of using an insider strategy. "What the Commission and staff are doing," he wrote, "will be useless if we do not catch on more broadly." Dutton recommended that reformers adopt an even more aggressive outsider strategy. He was chummy with plenty of journalists, and he believed that reformers had failed to give the press a clear and dramatic story line about the necessity of reform. "The real need is not just the usual press/TV releases," he wrote, "but several imaginative 'happenings' which indelibly get through to the country, conveying indignation, hope, expectation." To carry out this strategy, Dutton suggested that reformers consider nine tactics, such as getting "an articulate witness like Ken Galbraith to really scold the party" and recruiting senators who would deliver "a couple of fire-breathing speeches on the Senate floor in support of reform."

In trying to wrest control of the party machinery from the big-city and state bosses, Fred Dutton had one overarching goal: He wanted to change the Democratic Party's coalition. His goal was nothing less than to destroy the New Deal coalition, which had united the party around a broad, working-class agenda. In its place, he sought to create what he called a Social Change coalition, which would unite the party around the social, economic, and foreign policy concerns of young baby-boomers. "I'm a great believer in accelerating institutions, to the right or left," Dutton recalled. He was not one of those intellectuals who believed that the New Deal coalition had died already. In a book that he was wrapping up, which was published later as *Changing Sources of Power: American Politics in the 1970s,* he noted the "wobbling persistence of the Democratic coalition." He believed that the Democratic Party, in order to survive, had to embrace young people and students. In 1967 he had told Penn Kemble that "the coming of age of the World War II baby boomers" would "bring about in the years from 1968 to 1972 the biggest single revolution in U.S. voting."

Months before anyone had heard of Kevin Phillips' *The Emerging Republican Majority,* Dutton had already unveiled part of his agenda. He was a member of a commission subcommittee on party structure, which was to recommend how the Democratic National Committee should work with the state parties. The subcommittee chairman, LeRoy Collins, had written to the members to get their recommendations, and Dutton typed up a characteristically detailed response, dated April 22, 1969:

> With the profound alienation now apparent in this country, on the left, middle, and right, the party should harness the widespread want for involvement and participation by rank and file people in

the larger questions affecting their lives, including the full range of economic, social, bureaucratic, yes, and nuclear issues disturbing them. Fortunately, winning elections and giving expression to those insurgent impulses reinforce each other in the better educated, more affluent, and activist society. That is especially true among younger voters, black citizens, and college-educated suburbanites—three constituencies on which the Democratic Party must build as the lower middle class, blue-collar vote erodes. Some of that erosion is caused in a short-term sense by racial and generational tensions. But the traditional blue-collar base, while still very substantial politically, is disappearing over the long run by losing most of its children into a different political and social group with rising educational levels, affluence, and the greater cultural sophistication taking hold.

(Collins responded to Dutton's memo with a patronizing, three-sentence letter in which he said that Dutton's suggestions would "prove helpful.")

Others affiliated with the McGovern Commission also wanted to transform the Democratic Party. Anne Wexler and Eli Segal wanted to change the party's presidential nominating process. Their goal was to take control of the party machinery away from the bosses for the purpose of ensuring the nomination of a pro-peace nominee in 1972. "If you wanted to end the war, you had to change the [party] leadership," Wexler recalled. "So we came up with a way to pick our own delegates." To that end, they aimed to dismantle the boss nomination system, which since 1832 had enabled state party leaders to choose delegates and therefore the party's presidential nominee. In its place, they would build an activist nomination system, which would enable activists and voters to select the delegates and therefore the party's presidential candidate.

The leaders of the McGovern Commission were interested in more than trying to ensure that the presidential delegates who sat in the convention hall were elected through democratic procedures. They had their own agendas, which at times were unclear or concealed. Dutton, to his credit, was mostly upfront about his agenda. Although publicly silent about wanting to loosen the party's ties with blue-collar workers, he did speak at the November 19 commission meeting in favor of the soft quota for women and young people on the grounds that it would ally the party with the youth and women's liberation movements. As for Segal and Wexler, they hid their real agendas for years.

Meanwhile, most newspapers in 1969 described the goal of the McGovern Commission as opening up the party to participation by rank-and-file Democrats. The press never mentioned Dutton's statements. (Only two reporters, Carl Leubsdorf of the Associated Press and R. W. Apple of the *New York Times*, were present at the historic meeting.)

There were journalists who suspected that some commission leaders had ulterior motives; Robert E. Thompson of the *New York Herald-Examiner* wrote in June 1969 that a "relatively small, but highly determined, band of individuals" were trying "to convert the Democratic structure into a club restricted to the interests of the poor, the black and the young." But no journalists produced evidence to that effect.

The journalists missed a big story, because the agenda of the New Politics leaders was revolutionary. From 1932 to 1968, the Democratic Party had been united around the issue of economic inequality. The party had received the vast majority of its votes from two groups: Northern Catholics and Southern white Protestants. The party's presidential nomination process had been designed so that state party leaders would pick the nominee based on his ability to help the local ticket back home. Catholic bosses controlled the party's presidential wing and hence the party machinery. The party was a Catholic, Southern, and blue-collar party.

In the 1968 campaign, most Democrats recognized that the party had to change. The most important voice in this regard was Bobby Kennedy, the forty-two-year-old senator from New York. Kennedy believed that the party should reach out to new voters, but not at the expense of its old ones. He envisioned a "black-blue" or "have-not" coalition—an electoral alliance that added one new constituency, principally the young baby-boomers and opponents of the war, but did not downgrade the interests of two old constituencies, blue-collar workers and Catholics.

is: let them in. Give them the amount and kind of democracy that will tie them into the new Democratic coalition, but don't throw away the links and levers of the old coalition in doing so." Beer sent an amended version of his speech to Eli Segal.

Frustrated, Dutton changed course. In his letter to LeRoy Collins in April, he had rejected the use of quotas: "Whether special representation within party councils should be assured for substantial minority segments not able to rally a majority, as racial groups, younger people, and others, is a question on which I would like to hear more argument. Quotas are surely undesirable." But by the fall, he had embraced informal quotas. In April, Dutton had argued that Democrats must appeal to college-educated suburbanites, in addition to young people and blacks. By the fall, he was calling for "redistributing power" to the women's liberation movement.

Dutton changed his tactics not for ideological reasons, but for strategic ones. His long-term goal was to build a Democratic base among three constituencies while reducing the party's ties to blue-collar workers. But in the summer and fall, he worked with four people who also wanted to do more than democratize the party's nominating system: they wanted to achieve results at the 1972 Democratic convention. So while Dutton's main agenda was still to revolutionize the party over the long run, he allied with those who sought to change it in the short run.

—m—

THE THIRD SESSION of the 1968 Democratic convention in Chicago, on Wednesday, August 28, was bedlam. In the afternoon, the party's hawks and doves engaged in an unprecedented four-hour debate over the party's policy regarding the Vietnam War. In the evening, the Chicago Police and the National Guard went berserk, attacking thousands of antiwar protesters in the city's streets and parks with tear gas, clubs, and rifle butts.

Fred Dutton, one of the authors of the doves' plank, was nearly arrested by the Chicago Police. Jack Newfield of the *Village Voice* recounted the scene:

At the side entrance of the Hilton Hotel, four cops were chasing a frightened kid of about seventeen. Suddenly, Dutton moved out from under his marquee and interposed his body between the kid and the police.

"He's my guest in this hotel," Dutton told the cops.

The police started to club the kid.

Dutton screamed for the first cop's name and badge number. The cop grabbed Dutton and began to arrest him, until a *Washington Post* reporter identified him as a former RFK aide.

As an old man in 2003, eating lunch at the Prime Rib on Washington's K Street, Dutton mentioned that Norman Mailer had seen fit to include this scene in his book *Miami and the Siege of Chicago*. But the event had significance beyond its place in the work of a famous novelist. It crystallized Dutton's view of politics and of his place in the political world: The main dividing line in American politics was no longer between the poor and the rich or even the black and the white, but rather between the young and the old. And in this battle, he stood on the side of the kids.

Born on June 16, 1923, Frederick Gary Dutton was the son of a doctor from Julesburg, Colorado. During the Depression, the Dutton family had moved to California and Fred had graduated from the University of California at Berkeley and Stanford Law School. Having grown up affluent and educated, Dutton was never a Democrat of the blue-collar variety. Formerly the co-editor of the *Stanford Law Review,* he belonged to the intellectual wing of the party; his idol had been Adlai Stevenson, whose 1956 presidential campaign he had run in southern California. Nor did Dutton form close ties with union leaders or party bosses. Although he had befriended California chieftain Jesse Unruh, his interactions with most bosses had been negative.

Dismayed by the presidential wing of the party, Dutton blamed the bosses for creating the military-industrial complex. His own experience in wartime had been decidedly unromantic. As a twenty-two-year-old infantryman, he fought for two months in the snow at the Battle of the Bulge, was captured by German forces on January 5, 1945, and spent the next sixteen weeks in a German prisoner-of-war camp. In his mid-thirties, Dutton became a judge advocate general in the Korean War and spent time "fighting a desk" in Japan. When he joined the federal government as an aide in the Kennedy and Johnson administrations, he jumped at the chance to limit the military's reach. Aside from his work on the nuclear test ban treaty, whose passage he considered his greatest accomplishment, he had helped write the few peacenik speeches that Johnson delivered in the 1964 campaign. Dutton faulted Lyndon Johnson and Hubert Humphrey for the Vietnam War. According to *An American Melodrama: The Presidential Campaign of 1968,* Humphrey in July 1968 had tried to recruit Dutton for his presidential campaign. Dutton, disdainful of Humphrey's tepid stance on the war, turned him down. Before and during the Chicago convention, he spent weeks drafting the minority peace plank.

In addition to his moral qualms about the regular party, Dutton questioned the party's political future. He believed that the pocketbook issue, which had carried the Democrats into the majority, was now diminished. It had not helped Pat Brown in his race against Ronald Reagan. Nor had it helped Humphrey in his campaign against Nixon.

Despite his doubts about the party, Dutton was hardly a typical New Politics activist. In 1968, he had not sided with McCarthy, whose overriding issues had been party reform and opposition to the war. Rather, he had been the de facto campaign manager for Bobby Kennedy.

Dutton was also viewed as a regular Democrat, and an extremely able one at that. RFK had called him "one of the best political brains in America"; President Johnson got on his phone to solicit Dutton's advice; Pat Brown once told Johnson that Dutton was one of the party's best strategists. Their praise was understandable. Besides having worked in the Kennedy and Johnson administrations, Dutton had held numerous top jobs with the Democratic National Committee in 1964, including the job of writing the party platform. He had even worked in the final month of the 1968 campaign for Humphrey, after being assured of Humphrey's commitment to ending the war.

As a result of his impressive resumé, Dutton was an automatic choice for membership on the McGovern Commission.

Yet Fred Dutton in 1969 was anything but a Roosevelt or even a Bobby Kennedy Democrat. While he did not think of himself as a part of the New Politics or New Left movements, some members of the press, such as Richard Harwood of the *Washington Post*, identified him in 1968 as the chief theoretician of the New Politics, the intellectual counterpart to the student hero Allard Lowenstein. And they were right to do so.

Dutton sympathized increasingly with the New Politics. He had three teenage children from his first marriage, two of whom were college students. He had befriended Paul Schrade, the cofounder of the New Democratic Coalition who had been wounded by Sirhan's bullets in Los Angeles. And his outlook was secular; though his parents had been raised Christian, they had not brought up their children in the faith. An agnostic as an adult, Dutton believed in striving toward the goal of human autonomy. Writing in *Changing Sources of Power,* he expressed support for the secular aims of activist students: "Most of them also dispute the special emphasis on Christianity, the right of parents, teachers, and public officials to make decisions for others, and the essential decency of the present society."

What radicalized Dutton was his time on an unlikely training ground for leaders of the New Politics: the Board of Regents of the University of California, on which he had served since 1962. "So many [of the older Kennedy aides] really would have clung to the old politics as it was," Dutton recalled in a 1969 interview. "The idea of participation and involvement, the critiques of the New Left, they weren't very aware of them. I probably wouldn't have been except through my exposure out in Berkeley in intensive doses."

As one of twenty-two regents on the board, Fred Dutton championed the interests of students—not the sons and daughters of the working classes who attended junior and state colleges, but rather the elite students, the children of the professional and managerial classes. In accordance with the University of California's Master Plan for Higher Education, the UC schools were not like those in most state systems, but rather were comparable to Ivy League schools. The best-known campuses, Cal-Berkeley and UCLA, accepted only those students who had graduated in the top eighth of their high school class. They awarded Ph.D.s and took students from around the country. By contrast, the state colleges, such as San Jose State and Cal State Sacramento, accepted students in the top third of their graduating class and only from California.

When the student protest movements on the UC campuses began, Dutton did not view the students as spoiled children of privilege, as most Californians did. He saw them as victims of an oppressive political establishment. The kids in 1964 wanted free speech—and were forced to leave Sproul Plaza. The kids wanted to protest the war in the mid-sixties by occupying campus buildings—and were hit with billy clubs. The kids in 1969 wanted a park of their own—and the National Guard attacked them with pepper spray and tear gas. "I see the kids coming to us on the board and they can't get through to us," Dutton said in a June 1969 interview. "They get silence, so I've been getting an education myself—the popular word is radicalization—because I see the older society beating up kids for no reason."

Dutton supported the kids during the Free Speech Movement in 1964 and the various sit-ins of the late 1960s; and he made an unprecedented proposal in September 1967 to raise $40 million for the UC system, mainly from outside sources, while keeping student fee increases to a minimum. Dutton defended the students principally against Reagan, who in 1966 had made a campaign issue of "the mess at Berkeley." Dutton also became a spokesman for students' values. When the National Guard and thirty thousand students battled over the use of People's Park during Memorial Day weekend in 1969, he explained the students' actions to Nicholas von Hoffman of the *Washington Post.* "The park is cultural escalation. It's the kids telling us to keep our hands off their private lives, their shacking-up arrangements, their games," he said. "Harvard will have a park in eight months. This will be as important as the Free Speech Movement was. The park is symbolically very important."

Dutton viewed baby-boomers as the political wave of the future. "I believed, at least in '66—and I get it, I think, from being on the Board of Regents at the University of California— that tremendous change has gone on in the kids, and so forth like that," he said in an interview on November 18, 1969. "I think it's a healthy thing, a desirable thing. Even if it isn't, politicians better learn to channel it and direct it and exploit and prosper from it and so forth like that."

Dutton's political assessment was exaggerated, but it did spring from a coherent worldview. Like James Rowe Jr., he believed deeply in the modernization thesis: that affluence, education, and the media were bringing America into a new postindustrial age. Consequently, the nature of politics had changed; cultural and social issues now trumped economic ones. The nature of political expression had changed too. On a radio program marking the first anniversary of Robert Kennedy's assassination, Dutton said that "the newer political faces are all men who feel that it's better to stand up and say what they believe. We now have the politics of principle, I think, more than of pragmatism. We have the politics of confrontation rather than compromise and copping out.... " The younger men, he said, "feel that they must plunge into the hard questions, they must take on the Vietnam War if necessary, they must take on poverty."

Dutton knew how to build an alternative Democratic coalition. He had built one before, and not just with Bob Kennedy in 1968. In 1960, he had been the deputy national chairman of Citizens for Kennedy and Johnson, an organization that was independent of the Democratic National Committee. "Our primary function," he recalled in an August 1969 interview, "was to broaden the base, to pull in conservatives and independents and things like that." Eight years after his initial foray in coalition building, Dutton believed he had matured. He had developed intellectually, gained an understanding of history, and acquired a sense of where the country was headed.

Now Dutton was on the brink of revolutionizing the Democratic Party. And he would do so with an idea very different from those of Thomas Jefferson, Andrew Jackson, and Franklin Roosevelt. They believed that the heart of the party should be the working class. Fred Dutton believed it should be college-- educated young people.

—⚍—

AS A RESULT OF his experiences on the UC Board of Regents, Fred Dutton believed that the Democratic Party should do more than accommodate young people. He believed that it should scrap its broad working-class agenda. In its place, he argued, the party should create an agenda aimed at college-educated baby- boomers. In *Changing Sources of Power,* which he dedicated to "all the young people who will be voting for the first time in this decade," he explained why this was advisable:

> The hard fact is that the approach of the new generation contains irreversible pressures for a sweeping reappraisal of some of the most basic goals, methods, and power arrangements of liberalism and the national Democratic Party. At a deeper level than the histri- onics at the 1968 Democratic National Convention, bitter fights and basic changes in the Democratic coalition are likely inevitable during the seventies, with trouble-breeding dissatisfaction certain to persist whatever the outcome of the first round. No rhetoric or self-reassuring can extricate Democrats from the fateful family brawl they face sooner or later. One of the party's main con- stituencies for a number of decades has been younger voters, and it will soon be larger than ever before. Like all other political move- ments, the Democratic Party will have to go to this natural source of support, not wait for the increasingly independent young vote to come to it. The exhorting verbalisms and limp handholding of the past are simply no longer enough.

Dutton left no room for nuance or subtlety on the matter: If Democrats failed to change their political agenda, they would rue their decision for generations:

> The politics of the seventies offer one of those rare chances to rally a new following, or at least to provoke a different configuration, out of this immense sector of young voters who are still at an impressionable and responsive stage. If an exciting individual or

cause really stirs this generation, it could be activated in numbers that make irrelevant any past indicator of political participation among the young, and it would then become one of the few human waves of historic consequence. If this still un-marshaled mass is allowed to scatter, or a substantial part of it is politically turned off, it will pass as one of the great lost opportunities in American politics and history.... The full potential of the new generation of voters is perhaps best indicated by the fact that the opening of every major realignment in U.S. political history has been accompanied by the coming of a large new group into the electorate and a fundamental shaping of the voting populace.

In short, Dutton foresaw a Democratic Party in which young people's interests trumped those of blue-collar workers. His vision derived from the New Left, which had emerged after World War II as a response to the growing affluence of Western society. Where the Old Left had embraced unskilled workers or the proletariat, the New Left extolled students. The best-known New Left organization in the 1960s was Students for a Democratic Society. Although the New Left had failed to create a successful third political party, its supporters managed to build a mainstream spin-off movement, the New Politics movement.

Though not originally allied with either the Democrats or the Republicans, New Politics activists gained more clout in the Democratic Party. In 1967, Allard Lowenstein, a former president of the National Student Association, organized an effort to dump President Johnson from the Democratic ticket. In the same year, Lowenstein convinced McCarthy to challenge Johnson. After McCarthy lost at Chicago, the chairman of his Wisconsin campaign, Don Peterson, cofounded the appropriately named New Democratic Coalition. As the most prominent New Politics organization in 1969, the NDC sought to build an alliance of campus, ghetto, and suburb within the Democratic Party. "We will formulate criteria by which to test Democratic aspirants for public office," the organization's statement of political purpose declared. "Does the candidate oppose the foul, brutalizing, pointless war in Vietnam? Does he seek dramatic, remedies for the foul, brutalizing, pointless institutions of racism

and economic deprivation? Does he support the grape boycott? Does he oppose Gestapo attacks on the Black Panther
movement?"

Like other leaders of the New Politics, Dutton did not want
to purge Catholics and blue-collar workers from the Democratic
Party. He just wanted to relegate them to secondary status in a
new Democratic coalition—to make them reserves rather than
starters on the team. The Democratic Party, he wrote in his April
1969 letter to LeRoy Collins, must appeal to "younger voters,
black citizens, and college-educated suburbanites ... as the
lower-middle class, blue-collar vote erodes."

Even so, Dutton's vision departed dramatically from those of
most Democratic strategists. To be sure, there was broad recognition that after 1968 the party's coalition needed to include
young people. Among those who said so were Richard Scammon
and Ben Wattenberg in *The Real Majority: An Extraordinary Exam-
ination of the American Electorate,* Jack Newfield and Jeff Greenfield in *A Populist Manifesto: The Making of a New Majority,* Fred
Harris in *Now Is the Time: A New Populist Call to Action,* and
Michael Novak in *The Rise of the Unmeltable Ethnics: The New
Political Force of the Seventies.* But none of these authors argued
that the Democratic Party in so doing should dilute the influence of blue-collar workers and Catholics. Indeed, most party
strategists argued that the white working class should continue
to occupy a central place in the party's agenda. "The real division
in this country," Newfield and Greenfield wrote, "is not between
generations or between races, but between the rich who have
power and those blacks and whites who have neither power nor
property." In a similar vein, Novak called for an agenda aimed
at family and neighborhood concerns. Few Democratic thinkers
believed that catering to campus youth was the prescription for
the party's future.

Dutton justified his decision to choose young people over
blue-collar workers on two grounds. First, he portrayed young
baby-boomers as more moral than the white working class.
Emphasizing college students' commitment to individualism and
racial equality, he wrote in *Changing Sources of Power* that

the prospective political energy in this generation is suggested by the fact that even before coming to maturity, its vanguard members helped set the pace for the two predominant controversies of the last decade: the civil rights struggle and the Vietnam war protests. These young people have also forced the most searching reappraisal of higher education in the U.S. since the borrowings from the German universities in the last quarter of the last century. And the concern of this group with the college environment has been political as much as educational in nature.

Dutton regarded baby-boomers as egocentric but also "significantly more social and less economic" than previous generations. He believed they were best suited to solving the country's big problems—the population explosion, environmental pollution, and the specter of nuclear war.

By contrast, Dutton argued, the white working class unjustly opposed the social and cultural interests of college-educated young people:

> The principal group arrayed against the forces of change is the huge lower-middle-income sector—"working America," made up of almost twenty-five million white families whose breadwinners are typically white-collar clerks and blue-collar workers. The left has long held as a testament of faith that "the workers" are the main historical agents of social progress, but an important portion of this group is now providing the most tenacious resistance to further broadening the country's social, economic, and political base. Having gained a larger share of power institutionally during the last third of a century, this sector generally opposes—more accurately, is anxious about and therefore against—much additional change.

It is true that Dutton was no limousine liberal, oblivious to the interests of hardhats. He grasped that the working class continued to face economic anxiety, lacked adequate health care, and bore a disproportionate share of soldiers killed in Vietnam. But he contended that blue-collar workers nevertheless were intolerant and bigoted, treating "the beards and the blacks much as scapegoats have been used throughout history—viciously and indifferently at the same time."

There was another reason that Dutton elevated young people over blue-collar workers. He saw baby-boomers, ironically, as politically analogous to blue-collar workers and urban voters in the 1930s: that is, as the constituency that would make the Democrats the majority party. Twenty-five million new voters were eligible in 1972, another 16 million were by 1976, and an additional 18 million by 1980. Because they were more educated and affluent than their predecessors, Dutton concluded, they were more likely to vote. He did acknowledge that young voters, especially those 18 to 24 years old, were less likely to vote than their older counterparts, but he expected that their ranks would continue to grow. Yet he also recognized that because many baby-boomers were economically conservative and culturally liberal, they could move to the Republican Party en masse. Republicans, he wrote, "actually have a rare opportunity with the new voters as a result of the unmistakable individualism and resistance to big government among much of the new generation, including its most active members."

Blue-collar workers, on the other hand, were fading politically, Dutton said. For one thing, education and affluence were making them less likely to vote on economic issues alone. Dutton remarked that "a 'union man' not long ago connoted a craftsman or factory worker who lived in a crowded section of an industrial town, worked long hours, had little free time, and could generally claim only elementary school training. The union man of the 1970s must far more often be thought of as a leisure-seeking suburbanite with a high school education and a strong concern about his own identity and status." At the same time, he said in an August 1969 interview, education, television, and affluence were "wiping out the intermediate power brokers"— unions, political machines, and vast government patronage. In consequence, blue-collar workers were losing their affiliation with the Democratic Party. Some were becoming political independents. Others were splitting their votes between the two parties. "The Democrats are down from a clear majority during the Roosevelt years to around 45 percent; and that overstates the Democratic strength, since a larger percentage of registered Democrats than Republicans usually defects in elections nationwide," Dutton wrote, adding that the share of voters who considered themselves independents rose from one-fifth in the 1930s to more than one-fourth in the 1970s.

Most Democratic thinkers disagreed with Dutton's moral and political conclusions. Perhaps because they saw a broader spectrum of young people or wrote at a later stage of the counterculture, the strategists viewed 18-to-30-year-olds in less gauzy terms. Many young people, they argued, were more decadent and irresponsible than idealistic. Newfield and Greenfield, both of whom had supported the New Politics, argued that "those of us who have spent even a modest amount of time in the East Village, Taos, Berkeley, or Madison, Wisconsin, have seen a darker shade of greening: fifteen-year-old runaways strung out on dope; syphilis and gonorrhea becoming epidemic; heroin and methadrine addicts turning the countercommunities into jungles; minds destroyed by LSD; rock music and its artifacts controlled by conglomerate corporations and hucksters in wide ties and love beads; Abbie Hoffman ripping off his friends and companions out of book royalties."

As for Catholics and working-class whites, the strategists portrayed them as frequent victims of crime and poor workplace conditions. Indeed, several emphasized that Catholics should continue to play a large role in the party's affairs. As Newfield and Greenfield noted, "The Irish cop on the low end of the middle-income scale living in Brooklyn's Bay Ridge need not embrace the black family in Harlem or the Italian-American homeowner in Corona to know his kids are stuck with the same bad schools, dirty streets, and dangerous parks." Going further, Michael Novak argued that the Democratic Party should form a coalition of blacks and white ethnics that united the two groups' economic and social interests. "A coalition of blacks and ethnics will be inherently more stable than a coalition between intellectuals and blacks," he contended. "For the real interests of blacks and ethnics—homes, neighborhoods, services, schools, jobs advancement, status—are virtually identical; whereas the political interests of intellectuals are mainly those of a consciousness that can easily and often, as blacks well recognize, be false."

Other Democratic thinkers made political arguments on behalf of blue-collar workers. Where Dutton placed his hopes in the future, the strategists argued that working-class whites already made up a majority of voters. As Scammon and Wattenberg pointed out, most voters were "unyoung, unpoor, and unblack." Even Fred Harris agreed:

> Though some of the best progressive voices in America are among the affluent and most educated, and their support and ideas, as well as the energy and idealism of young people, are irreplaceable components in the construction or reconstruction of a Democratic majority, there simply cannot be a mass movement without the masses. And for the Democrats, those masses necessarily include both lower- and middle-income whites and blacks and brown people and other minorities. Without them, there is no way to count up a majority.

Dutton rejected such views as short-term political thinking. But he recognized that if the Democratic Party placed the interests of young people over those of working-class whites, the party would no longer be the Party of the Little Guy.

Dutton concluded that the party would need to adopt a new coalition. His preference was for a Social Change coalition, which would be composed of college-educated suburbanites, blacks, and liberated women, in addition to young people. Dutton acknowledged that these voting blocs would not merge automatically. Many white-collar workers would still vote Republican, just as many blue-collar workers would continue to vote Democratic. Even so, he expected that these two economic classes over time would change their political allegiances. "The seventies," he wrote, "should witness the steady growth of the social-change coalition even in the face of the built-in delays and undeniable reaction currently being felt."

Dutton saw college-educated whites as the gateway to the suburbs. He knew that Democrats could compete there. His friend and fellow commissioner Jack English had built a successful party in Nassau County, New York. Extending the party's reach to other suburbs was vital, Dutton recognized.

"Already, they wield the kind of political influence once held by the rural culture symbolized by the log cabin, then by the small town and then, with Franklin Roosevelt, by the big city," he stated. By 1980, two-fifths of the nation's population would reside in suburbs, up from one-fifth in 1940. He added that suburban voters also tended to be younger, better educated, and more prosperous than other Americans. "All economic and education projections," he concluded, "point to the rapid enlargement of the more 'liberated' sector."

Dutton viewed blacks as a natural partner with white liberals. "If Negroes have a broad-based potential ally," he noted, "it is the active vanguard of better-educated, young white Northerners coming of age." Dutton believed that unless a liberal candidate actively campaigned for their vote, too few blacks would show up at the polls. But if sufficient numbers of blacks did vote, they often put Democratic candidates over the top.

Dutton also ascertained that the ranks of "liberated" women would grow. "The much-publicized women's liberation movement is only the grossly exaggerated tip of a more fundamental and solidly based development," he wrote. "If the present trend continues, nearly 50 percent [of women] could be so employed by the end of the decade, and they would make up a third of the labor force."

Dutton believed that for this new coalition to take form, the Democratic Party would need to adopt a new agenda. To appeal to voters, Democrats could no longer focus on economic inequality. "Even in traditional economic terms," he wrote, "the great struggles of the past for working conditions, workmen's compensation, unemployment benefits, minimum wages, the right to organize and similar economic legislation have lost much of their pulling power." Instead, the party would have to campaign and govern on three other goals: opposition to the war, support for the post-civil-rights agenda of blacks, and support for most byproducts of the cultural revolution.

As for college-educated suburbanites, Dutton saw them as morally equivalent to blue-collar workers in the 1930s. They were making American life less repressive and more individualistic.

But unlike the white working classes, which had succeeded in extending economic opportunity, white-collar suburbanites were liberating the country culturally and socially:

> The cultural revolution since the mid-sixties has further aggravated the estrangement between the more prosperous sector on one side and the lower-middle class on the other. The middle and lowbrow cultures have been losing key battles to the avant-garde strain formerly confined mostly to artists and the wealthy. That culture has unquestionably been prostituted as it gained broader influence, often turning quickly into commercial clichés, a factor that only indicates the extent of its acceptance. In the most fundamental sense, this spreading cultural upheaval has become a powerful long-term generation of experimentation, protest, freedom, individualism and—the binding thread—change.

Using survey data from 1968, Dutton compared the views of low-income whites with those of college-educated whites on six questions: open housing, paying more taxes to reduce pollution, giving cities more money to tear down the ghettos, foreign aid, antiwar demonstrators, and whether "liberals, long-hairs, and intellectuals have been running the country too long." On each question, only one-quarter to two-fifths of poor whites gave a liberal answer, while more than half to two-thirds of college--educated whites did so.

Dutton's case for blacks was primarily moral. He saw blacks as victims of centuries of racism, bigotry, and oppression. To him, white fears about black crime were exaggerated and misplaced; he said that whites should be concerned far more about drunken drivers than black criminals. Though acknowledging that blacks were increasingly literate and prosperous, he emphasized that they continued to face disparities with whites in areas such as employment status, household income, and health. "The racial prospect is still grim," he concluded in *Changing Sources of Power*. "For both blacks and whites it is causing political and social discord, economic loss, physical violence, and a deepening pessimism that goes beyond will and moral character to challenge the American system's very capacity to do much about its most pressing human dilemma."

Blue-collar workers would not be the only losers in the new Democratic Party. Given the emphasis on cultural and social liberalism, Dutton recognized that Catholics could not be full members of a Social Change coalition. He did understand that Catholics were a key constituency of Bobby Kennedy's; in November 1969 he said that the "fundamental explanation" for Kennedy's loss in the Oregon primary was that "there was not a big black population, not a big Catholic population, not problems, things like that." He also acknowledged in *Changing Sources of Power* that "the Catholic vote" had consistently supported Democratic presidential candidates since the 1930s. But Dutton believed that on moral and political grounds the Democratic Party should loosen its ties with Catholics. (He was not operating from any anti-Catholic motives; his father was baptized into the faith.)

Citing figures from the 1966 and 1968 elections, he contended that too many Catholic voters had swung toward the Republicans in bellwether states. Although these Catholics had defected in opposition to liberal racial policies, Dutton believed that Catholic voters would also leave the party in opposition to the youth movement. "The net effect of these groups in relation to the dynamic of social change has become vastly different from thirty or sixty years ago," he wrote, referring to white ethnics who opposed racially integrated neighborhoods and the permissive youth culture. "Then they were a wellspring of cultural diversity and political change; now they constitute an important bastion of opposition. They have tended, in fact, to become a major redoubt of traditional Americanism and of the anti-Negro, anti-youth vote."

—⟋⟍—

ON THE SAME DAY that Fred Dutton emerged as a symbolic champion of young baby-boomers, Anne Wexler lost her sympathy for the party bosses. Even after the Connecticut Democratic convention in June 1968, Wexler had maintained respect for party leaders, especially for John Bailey. But on the Wednesday of the Chicago convention, her lingering respect for them turned to disgust. In the afternoon, after the minority peace plank was defeated on the convention floor, Wexler felt betrayed. She believed like other McCarthyites that the bosses had torpedoed all their efforts. Leaning on the shoulders of one of the British authors of *An American Melodrama,* Wexler sobbed, "They got us in a corner and did this to us." In the evening, after Senator Abraham Ribicoff denounced the "Gestapo tactics" of Mayor Daley's police, she exulted that her fellow Connecticut Democrat had stood up to a major party boss. On the bus home from the convention that night, Wexler, a dignified woman with a bouffant hairdo and a degree from Skidmore College, talked like a battle-hardened campaign veteran: "I'm going to get everyone to work their guts out for Abe for what he said tonight."

Even before Chicago, Wexler and Segal had discussed overthrowing the bosses. *The Democratic Choice,* the report of the commission that both had helped bring into existence, had noted the discontent of antiwar forces with the party chieftains: "As delegates assemble for the 1968 Democratic National Convention, the demand for more direct democracy and the call for an end to 'boss control' of the nominating machinery can be heard, with an intensity not matched since the Progressive Era." But the Wednesday of the Chicago convention was a conversion experience for Wexler, as Tuesday had been for Segal. They changed overnight from peace Democrats to New Politics Democrats. Wexler became an at-large member of the New Democratic Coalition. Segal by his own admission became a reform Democrat.

As devotees of the New Politics, Wexler and Segal worked for the same overall agenda as Fred Dutton. Although there is no record that they agreed to build a Social Change coalition, they aided his cause indirectly. (All three had been affiliated with the Harold Hughes Commission.) They worked to create a presidential nomination process in which the issue of economic inequality took a back seat to that of opposing the war. In practice, their efforts changed the priorities of the presidential wing of the Democratic Party. The interests of blue-collar workers—the "little people" in Franklin Roosevelt's phrase—would no longer occupy pride of place. Instead, those of baby-boomers and college-educated liberals would take center stage.

Wexler and Segal aided Dutton's agenda in three ways. First, they sought to depose the bosses, who helped protect the party's working-class agenda. Reducing the power of the bosses meant reducing the power of their blue-collar and Catholic constituents. To be fair, Wexler and Segal's goal was broadly similar to the mandate of the McGovern Commission: to create a largely "unbossed" presidential nomination system. At a minimum, state Democratic leaders would have to do two things: choose their delegates in the calendar year of the convention and not impose the unit rule on their delegations. But the commission ended up requiring much more.

Eight of the McGovern Commission's final eighteen recommendations were designed to ensure the participation of Democratic voters. The most important requirement was guideline A-5, which mandated that state parties provide adequate information to the public about when and where their presidential delegates would be chosen. The staff discovered that ten states had no written rules at all about the delegate selection process, while another ten states had rules that were virtually inaccessible. Another key requirement was guideline C-1, mandating that states identify which presidential candidate a delegate supported. Ten states, including the boss-dominated parties in Illinois and Pennsylvania, had failed to do this in 1968.

Wexler and Segal, as well as Ken Bode, fought for most of those eight requirements. On July 13, Segal wrote a one-page memo to Bode in which he expressed concern about "inadequate state provisions for voting hours and allowing workers to secure leave from their jobs in order to vote."

But Wexler and Segal were not exactly Jacksonian or Jeffersonian Democrats. They viewed direct democracy as unrefined and liable to be swayed by the passions of the mob. For example, *The Democratic Choice* supported a variety of delegate-selection methods, on the grounds that "no particular mechanism, such as the presidential primary, is necessarily the best or the only way to guarantee the people's right to participate in the process of

choosing delegates, or their right to have their preference represented by the delegates who are chosen." The commission consultant Alexander Bickel, a former member of the Harold Hughes
Commission, was also skeptical of direct democracy. In 1968 he
had written a slim book, *The New Age of Political Reform,* arguing
that direct democracy neglected the importance of debate and
compromise. As a result, Segal and Wexler merely urged state
parties to provide for easy access and frequent opportunity for
party enrollment by unaffiliated voters and non-Democrats, a
toothless recommendation that the commission adopted.

The second way that Wexler and Segal helped Dutton's
agenda was in aiming to shift power from the bosses to *activists,*
from the pros to amateurs, from the politicians to true believers.
Both recognized that the activists were more likely than ordinary Democratic voters to agree that opposing the war was more
important than upholding the party's working-class agenda.
Since the Montgomery bus boycott in 1955, activists had capti-
vated the liberal imagination with their opposition to racial segregation and the military-industrial complex, rather than
economic inequality. (Jack Newfield in 1966 wrote a reverential
book about New Left activists titled *A Prophetic Minority.*) *The
Democratic Choice* implied that liberal enthusiasts had different
priorities from those of ordinary Democratic voters: "Issue-
oriented individuals who rank relatively abstract ideological
questions high among the criteria by which they approve or dis-
approve of candidates have become a substantial part of the electorate, as the Vietnam War has shown."

Segal and Wexler's decision flowed naturally from their ideology. They believed in participatory democracy, which relies
heavily on activists. Although similar to direct democracy, participatory or grassroots democracy differs in one crucial respect:
Whereas direct democracy lodges power in voters, participatory
democracy lodges power in enthusiastic voters or activists. In
states that hold caucus elections, citizens cannot simply show
up at a polling booth to cast a ballot for a candidate, as they can
in a primary election. They must also deliberate with others face
to face about which delegates and candidates should be chosen.
"I prefer a system where people get together and talk about the

candidates," Segal said in a 2003 interview. "I think that pro-
duces a higher-quality nominee." Interestingly, Wexler did not
anticipate that activists and affluent voters would dominate the
primary-and-caucus system. "What you have now, what the
reform created, is hardcore committed ideological folks [who
participate] and people in the middle," she said, chuckling rue-
fully, "who don't really do much."

Indeed, Wexler and Segal showed their greatest concern for
the participation of Democratic activists. On this matter, they
found the strongest resistance from the commission members,
most of whom were not allied with the New Politics. So Wexler
and Segal joined forces whenever possible with members of the
executive committee. They won six key victories. The commission banned state parties from imposing the unit rule on delegates (guideline B-5); banned the use of ex officio delegates
(C-2); required state parties to choose three-quarters of their
presidential delegates at the district level or below (B-7); and
required any slate-making body to provide adequate public
notice, easy access to participation, and the right to challenge
the result (C-6).

Third, Wexler and Segal aided Dutton's agenda by never
putting their collective foot down on his proposal to require soft
quotas for minorities, women, and young people as delegates.
Segal viewed himself as a change agent, not a rock thrower. "It
has always intrigued me," he wrote to Senator Bayh, "how prepared we are to overlook the fact that the 'founding fathers' were
first and foremost political animals—devising a scheme which
was *workable* in the context of the late 19th century, and not a
scheme which was *ideal.*" Writing to the executive editor of
Harper's magazine with a proposal to write a story about the
state of American political parties in 1969, he summarized his
goals for the commission and his view of politics: "Party reform
is dictated by expediency as much as by conscience."

Segal was pragmatic on the issue of soft quotas for delegates.
Like McGovern, he voiced opposition to hard racial quotas at a
commission meeting in September. But he was not necessarily
opposed to soft or informal quotas for certain groups. On June
12, he concluded in a draft report that "while it is necessary that

minority groups such as racial, religious, ethnic, and economic groups be fairly represented, practical considerations preclude that minorities always have delegates in proportion to their numbers." And at a commission meeting in September, he declined to comment when member Will Davis proposed that the commission repudiate quotas. "As sure as we're sitting here today, you're going to have challenges at the next national convention against state delegations that do not meet a rigid quotas system," Davis said. "If states are not going to be subject to that sort of test, then we ought to tell them that." The staff and other commissioners said nothing.

—॥॥—

WAKING UP LATE ON the morning of July 20, 1969, with the sunlight streaming in on his face, George McGovern felt that he might well be the Democratic Party's presidential nominee in 1972. As he recalled in his autobiography, *Grassroots*, McGovern was staying at the home of Henry Kimelman, a friend and political contributor, in the Virgin Islands. After his brief bid in 1968, McGovern assumed that he would run for president again. In fact, he and Kimelman had been talking about his presidential prospects for several days when a friend arrived on July 19. She said that Senator Ted Kennedy had been involved in a serious accident; his car had gone off a bridge and the young woman accompanying him had drowned. With the party's presumptive nominee effectively out of the race, McGovern liked his chances of winning the nomination. After flying back to Washington, the forty-seven-year-old senator told his aides, "It's a whole new ballgame."

McGovern asked Kimelman to host a small dinner for a dozen or so Democrats at his home on California Street. He wanted to ask them what type of campaign he should mount for 1972. Of those invited, four were apostles of the New Politics—Allard Lowenstein, Blair Clark, David Mixner, and Fred Dutton. McGovern's chief conclusion after listening to his guests on August 4 was that he needed to widen his base of supporters. In a letter to Arthur Schlesinger Jr. dated August 8, he said, "I intend to do what I can to broaden my understanding in those areas where I am weak and seek to increase my national constituency." Other participants at the dinner were more forthright. "He told the group he was interested in the Democratic presidential nomination in 1972," one of the men said to the *Boston Globe.* "He was told that if he thinks that Muskie was the established candidate of the party then he must become the 'high risk' candidate, one who would speak as a reform candidate in the party, who would represent the liberals of the party." On September 29 in Nashua, New Hampshire, McGovern announced, "If no one speaks out against the issues as I have, then I shall seek the nomination."

George McGovern's decision to add to his political base may not sound like an important event in the history of the Democratic Party. But it was important because he was agreeing to help Fred Dutton build a Social Change coalition.

Until that dinner at the Kimelman home, McGovern had been more of a populist-intellectual Democrat than a Eugene McCarthy Democrat. He had never been really trusted by McCarthy supporters. After Bobby Kennedy was assassinated, McGovern not only refused to endorse McCarthy but ran against him. "Worst of all," recalled Lanny Davis, a McCarthy backer, in his book *The Emerging Democratic Majority,* McGovern appeared "on the platform with his arm around Hubert Humphrey the night he was nominated in Chicago—just at the time that Mayor Daley's police were at the height of their police riot on the streets of Chicago." McGovern was well aware of the McCarthyites' anger toward him. "I never had the slightest doubt who I'd support, Humphrey or Nixon. The McCarthy people felt differently. They thought the system was stacked against them."

Davis's perceptions were not far off. McGovern had not thought of himself as a reform Democrat. When asked by DNC chairman Fred Harris on January 31 whether he would be willing to head the reform commission, McGovern said that he needed to mull it over. "I didn't think [party reform] made much difference," McGovern told Byron Shafer in *Quiet Revolution.* "Procedural questions were always secondary to merging opposition in Congress and in the country to the war."

McGovern took the job after Richard Wade convinced him that he could build a constituency among not only antiwar Democrats but also regular Democrats. McGovern believed he could balance the interests of these divergent groups. At a public commission hearing in Washington on April 22, he had said, "procedural reforms can never substitute for our party's position on policy and the issues." When asked on NBC's *Meet the Press* on July 6 whether the Democratic Party should become more liberal, McGovern issued something less than a call to arms. "I think on balance it would serve the national interest and serve the interests of our party ... if we move more in the direction of a unified party where we can expect the overwhelming majority at least of our membership to follow the party's platform and program."

George McGovern's political career was devoted to one overarching principal: to end American militarism abroad in general and the Cold War specifically. He had been a delegate at the 1948 convention that nominated Henry Wallace, the vice president under Franklin Roosevelt who called for sharing nuclear secrets with the Soviet Union and international control of nuclear weapons. In the late 1940s, McGovern had called for China to be admitted into the United Nations. He believed that President Eisenhower had "hit the nail on the head" in his 1961 farewell address when he warned against the military-industrial complex. And as early as 1963, he had condemned U.S. military involvement in Vietnam.

After the August 4 dinner, McGovern embraced the New Politics coalition and nominating system as the means to end the American military presence in Southeast Asia. He adopted Dutton's view that young people were a more important constituency than blue-collar workers and Catholics. Speaking at the American Psychological Association convention on September 3, McGovern favorably compared the peaceful conduct of those who attended the recently concluded Woodstock music festival with those who had attended an NFL football game between the New York Giants and the New York Jets:

> The Woodstock festival should be a lesson to the nation. We should learn first that the youth rebellion doesn't mean disruption.

For three days in Bethel was the third largest city in New York State and there were virtually no crimes of violence. Second, Woodstock was a lesson in love. It was a demonstration of the unity of our young people: that they are, in the words of singer Janis Joplin, "a whole new minority group." They are in their phrase, "together," and yet are they quite apart from the rest of our society.

In September or early October 1969, McGovern wrote a draft of a revealing and little-noticed article for *Playboy*. Besides quoting Dutton, who was identified as a member of the "California Board of Regents," McGovern argued that the Democratic Party should alter its coalition, putting young people at the heart of it:

> If there is to be a new direction in American society, it must begin with a new combination of voters interested in providing that direction. It seems to me that the most important challenge now before the youth of this country is to work toward forming such a new coalition—a coalition of the young, the poor, and the oppressed minorities, of the workingmen left in the wake of a changing technological society, of the educated affluent who now recognize that the goals of society are out of joint. A voting "coalition of conscience" needs to be formed and mobilized. The energy and inventiveness of young people are absolutely indispensable to the success of such a coalition.

McGovern later boasted of visiting more college campuses in 1969 and 1970 than any other senator in history. In mid-October, he and Allard Lowenstein were the keynote speakers at the organizing convention of the New Democratic Coalition of Missouri.

To be sure, McGovern endorsed keeping blue-collar workers in his "coalition of conscience." But the white working class was never going to be more than a minor player in this new coalition. Compared with Bobby Kennedy's black-blue coalition, McGovern's "coalition of conscience" gave the working class far less status. McGovern accorded no special significance to blue-collar workers, who had been the heart of the Democratic Party since Andrew Jackson founded the party. By contrast, Kennedy assigned coequal status to blue-collar workers. McGovern exalted young people in general and baby-boomers specifically, who were enjoined to form the "coalition of conscience." By contrast, Kennedy assigned secondary status to young people and baby-boomers, largely because most were prospering in the affluent society. McGovern made no mention of white ethnic or Catholic voters, a key Democratic constituency since the 1840s. By contrast, Kennedy reached out to white ethnic voters, visiting their churches and clubs. Finally, McGovern included "the educated affluent" in his coalition. By contrast, Kennedy made no mention of educated affluent voters, except when he criticized them.

McGovern's embrace of a Social Change coalition was important not just in the long run. It had one major short-term consequence: McGovern, the chairman of the Commission on Party Structure and Delegate Selection, failed to stop the New Politics activists when they proposed soft quotas for minorities, women, and young people. The informal quotas clearly violated the commission's mandate, which had said nothing about guaranteeing representation to any group.

McGovern could have ruled the proposals out of order. After all, the leaders of the Lawrence Commission had come out against quotas. David Lawrence, at a reform commission hearing on October 6, 1965, said in his opening statement, "It is not the function of this committee to dictate the composition of any state delegation in the 1968 Democratic convention. To do so would violate the fundamental principles of our Party." Another opponent of quotas was Berl Bernhard, the executive director of the Lawrence Commission. After Lawrence died in November 1966, Joseph Rauh proposed that the Lawrence Commission adopt a soft or implied quota. "Where blacks constitute 20 percent or more of the voting age population of any state, and blacks constitute less than 10 percent of the delegation certified by the state democratic party, this shall be deemed prima facie evidence of discrimination on grounds of race or color," he wrote on February 1, 1967, adding that the state party would have to explain why few blacks were chosen. Bernhard recognized the dubious nature of the proposal and said so. "This is trouble. It is reverse discrimination," he wrote on April 4, 1967, to Walter Giesey, Lawrence's former executive assistant and an aide to the commission. "Instead of tying it to percentages, it should be tied to procedures." Bernhard's argument prevailed.

Nonetheless, McGovern failed to prevent Ken Bode and Fred Dutton from sponsoring the soft quota proposal. He had hinted that he might support informal quotas. In the *Playboy* article he wrote,

> It is not enough, however, to urge participation. In too many cases, the institutions by which change is engineered have fossilized beyond the point where they provide any meaningful channels for the hopes of the young. My party—the Democratic Party—is a case in point. Through the Reform Commission, which I chair … we have been laboring to correct that situation, to avoid a repetition of the 1968 experience, in which the constructive energy of the young encountered so much frustration.

Indeed, at the November 19 meeting of the commission, McGovern voted for Dutton's proposal. As for the proposal by Austin Ranney and Senator Birch Bayh to add informal quotas for minorities, McGovern merely voted "present."

—⟋⟍—

ON SEPTEMBER 24, 1969, in Room 3106 of the New Senate Office Building, the McGovern Commission convened for the second day of its two-day meeting. Fred Dutton sponsored two major proposals related to women and young people. One proposal prohibited state parties from discriminating against women in party affairs, and the other gave membership and full political status to citizens 18 through 20 years old. Although both passed easily and with little debate, the youth resolution was far-reaching. It allowed 10.3 million young people to run as delegates and vote for delegates on the county and state levels. It carried the threat of enforcement by the national party. It was approved months before Congress had voted to approve what became the Twenty-sixth Amendment to the Constitution, which extended voting rights to 18-to-20-year-olds, and nearly two years before the Twenty-sixth Amendment was ratified. The *New York Times* wrote that the youth resolution could "remake the face of the party," allowing young people and college students to take over some Democratic organizations.

Ken Bode was not impressed. A short, slight man of birdlike appearance and medium-length brown hair, Bode was the thirty-year-old director of research for the commission. He wanted to do more than prevent discrimination against women and enfranchise young people in the Democratic Party. He wanted to ensure the nomination of a pro-peace Democratic candidate in 1972.

When Bode was hired in the spring, he seemed to be the perfect match for the job. He had practical political experience. He had worked for the Democratic National Committee in 1964; in fact, he had carried the valise of John Bailey as he traveled around the country; and he had worked for the Kennedy, McCarthy, and McGovern presidential campaigns in 1968. And he had academic experience. After earning his Ph.D. in political science in 1966, Bode had been a peripatetic academic, teaching at Michigan State University and the State University of New York at Binghamton.

In his first four months as the commission's research director, Bode worked toward the benign goals of the New Politics movement—openness, representation, and participation. An advocate of one-man, one-vote, Bode on August 19 finished a long memo, complete with five pages of statistical tables, about applying the principle to New York State's presidential election. Early on, Bode did not express great interest in demographic quotas. While he referred in a June 26 letter to "compiling data on minority group representation of both parties at the 1968 Convention," the topic was not central to his research. On July 17, Joseph Gebhardt, an intern whom Bode had handpicked to lead the behavioral research staff, asked the interns to compile detailed data on the delegate selection process in all states. Of the fifty-seven questions on the list, none had addressed the racial, ethnic, gender, or age make-up of a state's delegation.

But Ken Bode was not concerned mainly with opening up the party to democratic participation. Like Fred Dutton, he detested the war and the Democratic leadership. At the convention in

Chicago, working for McGovern's floor operation, Bode had watched in horror as Dutton's minority peace plank went down to defeat. In an unpublished account he wrote years later, Bode favorably quoted playwright Arthur Miller's remark that the convention had made a "mockery of a majority of Democratic voters who had so little representation on the floor and on the platform of this great convention." The Democratic Party leadership, Bode added, had exerted "heavy-handed discipline," while the delegates had given their "passionate consent" to the bosses.

More than a year later, Bode was well aware that the peace movement had made progress. He knew about the Vietnam Moratorium Committee and the New Mobilization to End the War in Vietnam, two organizations which had scheduled massive antiwar demonstrations for the fall. Both had their headquarters at 1029 Vermont Avenue NW, less than two miles from his office at the Democratic National Committee in the Watergate office complex. Eli Segal was the chief counsel for the moratorium; one of the commission's summer interns, Rick Stearns, had also been an intern for the moratorium; and commissioner David Mixner was one of the moratorium's three cofounders. The moratorium called on Americans to take a day off from their regular jobs on Wednesday, October 15, in order to work to stop the war. "During the summer, the moratorium grew and grew," Mixner recalled in his autobiography, *Stranger Among Friends*. "Our offices expanded to two floors, we had regional offices around the country, our staff had grown to dozens, and thousands of small contributions arrived in each day's mail." More than a million people participated, making the event one of the largest antiwar demonstrations in American history.

In contrast to the success of the broader antiwar movement, Bode believed that the McGovern Commission had done nothing to end the war. On August 11, staff director Bob Nelson had written a confidential memo to McGovern and Dutton in which he informed them of the panel's sorry financial shape. "Underscoring the urgency of calling potential contributors to the commission is the fact that when I finish writing the checks for the interns tomorrow, we will have exactly $193.13 left in our bank account!" Nelson confided. "We have hopes of raising a substantial amount from [a fundraiser on September 7]. However, it is the next month which gives me most concern." In fact, the commission was so broke that it was unable to pay the court reporters who had transcribed the field hearing in Portland, Oregon, their fee of $630. Even Segal, an optimist by nature, expressed doubts about the commission's prospects for success. "The commission," he wrote in an August 26 letter to his friend Simon Lazarus, "is proceeding at a pace which could best be described as 'sluggish.'" Recalling his mindset decades later, Bode was more blunt: "We thought, God*damn!* We're not getting anywhere with this war!"

Frustrated with what he perceived to be the commission's lack of success, Bode changed his tactics. He and his interns were already counting up the number of delegates to both 1968 conventions who were racial minorities. Why not look at other types of people? After all, as he wrote turgidly in his Ph.D. dissertation, "typological classifications constitute meaningful independent variables relevant to attitudinal cleavages."

Bode knew that young people were more likely to oppose the war than others. As a young associate professor at Michigan State University, he and another academic in November 1966 had completed a twenty-one-page paper on the political knowledge and views of high school seniors in Ingham County, Michigan. What they found, not surprisingly, was that the young people were significantly more likely to favor extending the franchise to eighteen-year-olds than their older counterparts. While 63 percent of the country's high school seniors supported lowering the voting age to eighteen years of age, only 35 percent of Michigan residents did in a statewide referendum.

Bode also knew that women were more likely to oppose the war. During the last days of the 1968 campaign, polls showed that women had surged toward Humphrey because of a last-minute U.S.-brokered bombing halt. The political scientist Jeane Kirkpatrick confirmed this tendency in her seminal study of both 1972 conventions, *The New Presidential Elite: Men and Women in National Politics.* "The single exception to [the] general pattern of similarity in issue orientation of the sexes concerns opinions on military policy," she wrote. "Women were somewhat less likely than men to support the resolution of problems by force. Consistent though not large sex differences existed on whether the United States should withdraw all troops from Asia."

So Bode came up with an idea. "There was a cleavage in society," he recalled. "People under 30 were fighting this war, and we said, 'Count the number of people under 30 and women who were delegates to the '68 convention.'" What Bode's staff found was that only 13 percent of the delegates to the 1968 convention were women and 4 percent were younger than thirty. Bode drew up a proposal: States would be required to pick as delegates a certain percentage of women and of people between eighteen and thirty years old.

There are many demographic groups in America—ethnic minorities, racial minorities, old people. Why did the McGovern Commission focus on women and young people? Historians and political scientists have either guessed or avoided giving an answer. "This is not the time or place," Kirkpatrick wrote in *The New Presidential Elite,* "to pursue the very interesting question of how these groups came to be the beneficiaries of 'quotas' within the state delegations...." The leaders of the McGovern Commission claimed that women and young people had faced discrimination in the 1968 Democratic campaign. In *Mandate for Reform,* the commission's document published in April 1970, the authors lumped together blacks, young people, and women as victims of bias in 1968. The report added that "the commission found that each of the groups (blacks, women, and youths) was significantly lacking in representation."

In truth, Bode drew up the soft quota for women and young people for reasons having nothing to do with discrimination. When the research staff compiled a list of the eighteen abuses most commonly alleged at the hearings, none mentioned discrimination against women or young people. Bode focused on these groups primarily for one reason: He wanted to ensure the nomination of an antiwar Democratic candidate in 1972. "Can you imagine the '68 convention voting down a peace plank if a third of the delegates had been under 30?" he said to the *New*

York Times Magazine in 1972. An intern named Alex Sanger confirmed Bode's version of events. "This was most definitely part, the strategic part, of the antiwar strategy—to get Richard Daley less representation on the floor," Sanger said.

According to Austin Ranney, a commissioner who got to know him personally, Bode was seeking to get McGovern elected president. "It was widely believed, and I was one who participated in the belief, that he was more concerned with George McGovern as a presidential candidate than types of reforms the McGovern Commission was contemplating. In other words, he had an agenda. Really, more specifically, it was to get George McGovern elected. Any antiwar Democrat would have been good, but McGovern was the best," Ranney said in a 2003 interview. "He was more of a manipulator than a friend or enemy. This was not done out of lofty motives or the good of his conscience. It was more personal ambitions that he worked to get McGovern elected and he would have a prominent role in a McGovern administration."

Ken Bode was not the first to manipulate the composition of presidential delegations for political ends. Vice President John "Cactus Jack" Nance Garner, aware that a majority of the delegates to the 1936 Democratic convention were federal officeholders, contrived the Hatch Act in order to reduce President Roosevelt's power at the 1940 convention. But Bode's proposal qualified as a genuinely radical idea. Among those who had testified at the hearings, only Don Peterson and Paul Schrade of the New Democratic Coalition had supported quotas, formal or informal.

Joseph Gebhardt said that the quotas represented a tension or conflict with the McGovern Commission's mandate. But in truth, the soft quotas were a repudiation of the commission's purpose, a complete violation of its aim. The activists' main line of attack against the bosses had been that the bosses were undemocratic—that they stacked the election process to get the results they wanted. Now the activists were being equally undemocratic: stacking the election process to get the results they wanted.

The transformation did not take long. On March 1, the McGovern Commission spelled out its democratic mandate: The party's voters would have a "full, meaningful, and timely *opportunity*" to participate in the selection of delegates (emphasis added). On November 19, the day the commission adopted the informal quotas for women and young people, the activists pursued results-oriented goals. In less than nine months, the activists had abandoned democracy in favor of their policy aims.

The activists had become bosses. One elite had replaced another. And the consequences of this coup d'état in the Democratic Party would soon be apparent.

SIX

Enter the Sisterhood

Easing into the elevator, the feminist leaders knew they had only one ace in the hole. It was November 18, 1971, and the women were inside the Watergate office-hotel complex at 2600 Virginia Avenue NW, the headquarters of the Democratic National Committee. They had come to increase the number of women as delegates to the party's 1972 convention, and they realized that most of their cards were weak. Their nonpartisan organization, the National Women's Political Caucus, had been founded 130 days earlier. They had no real legal backup, they had chapters in only half a dozen states, and their employees did not receive regular paychecks. But their infancy, lack of support, and meager funds were not so important. After all, they had guideline A-2 of the McGovern Commission: the requirement that state Democratic parties must choose women and young people as delegates in "reasonable relationship" to their presence in the state's population. It was enough to get them a meeting with the leaders of the national Democratic Party.

On the sixth floor, the feminist leaders filed in through the glass doors of the DNC headquarters at around 6 or 7 P.M. They included Anne Wexler, the chief of consultants to the McGovern Commission, and Phyllis Segal, the wife of commission counsel Eli Segal. Smiling and shaking hands, they met their six hosts, including Representative Don Fraser, the new chairman of the McGovern Commission, and Robert Nelson, the commission's staff director. After sitting down at the table, the feminist leaders played their ace. "You have this rule," Doris Meissner, the NWPC executive director, recalled saying. "Something must be done about it." Her colleagues agreed. If Democratic officials did not implement guideline A-2 fully, the women would not let them forget it. They would tell the national press. They would file lawsuits.

Feminist leaders had previously threatened Democratic officials for what they perceived as abandoning guideline A-2. The main instigator had been Representative Bella Abzug of New York, a large, blustery woman famous for her Bronx accent, profanity-laced exchanges, and wide-brimmed, floppy hats. After winning election in 1970, Abzug had become a cofounder of the NWPC. On July 15, she had written to Fraser demanding that his commission enforce guideline A-2:

> I strongly urge the McGovern-Fraser Commission to take immediate action that will clarify for state parties their responsibility for meeting these Guidelines. The Commission should provide them with guidance as to what is meant by "reasonable representation" (in terms of acceptable percentages) and should explicitly define the responsibility of each state party for living up to these standards. The National Convention is less than a year away, and it is disturbing that so little has been done to implement the work of your Commission.

Fraser complied happily. The son of the dean at the University of Minnesota Law School, the forty-seven-year-old was an original member of the Harold Hughes Commission and was married to the feminist Arvonne Fraser. After McGovern resigned from the commission to run for the presidency in January 1971, Fraser had become the new chairman, and he agreed with the feminists' political and legal goals. On July 23, he wrote to Abzug as if her letter were manna from heaven:

> Thank you so much for the letter concerning the importance of achieving compliance by the states of Guidelines A-1 and A-2 to provide for fair representation of minorities and women. Your letter correctly identifies the need to encourage the states to come into full compliance with these Guidelines. In fact, the progress we

are able to identify is encouraging, but our goal is to achieve compliance by all of the states. Therefore, any encouragement which
your organization or state affiliated groups can give to party officials to complete their reform efforts will be in our mutual interest.

Emboldened, the NWPC leaders pressed their cause with
DNC officials. At the November 18 meeting, they sought to take
full advantage of guideline A-2, demanding that each state delegation be no less than 50 percent women. What would happen,
one woman asked, if a state party had barely any women on its
delegation? Fraser replied, "If the delegation was so badly unbal-
anced, you've got a prima facie case." Seizing her opportunity,
Representative Patsy Mink of Hawaii responded, "Why don't you
put that in writing?" DNC staff member Bill Welsh's jaw dropped.
Meissner was stunned, too. "We would have gone for 10 percent,"
she told Byron Shafer for his book *Quiet Revolution,* "but they gave
us 50 percent and allowed us to make the challenges."

The feminist leaders benefited greatly from guideline A-2 of
the McGovern Commission. As Ken Bode and Fred Dutton had
predicted in 1969, this rule was the golden ticket that allowed
activist women to board the Democratic train. Meissner said,
"When we went to the Republican chairman, there wasn't anything like A-2 to go on. We couldn't say, 'It says you must do
this, and if that doesn't mean that, what does it mean?' We got
a little from the Republicans on the Democratic shirttail, but
that was all." She later added that the soft quotas were "a way
to seek to reform the existing structures within rather than challenging them from the outside."

Other documents from the National Women's Political Caucus support Meissner's account. In early 1972, for instance, the
NWPC sent its members a communication in which it stated
emphatically, "THE DEMOCRATIC PARTY HAS NOT ONLY REC-
OGNIZED THE RIGHT OF ALL WOMEN TO FULL PARTICIPA-
TION IN THE POLITICAL PROCESS ... *BUT IT IS DOING
SOMETHING ABOUT IT!"* By contrast, an NWPC newsletter
from February 1972 noted, "The Republican party has not formally agreed to implement a proposal for equal representation of
the sexes."

In the early 1970s, feminists were clearly an emerging political force. On August 27, 1970, the fiftieth anniversary of women's suffrage, feminists held a march for women around the country. In the summer of 1971, feminist leaders formed the NWPC, an organization dedicated to putting women in positions of political power. But it was unclear which direction the NWPC would go.

Would feminists align with the Democratic Party? By any objective standard, the odds looked bad. Catholic bosses dominated the party's presidential wing. Union workers and lower-class women supported protective labor legislation, which feminists opposed on the grounds that women were treated differently from men. Democrats had a lower share of female delegates (13 percent) at their 1968 convention than the Republicans (17 percent). The party did support birth control in its 1968 platform, but so did the Republican Party.

Would feminists side with the Republican Party? The prospects were more encouraging. The party's presidential wing included an Eastern Seaboard establishment and Western economic conservatives, both of which were congenial to feminist interests. Republicans had a longer history of supporting the Equal Rights Amendment. Republicans were friendlier to feminist interests on abortion. President Nixon in 1969 had signed an executive order allowing military hospitals overseas to perform abortions. And more generally, the Republicans had far more women in their leadership ranks than did the Democrats. As Meissner said, "There were Republican women who were very highly placed in their own party structures.... Anne Armstrong was executive director of the RNC, and she was in the Nixon White House. Mary Crisp, Ellie Peters, Virginia Allen—there were no counterparts in the Democratic Party. There was *nobody* on the Democratic side who had risen to that stature."

Or would feminists form their own party? The question was fiercely debated in the summer and fall of 1971. The ideological feminists, who usually came from the National Organization for Women and other women's rights groups, wanted the NWPC to form their own party. The pragmatic feminists, who usually were public officials, wanted the NWPC to align with one of the two parties.

Feminists chose none of those options. Instead they boarded a new train, a reformed Democratic Party, with new conductors—secular activists. The feminists did so mainly because of the McGovern Commission and guideline A-2. And they learned the value of this rule from three people affiliated with the McGovern Commission: Phyllis Segal, Ken Bode, and Fred Dutton.

—ᴡ—

ON APRIL 6, 1971, Representative Martha Griffiths of Michigan walked onto the floor of the U.S. House of Representatives. A vivacious fifty-seven-year-old, Griffiths was establishing herself as a legend among feminists. She had helped extend the antidiscrimination measures of the 1964 Civil Rights Act to women and she used a parliamentary device to get the Equal Rights Amendment out of the House Rules Committee, where it had been bottled up for decades. On this Monday afternoon, Griffiths walked to the lectern on the Democratic side of the aisle to mention an exciting new paper by a congressional aide. "Mr. Speaker," she said, "sex discrimination pervades the institutions of our society, and political parties have not escaped its curse. At this time, I would like to insert in the Record an excellent analysis of present discrimination against women in American political parties, written by Phyllis N. Segal of the Georgetown University Law Center."

The 4,000-word paper was titled "Women and Political Parties: The Legal Dimension of Discrimination." It was a direct product of the McGovern Commission. Phyllis Segal had based much of her research on *Mandate for Reform,* the official interim report of the commission released in April 1970. "I used the data from the McGovern Commission and beyond that, from the Democratic and Republican parties," Segal said in a 2003 interview. For example, she noted that only 13 percent of the Democratic delegates in Chicago were women.

Phyllis Segal's research impressed Bella Abzug. On July 15, four days after the first meeting of the National Women's Political Caucus, Abzug cited Segal's paper and statistics on the House floor. Abzug decided to give Segal's research an institutional focus. And in October 1971 the NWPC created a Task Force on Delegate Selection. "Such a campaign," the task force's resolution stated, "would have the purpose of developing and implementing a strategy to place media and organizational pressure on both political parties in as many states as possible to ensure the National Party guidelines recommending full participation of women are carried out in good faith and, if they are not, to mount challenges to party delegations that are not in compliance.... The council accepts this as a PRIORITY campaign." In need of a person to head the task force, Abzug hired Segal.

Although the task force was ostensibly concerned about female representation in both political parties, it focused on the Democratic Party. On November 8, 1971, Meissner wrote to the DNC chairman, Lawrence O'Brien, to request a meeting. O'Brien agreed, and the five members of the Task Force met with DNC officials ten days later.

In addition to using the McGovern Commission's research and soft quotas, feminists enlisted two key players affiliated with the commission. They needed consultants to advise them on the language and formula by which they could petition Democratic officials. They needed leaders of the McGovern Commission.

The women's first major adviser was none other than Ken Bode. After leaving the commission to serve as a legislative aide for McGovern, Bode had formed the Center for Political Reform, which pressured party officials to implement the commission's reforms and rules changes. Bode also co-chaired the Convention Task Force of Americans for Democratic Action. Seeking to build ties with the NWPC, he created the Reasonable Representation Project, the focus of which was the proposed soft quotas for minorities, women, and young people.

Bode recruited Phyllis Segal and Anne Wexler. On November 8, the Reasonable Representation Project came up with a "20 percent deviation" formula to judge whether state parties were complying with the McGovern Commission's proposals. For example, if women made up 50 percent of a state's population, 40 percent of the state party's delegation had to be women.

There were plenty of Democrats who opposed Bode's reinterpretation of guideline A-2. One critic was Carl Auerbach, a professor of law at the University of Minnesota. On January 21, 1972, Auerbach wrote to Bode personally to condemn his efforts:

> I am very much disturbed by your intimation that challenges will be made to the credentials of state delegations which bring a "diminished proportion of persons between the ages of 18–30 [and women] to Miami in July." I am astounded that you can say Guideline A-2 "explicitly requires" that persons between the ages of 18–30 [and women] be represented in 1972 delegations in proportion to their presence in the voting population of each state. Surely I need not remind you that Guideline A-2 merely requires state parties to take "affirmative steps to *encourage* representation … of young people … and women in *reasonable* relationships to their presence in the population of the state and expressly adds that this is not to be accomplished by the mandatory imposition of quotas." … No matter how democratic one's selection *process* may be, it cannot *assure* that the *outcome* will accord proportional representation to every faction seeking a particular objective…. If challenges will nevertheless be filed because state delegations are not as precisely proportioned as you seem to think essential, the 1972 Convention will be as great a shambles as the 1968 Convention.

The feminists' second major adviser was Fred Dutton. In the summer of 1971, while working at his law office downtown, Dutton received a phone call from Bella Abzug. She had founded the antinuclear group Women Strike for Peace in 1961 and had worked with Dutton nearly a decade earlier on the nuclear test ban treaty. Would he help the NWPC?

In mid-July, Dutton drafted a letter on the organization's behalf. At issue was what constituted a "reasonable" share of women delegates. Was it a quarter, a third, or a half? Dutton's answer was more uncompromising than Bode's: Half of the delegates must be women.

My brief takes the position that when the commission and then the DNC voted that women shall be represented in reasonable relationship to their proportion of the population, that means that they are entitled to an absolute majority. They constitute 52.2% of the adult population of this country 18 or over, according to the 1970 census. A majority cannot be made into a minority in a popularly based political process without violating a very fundamental concept. The violation would be quite unreasonable.

As a result of the meeting on November 18, 1971, DNC officials repeatedly acquiesced to the feminists' demands. On December 8, O'Brien sent written instructions about the new rules to all fifty state parties: "I want to underscore those points in Congressman Fraser's letter that emphasize the importance of each state's taking specific, affirmative actions to encourage the representation and involvement of women, minorities, and young people in the selection of delegations to the 1972 Democratic National Convention and as members of the delegations." He added that by mid-January 1972, the state chairmen should send him "a report on the affirmative steps being taken by the state party to fulfill the provisions of A-1 and A-2."

Feminist leaders viewed the state parties with distrust. On April 3, Meissner wrote to O'Brien complaining that only four states had submitted affirmative action programs to the DNC. "If the Democratic National Convention were to be held tomorrow, there would be only 22% women delegates—a far cry from the 50% figure which we both agree is suggested by the guidelines," she wrote. O'Brien, showing little of the grit that had endeared him to Lyndon Johnson and Robert Kennedy, indicated that he was ready to address Meissner's concerns. "I should be most interested in receiving from you as soon as possible a memorandum specifying what the Caucus has done and is doing to encourage and assist women to take part in the delegate selection procedure," he wrote.

The feminists' alliance with the McGovern Commission bore fruit. At the 1972 Democratic convention, 40 percent of the delegates were women. Four years earlier, it had been 13 percent. The share of women delegates had more than tripled.

Germaine Greer, author of the feminist tract *The Female Eunuch*, could not conceal her joy about the increased presence of female delegates to the 1972 Democratic convention. On a visit to the NWPC meeting in the Napoleon Room at the Deauville Hotel on the morning of Sunday, July 9, she walked in while Gloria Steinem was speaking. Greer recalled that Steinem "spoke of councilmen being ousted by housewives, of women forming 46 percent of the attendance at precinct meetings in one state. 'The political process has been changed,' she sang, 'and it will never be the same again.' Women had challenged their way to being 40 percent of the delegates, with 38 percent of the vote; they had made the McGovern-Fraser guidelines work for them."

—◊◊—

INSIDE THE JAPANESE-STYLE home of George McGovern, feminist leaders sat on the low, formal furniture or on a wool carpet woven to look like an authentic rice-straw tatami. It was after dark on June 26, 1972, the first day of the party's Platform Committee meeting. Two dozen members of the National Women's Political Caucus were waiting to lobby McGovern about their issues. After he walked into the room, the women got down to business: What did he think of making abortion legal nationwide? While McGovern and a few women exchanged their views, Gloria Steinem sat up straight against a sliding glass door, with her long brown hair spilling over purple-tinted aviator glasses. The thirty-eight-year-old magazine writer proposed that McGovern run on a platform in favor of abortion rights. On this issue, she told the antiwar candidate, there was no compromise. "We women look at this subject as our Vietnam," she said, "since there are more women dying from butchered abortions than servicemen killed over there."

Steinem was not speaking just for herself. In mid-1972, many feminist leaders viewed the legalization of abortion as their top priority. Of course, abortion had been central to third-wave feminism since its inception. "Free abortions" had been one of the four main planks of Women Strike for Equality, the name of the famous national march on August 26, 1970, and government-subsidized abortions had been listed as a basic human right by the National Women's Political Caucus upon its founding. But after the U.S. Senate passed the Equal Rights Amendment in March 1972, thereby leaving the amendment in the hands of the state legislatures, many feminist leaders were most interested in legalizing abortion. Bella Abzug, who had called the legalization of abortion a "transcending point of view," introduced legislation in Congress to void all state laws that barred or limited abortion.

In the hope of convincing the Democratic and Republican parties to endorse abortion rights, the NWPC drew up a plank. It read, "In matters relating to human reproduction, each person's right to privacy, freedom of choice and individual conscience shall be fully respected, consistent with relevant Supreme Court decisions." Although the proposal did not refer to the word abortion, its overriding goal was to eliminate legal protection for unborn infants. And at the Democratic Party's Platform Committee hearings, a sufficient number of Democrats approved the abortion plank, meaning that the delegates in Miami Beach would have to vote on the issue.

Feminist leaders sought the same destination that Fred Dutton envisioned. He wanted to destroy the old Democratic Party, a party whose ultimate destination was human equality. In its place, he wanted to build a new Democratic Party, a party whose ultimate destination was human liberation. Now, two and a half years after Dutton had urged his fellow commissioners to embrace the women's liberation movement, feminist leaders were onboard and working to reach the same station.

Feminist leaders had matured in a paradoxical era in American life: While millions of women were college graduates, many were barred from the professions. Abzug, after serving as an editor for Columbia University's law review, could not find work as a lawyer. Steinem, a graduate of Smith College, for years could not land assignments from national magazines or jobs in New York. Women had not been treated as individuals, as persons with the same rights as men, but as members of a group. How would they respond?

The answer was shaped not only by their upper-class status, but also by their secular outlook. While growing up, Steinem had been taught theosophy or New Age religion. Abzug had studied Reform Judaism in graduate school. Both believed that women should be treated no differently from men, whether they were going to school, applying for a job, or having sex without commitment or responsibility. The right to abortion, therefore, was necessary to ensure equality. Steinem, who had had an abortion herself in England in 1956, said that her commitment to abortion rights began after she attended a hearing in New York City on abortion reform in February 1969. As her biographer Carolyn G. Heilbrun described Steinem's thinking, "All the humiliations of being a woman, from political assignments lost to less-experienced male writers to a 'lifetime of journalists' jokes about frigid wives, dumb blondes, and farmers' daughters that I had smiled at in order to be one of the boys' sharpened into focus, their meaning revealed."

By contrast, many Democratic women were "difference" feminists, holding that women should be treated equally but valued for their contributions to family life and the nurturing professions. A good example is Ella Grasso of Connecticut, a Catholic Democrat who rose through John Bailey's organization. After winning election to Congress in 1970 and 1972, Grasso was elected governor in 1974, becoming the nation's first woman to do so in her own right, and she made Medicare coverage available for hospice patients. In each of her races, Grasso campaigned and governed on a pro-life platform, disagreeing publicly with *Roe v. Wade* and signing legislation to end Medicaid funding for abortions. "I'm opposed to abortion," she once said, "because I happen to believe that life deserves the protection of society."

In contrast to Grasso, liberation feminists usually were secular professionals. To be sure, feminist leaders were sensitive to the charge that theirs was largely an upper-class, secular movement. At the NWPC's inaugural meeting in July 1971, Abzug said that "it is certainly not my purpose to replace or supplement a white, male, middle-class elite with a white, *female*, middle-class elite." Feminist leaders sincerely tried to speak for most women, but they tended to focus on the concerns of professional-class women.

For example, support for unfettered abortion rights was most popular among the college-educated and affluent. In *Science* magazine, February 12, 1971, the esteemed UC Berkeley sociologist Judith Blake, a self-described foe of "repressive ... pronatalist policies," published a comprehensive survey of polls regarding American attitudes toward abortion during the 1960s. When women were asked whether they favored legalizing abortion if the parents can't afford another child, two-thirds on average said they did not. "The net result," Blake concluded, "is that at all educational levels (but particularly at the college and grade-school levels), women now object to abortion for economic reasons decidedly more than men." She argued that abortion-rights supporters should not try to lobby the lower classes and women: "Rather, it is to the educated and influential that we must look for effecting rapid legislative change."

At the 1972 Democratic National Convention in Miami Beach, feminist leaders made their case for the abortion plank primarily in terms of property rights. They had ditched Steinem's argument that abortion should be legalized so as to prevent women from dying as a result of illegal abortions, perhaps because so few were dying. Instead, they contended that women had a right over their own flesh. As Abzug had said in May, her legislation "would guarantee women the freedom to choose for themselves whether they wish to have children and end forever the humiliation of not controlling their own bodies."

The debate over the abortion plank ran from 2 to 4 A.M. on Wednesday, July 12, the second session of the convention. The three delegates who spoke in support of the plank portrayed their cause as one of privacy and pluralism rather than equality. They recognized that most Democratic delegates at the time rejected the argument that in order for women to be treated as equals, they needed to have the legal right to abort an unborn infant. So they made a relativistic argument: the government should stop regulating people's reproductive lives.

Jennifer Wilke, a delegate from Alaska who had devised the language of the abortion plank, spoke first. "This minority report asserts that abortion is only one aspect of reproductive rights, which must be a matter of individual conscience," Wilke said. "The freedom to make difficult moral choices based on personal values and the freedom of all people to control their own fertility must be an essential human and health right."

The second speaker was Frances "Sissy" Farenthold, who had exceeded expectations in her losing 1972 bid for governor of Texas. A forty-six-year-old Roman Catholic, she had graduated from Vassar College and the University of Texas Law School. She cast the abortion issue mainly in liberationist terms:

> I do not lightly nor naively suggest [the plank's] inclusion in our platform, nor am I an individual proponent of abortion. But ours is a pluralistic society. And I believe that the Democratic Party has an obligation no matter what the background of the individual candidates to include this issue as a fundamental right.... I say that there has been an intrusion by the states on a fundamental moral question. I say that we should begin to put an end to this cruel, capricious, and unconstitutional interference in a fundamental human right.

The female speakers recognized the plank's ideological significance: The Democratic Party was venturing onto a new track. The values of an upper-class, educated, and secular constituency were making inroads into a Catholic, urban, blue-collar party. Eleanor Holmes Norton framed the debate most succinctly. A former legal aide to Joseph Rauh in his dispute over the seating of the Mississippi Democratic delegation in 1964, Norton was now a thirty-five-year-old delegate from New York. She recognized that if a majority of delegates adopted the abortion plank, the Democratic Party would no longer be the party it had been. "In the name of moderation and accommodation," Norton said, "in the name of the new spirit of reform, in the name of the new Democratic Party, let us be true to ourselves and approve the minority plank."

—m—

THE PRESIDING PARLIAMENTARIAN in the convention hall those early morning hours on Wednesday was Joseph Califano Jr., a forty-one-year-old Roman Catholic. He listened as the delegates debated and voted on two unprecedented issues: Should the Democratic Party embrace abortion rights (Minority Report no. 7) and gay rights (Minority Report no. 8)?

For years, Califano had vaguely supported the rules changes proposed by the McGovern Commission. He had seen them as similar to the Catholic Church's decision to stop using Latin at Mass in favor of the local vernaculars. In an article for the *New Democrat* magazine of March 1971, he said the proposals represented "essentially liturgical" rather than revolutionary changes. Perhaps because he had traveled around the world in 1969 on a research grant to study the causes of student unrest, Califano believed that the reforms would open up the Democratic Party to young people. "The only ideological base they reflect is the need to increase the democratic responsiveness of the 1972 convention delegates," he declared in an October 1970 speech at the University of North Carolina. "Their concern with the ideological commitment or vision of the Democratic Party in the seventies is marginal at best."

Califano was the general counsel to the Democratic National Committee in 1970. Yet even if he had suspected that antiwar liberals were attempting to hijack the party machinery, his hands were tied. The DNC could not override the recommendations of the McGovern Commission. Only the Credentials Committee of the 1972 convention could do so. Given that many state parties in 1970 had already reformed their delegate selection methods, the McGovern Commission guidelines were in effect party law.

Standing on the convention podium Wednesday morning, Califano realized how wrong he had been. It wasn't just that most big-city mayors—Daley of Chicago, Kevin White of Boston, Frank Rizzo of Philadelphia—had boycotted the convention. The reformers' changes had not been merely liturgical after all. Below him on the floor, the delegates were considering two cultural issues that their predecessors had never even contemplated. "As I watched and listened, the convention was moving the Democratic Party from the harbor of economic issues like full employment and health care for all into the turbulent seas of cultural revolution likely to infuriate and alienate many middle-class Americans who had been the backbone of the party from Roosevelt through Johnson," Califano recalled in his memoir, *Inside: A Public and Private Life.* "How will they react . . . to the effort of many delegates to establish cultural issues like abortion rights and gay liberation as litmus tests for what constitutes a national Democrat?"

Another doubter was Ben Wattenberg. Besides being the co-author of *The Real Majority,* Wattenberg was a member of the party's Platform Committee. At the committee's hearings in late June, he recoiled as committee members approved minority reports in favor of forced busing, amnesty for draft dodgers, and legalization of drugs and abortion. McGovern's supporters "just lost Michigan today with their busing plank," Wattenberg told Theodore White in *The Making of the President, 1972.* "No one seemed impressed by the fact that in Macomb County [a working-class suburb of Detroit] they voted against busing in a referendum last fall by fourteen to one."

Califano and Wattenberg were big-city white ethnics who had grown up in the 1930s and 1940s and served as top aides in the Johnson White House. They intuitively understood a political truth that the New Politics activists did not: a culturally liberal agenda was profoundly alienating to the heart of the Democratic base—Catholics and blue-collar workers. They were not alone in this view. McGovern's lieutenants, who had seen their candidate hemorrhage support in the primaries after being attacked for his cultural views, tried to defeat the minority reports on abortion and homosexuality for that reason. But unlike McGovern's aides, Califano and Wattenberg recognized that moving away from the party's working-class agenda invited electoral defeat and moral decline.

In 1972, eviscerating the nation's abortion laws was broadly unpopular. Pro-choice feminists struggled to get elected. After Abzug unveiled her abortion-rights law in May, she faced a tough primary election in June because of redistricting. Her opponent was Representative William Fitts Ryan, a pro-life Democrat who opposed the war. Abzug lost by more than a 3-to-1 margin.

When the Platform Committee held hearings around the country in the spring, right-to-life groups urged the party to adopt a pro-life position on abortion. Perhaps the most energetic organization was Women Concerned for the Unborn Child. A nonsectarian group from southwestern Pennsylvania, the nonprofit had three thousand members at a time when only thirteen states had changed their abortion laws. "Catholics don't own the fight against abortion, and are not unique in the value they place on every single human life," the group wrote in its mission statement.

The organization overstated its case somewhat: Catholics were more likely than other Americans to support legal protections for unborn infants. Surveys by the sociologist Judith Blake in 1968 and 1969 found that Catholic disapproval of abortion for economic reasons was 10 percentage points higher than for non-Catholics—74 percent as against 64 percent. In addition, Catholics were slightly more likely than non-Catholics to reject abortion if the parents don't want another child—85 percent as against 79 percent.

According to Blake's research, a strong majority of *non-Catholics* opposed abortion for economic reasons. But opinion varied significantly in relation to education: More than two-thirds of men with a grade school or high school education opposed legal abortion for economic reasons, while less than half of men with a college education did. Among women, three-fourths of the less educated were opposed to abortion for economic reasons, while 61 percent of all women were opposed. Blake concluded, "it is clear that opinions concerning pregnancy termination are changing rapidly over time, though not equally by educational level. The class with a college education has changed most rapidly, while the class with only an elementary education showed the least change. Because of this differential rate of change, social class differences have widened."

The opposition of Catholics and blue-collar workers to abortion was significant. It underlined the extent to which an upper-class, secular movement was trying to take over the Democratic Party.

What Catholics and blue-collar workers grasped were the moral implications of legal abortion. Both recognized that eliminating the legal protections for unborn infants consigned many of them to a violent death. At the convention, St. Louis attorney Eugene Walsh, a national committeeman from Missouri, spoke out against the abortion plank. His speech was an eloquent summary not only of the right-to-life position, but also of the contradiction between the abortion license and the underlying social vision of the Party of the Little Guy:

> The Democratic Party has no place or kinship with a plank that would approve the slaughter of the most innocent, the most helpless, and the most precious of all creatures, the unborn young whose right to live is not mentioned in the minority report.
>
> I submit this right to live is superior to those mentioned rights of privacy, choice, and conscience.
>
> Should this party, with its long history of espousal in advancement of the rights of children in child labor legislation, in providing all of the forms of social security to the parentless child, in seeking the finest in health and nutritional care for our young, in expending its revenues for the great programs of the education of its offspring, shamefully betray the Franklin Roosevelts, the Harry Trumans, the John Kennedys, the Lyndon Johnsons, and the countless members of the Congress and the state legislatures of our party who dedicated so much of their lives and efforts to secure the rights of the children in America?
>
> ... Life is worth living, Mr. Chairman, and life is not perfect, but this party from its inception has an illustrious history of trying to improve the quality of life in our country and all of the world and has been devoted to the young and the old.

A debate on the party's position on abortion was the last thing that McGovern's strategists wanted. To win in November, they recognized, McGovern would have to win among Catholic voters. In mid-June, two campaign aides sent McGovern a three-page memo spelling out the importance of this traditionally Democratic constituency:

> The Catholic-ethnic vote is centered in eight key industrial states (New York, Pennsylvania, New Jersey, Illinois, Ohio, Michigan, California, and Texas) which have 230 of the 270 electoral votes needed to win. This is the blue-collar vote in these states and it is the dominant vote. There are Republican governors in five of the

states and the elections of Callahan in New Jersey and Buckley in the state of New York have been based quite directly on large eth- nic-Catholic switch overs from the Democratic to Republican col- umn.... For you to beat Nixon on the Catholic vote (which we again emphasize as being ethnic and blue-collar) we believe you must speak directly and often to the concerns of these people, espe- cially in terms of their two overwhelming concerns, *family* and *neighborhood.*

So when feminists at the Platform Committee hearings introduced a new version of the plank, McGovern lieutenants lobbied committee members to ensure its defeat. McGovern aide Ted Van Dyk told reporters that their efforts would prevent Catholics from bolting the ticket in November. Even when another McGovern aide, Shirley MacLaine, offered a milder plank in support of legal abortion, she felt relief after it, too, was beaten. "It worked," she told reporters afterward. "We're not going to say anything to hurt George's chances."

To MacLaine's dismay, feminist leaders succeeded in winning enough support on the Platform Committee for a minority report in favor of abortion rights. But at the convention, McGovern lieu- tenants walked from delegate to delegate lobbying them to oppose the measure. "We were very afraid, or we believed, that the plank would have passed if we hadn't taken a strong position against it," said McGovern's deputy campaign manager, Rick Stearns, as quoted by Susan and Martin Tolchin in *Clout: Wom- anpower and Politics.* "I was surprised when it was defeated so heavily. If we had just left things alone, it would still have been defeated, but it would have been defeated by a more respectable margin, and the women would have been less upset." Stearns' tactics worked: The abortion plank failed, 1,101 to 1,547.

—⅏—

IN THE MIDST OF the debate over the abortion plank, Bella Abzug heard about the McGovernites' tactics. Her response recalled Richard Daley's more animated exchanges four years earlier. Charging up to the first row of the California delegation, Abzug accused Shirley MacLaine of betraying the feminist movement. With an occasional "Listen, God damn it," Abzug told MacLaine, "A sister never goes against a sister. This cannot be tolerated!" After New York delegates pulled their support for the plank, Abzug shook her fist and threatened them. "I ask you don't distort the vote and sabotage our law in New York. You McGovern people should hold the line. Those of you who keep this up, we're going to pull you and have it on record!"

Gloria Steinem, for all her feminine pulchritude, was more imperious than any old-school political boss. She was not a delegate at the convention, but she grew livid as Eugene Walsh spoke on the podium. "They put a right to lifer on, and they promised they wouldn't," she told a reporter. Walking up to McGovern's campaign chairman, Gary Hart, Steinem said in tears, "You promised us you would not take the low road, you bastards."

Feminist leaders had tried to muzzle intraparty disagreements about abortion before. During the June 26 meeting at McGovern's house, a woman from New Jersey openly questioned the leadership's authority. "There are some of us who don't feel as strongly as Gloria and Betty on abortion," she told the group. According to Shirley MacLaine, Steinem told the woman, "We don't need to discuss that." In addition, the National Women's Political Caucus acknowledged in its internal documents that support for legal abortion was less than unanimous among its own members. According to undated guidelines for forming state caucuses, the organization cited abortion as first among the issues that could polarize members. "All women are not in favor of abortion, in several states women fighting against abortion are members of the state organization," it read. "It's a hot item and what we are trying to do is focus on the ways in which we are alike, not on the ways in which we are different."

Feminist leaders wanted support for abortion rights to be more than a key position for national Democrats. They wanted it to be a mandatory position, a litmus test. When their efforts failed, they retaliated. The next night, they marshaled their forces in support of Sissy Farenthold for vice president. Steinem gave the nominating speech for her. Because of their efforts, which dragged on for three hours, McGovern did not begin his acceptance speech until 2:48 A.M. EST, which meant that the party's presidential nominee commanded a primetime audience only on the island of Guam.

Feminist leaders also responded by lobbying the Republican Party to adopt the abortion plank. Jill Ruckelshaus—the wife of William Ruckelshaus, who administered the Environmental Protection Agency—was a well-known proponent of legal abortion. At the 1972 Republican National Convention, in closed session, the NWPC cofounder Betty Friedan testified at length in support of the abortion plank. Friedan later urged the Republican women, "I am here now to raise the issue to urge women to fight for the right to control their own bodies, to fight for the right not to die by a coat-hanger abortion." Her efforts failed. The Republicans did not adopt the abortion plank.

The two setbacks did not discourage the feminists. After the Democratic convention, many leaders of the women's movement vowed to change their tactics. No longer would the national party remain neutral on the most important issue of all, the right to abort an unborn infant. North Carolina state chairwoman Martha Kay Clampitt told her friends that the abortion fiasco would not be repeated. On the airplane home from Miami Beach, Clampitt talked to Terry Sanford, former governor of North Carolina. Sanford had been Hubert Humphrey's first choice for DNC chairman in 1969 and was considering a presidential run in 1976. "You understand, Terry, if it comes to a case of your interests or women's interests, which one it's going to be, don't you?" Clampitt asked. Sanford replied, "Yes, I understand."

SEVEN

The Emerging Democratic Minority: McGovern's Campaign Shows the Way

O n June 11, 1970, Gary Hart walked into Room 362 in the Old Senate Office Building. He had flown in from Denver, where he had a private law practice. After organizing a McGovern Commission hearing in the city a year earlier, the bushy-haired, thirty-five-year-old had gained McGovern's trust. For the past two and a half months, Hart had organized Western party leaders and workers in behalf of McGovern's nascent presidential bid. Now he was inside McGovern's Washington office. The two men were about to embark on a campaign-related trip to New Hampshire, which in less than two years would hold the nation's first presidential primary.

Curious about the senator's future commitments, Hart talked with McGovern's secretary, Patricia Donovan, who opened her red daybook for September and October. Inside was nothing but blank pages. Hart was stunned. "After talking to Pat and others on the Senate staff, it became clear that no long-range, coherent planning for a Presidential campaign was taking place on a national basis," Hart wrote in his 1973 book, *Right from the Start: A Chronicle of the McGovern Campaign.* "Immediately, the efforts I had been making in the West seemed isolated, detached, and unrelated to any grander plan."

Hart's doubts were renewed the next day, when he and McGovern landed at the airport in West Lebanon, New Hampshire. A lone student picked them up and drove them several miles into Hanover in an old jeep. McGovern sat in front, while

Hart was in back sitting atop their luggage. "Somehow this did not conform to my preconceptions of a Presidential campaign," Hart wrote. "Where were the jubilant crowds, the banners and balloons, the eager supporters pressing to get closer to the great man? And most of all, where were the limousines?"

Many presidential candidates begin with shoestring budgets and more prayers than plans. But McGovern's woes underlined a larger problem. By the standards of every known political law, George McGovern stood almost no chance of winning the 1972 Democratic presidential nomination. His bid was one of the longest of long shots, the political equivalent of the Chicago Cubs winning the World Series. Celebrated odds-maker "Jimmy the Greek" Snyder would later announce that the odds against McGovern earning the nomination were 200 to 1.

McGovern, a man of indomitable will, rejected the odds. But he recognized that in his path for the Democratic nomination were innumerable political hurdles.

McGovern's ties with blue-collar Democrats were frayed. To be sure, he had won four elections, twice as a congressman and twice as a senator. But his popularity with South Dakota farmers had not carried over to industrial laborers. After his meeting with potential presidential advisers in August 1969, Charles Guggenheim, a filmmaker and a key aide in McGovern's successful bid for the U.S. Senate in 1962, wrote a memo to McGovern expressing concern about his tenuous relationship with the little people. "The necessity to turn your concerns to the 'forgotten man' in America cannot be overemphasized," Guggenheim wrote. "You enter national politics with your own coalition, but it does not include the people who won for Bobby in Indiana, Nebraska, and South Dakota and defeated him in Oregon. It does not include the people that Norman Rockwell painted. It does not include those people you must have to win outside the glandular and issue-oriented constituencies of the American seaboard."

Furthermore, McGovern's relationship with the leaders of organized labor was equally strained. Though McGovern usually voted for pro-labor legislation, he had incurred the wrath of George Meany, president of the AFL-CIO. In the early and mid

1960s, McGovern criticized unions that refused to send grain shipments to the Soviet Union, and he voted against a motion to shut off a conservative filibuster of a right-to-work section of the Taft-Hartley Act. In 1969, McGovern's chairmanship of the reform commission made him persona non grata at AFL-CIO headquarters.

McGovern's ties with Catholic Democrats were thin, too. He did correspond with a number of priests about the war. But as a senator from a heavily Protestant, rural state, he was detached from the Catholic party bosses and rank-and-file voters. And given the longstanding battle between reform Democrats and Catholic bosses, his chairmanship of the reform commission was no help.

McGovern's identification with the antiwar movement was hurting him with the American public at large. It wasn't that the war was popular. It was that the antiwar movement was even more unpopular, as McGovern well knew. In the fall of 1969, over lunch with James E. Solheim, the editor of *Event* magazine, a publication of the American Lutheran Church, McGovern confided that he had agonized over whether to participate in one of the antiwar events because of its association with student radicals and the New Left.

McGovern's top issue, the Vietnam War, was losing political steam. "The Indochina war is not an issue," said George Mitchell, a member of the McGovern Commission and Maine's Democratic national committeeman, to the *New York Times* in October 1970. "I think he [President Nixon] has skillfully defused it. His turning it around and bringing the soldiers back home has taken the heat off the subject. The ceasefire effort has merely helped the cooling-off process along."

McGovern's national recognition was minimal. He had been in demand as a public speaker in the last two years, but that appeal had not extended to the masses. According to several polls in 1970, McGovern's name was recognized by only 3 or 4 percent of the public. Also, with his nasal Midwestern monotone and deadpan features, he was unlikely to increase his visibility based on charisma.

McGovern's profile among Democratic voters was low. Doubtless he had impressed many Democrats during his eighteen-day presidential run in 1968, especially when he delivered a calm, articulate, good-natured performance before the California delegation at Chicago. But few Democrats regarded him as their ideal nominee. According to a Harris survey in December 1970, McGovern had the support of 2 percent of Democratic voters for the party's nomination. Not only did he trail Muskie, Humphrey, and Kennedy, but he also trailed John Lindsay, mayor of New York City and a registered Republican whose aides had mentioned him as a possible candidate. After McGovern formally announced his presidential campaign in January 1971, the *Washington Post* ran a profile of him with the headline "How 'Serious' Is McGovern's Candidacy?" His friend and mentor Hubert Humphrey admitted, "I quite honestly did not take him seriously as a presidential candidate."

McGovern's political record differed from those of his Democratic rivals in only minor ways. He steadfastly opposed the war and the military-industrial complex and supported the food stamp program. Otherwise, he was actually less liberal than the other presidential contenders. Americans for Democratic Action, the premier liberal interest group of the time, gave him a lower liberal rating than Muskie, Humphrey, and Kennedy. The only major Democrat who rated less liberal than McGovern was Senator Henry "Scoop" Jackson of Washington State.

Even the party's top antiwar activists considered McGovern's chances to be dubious. In 1971, Anne Wexler signed up for Muskie's campaign, as did Harold Ickes and Lanny Davis, two young stars of the McCarthy campaign.

Wexler had witnessed firsthand the unsuccessful 1970 Connecticut Senate campaign of Joseph Duffey, the young Protestant minister who had negotiated with John Bailey in 1968. Duffey's candidacy became a magnet for young antiwar activists, including Bill Clinton of Yale Law School. Wexler, who divorced her husband and married Duffey, saw McGovern as similar to her future husband: an ideal liberal candidate who couldn't win in November. "It was a hard decision on the basis of my personal relationship with McGovern," Wexler said in a 1972 interview with the *New Democrat* magazine. "[But] we had fought a very, very tough Senate campaign for all the things I think are important and with a candidate I thought far superior ideologically, politically, intellectually, morally to any other candidate who had been in the race for Senator. And we were badly defeated.... So, this time I thought, hell, if we are going to win, we have to win with a candidate who has a broader appeal."

A month after Gary Hart's trip with McGovern to New Hampshire, his gloom about the candidate's prospects had still not lifted. "The prospect for organizing a Presidential campaign from scratch seemed overwhelming," he wrote. "There was no guidebook or set of rules. There were few advisers to suggest the way. There was despair at ever having the resources and staff to mount a serious national effort." On July 15, McGovern opened his first presidential campaign headquarters on the first floor of a corner townhouse at 201 Maryland Avenue NE. In the evening, Hart and two campaign workers carried three cardboard boxes down the street from McGovern's Senate office to his new campaign office. Walking down the block, in the heat and mugginess of a Washington summer, Hart joked about the lack of press for the occasion: "I always thought Theodore White covered events like this."

Despite Hart's doubts and the odds against the South Dakota senator winning the party's nomination, McGovern grasped that he enjoyed a major advantage over his rivals. It wasn't that he had been a war hero, as a bomber pilot during World War II. It wasn't that he had been a presidential candidate in 1968 and was supported by some Kennedy aides. It wasn't that, as chairman of the Senate Select Committee on Nutrition and Human Needs, he was gaining renown as a champion of the poor and hungry. It wasn't even that he had been a vocal critic of the Vietnam War all along. McGovern's main advantage was the McGovern Commission. As its chairman, he recognized that the Democratic train would travel down a new nomination track, one dominated by an insurgent group of passengers.

McGovern's presidential bid was the second result of the McGovern Commission. If the old system had remained, McGovern would have stood little chance of gaining the party's nomination. His ties to traditional Democrats were too thin and frayed. But under the activist system, he had a real shot at winning. Although McGovern has said in recent years that he could have won the nomination under any system, he did not reach that conclusion in early 1972. After losing the Iowa and Arizona caucuses he said, "Under the old system, where convention delegates were mainly chosen by party leaders, I would have had no chance. Ed Muskie would have the nomination by now."

Understanding the task in front of him, McGovern in the summer of 1970 invited a handful of aides to his farm, Cedar Point, on the Eastern Shore of Maryland, for a strategy meeting. Along with his wife, a secretary, and a longtime aide, he brought Hart and two other party workers with ties to the reform commission. One was Richard Wade. The other was Rick Stearns, who in between interning for the commission and the Vietnam Moratorium had been writing a thesis at Oxford University on the Democratic Party's nomination process.

Over the weekend of July 25 and 26, the group discussed when McGovern should announce his candidacy. Should he do so after the debate on the McGovern-Hatfield amendment to end the war in late summer, before the November elections, or after the midterms? McGovern's decision was determined by one consideration: that he be the candidate of party activists, especially those based in the universities. According to Hart, McGovern said that "for a year and a half he had sensed, more than any time since he had been in public life, a wide-spread need for leadership, particularly among activists in the Democratic Party." McGovern added, "[T]he first person who announces loud and clear is going to be relieved that somebody will take Nixon on. Anyone who waits beyond, say, November 15 is going to be the second guy."

McGovern would be the liberal-issue candidate. He couldn't be the pragmatic liberal candidate; Muskie had won that distinction already. He couldn't be the charismatic liberal candidate; John Lindsay was that man. McGovern would be the candidate of the college students, the New Politics activists, and the antiwar protesters.

After a few more threads of discussion, the group turned to McGovern's strategy with party regulars. If McGovern championed liberal activists, why would party bosses support him? Wouldn't party regulars endorse a more traditional Democrat like Humphrey or Muskie?

The group answered the questions easily: McGovern would argue that his reform commission defused the possibility of a third or fourth party emerging in 1972. "My one unique position with reference to the potential competition," McGovern said, "is to be to the left of them all, but to make clear to the party pols and organization Democrats that they're not going to find me leading a fourth party or my candidacy producing pickets outside the convention hall. [It's] conceivable that while I might be the most left-leaning candidate, I am also the most reconciling candidate."

McGovern had said before that his reform commission could prevent college students and upper-class voters from bolting the Democratic Party to form a third or fourth political party. In an early 1970 interview with Theodore White, McGovern had laid out the following scenario, as White characterized it: "The Reform Commission he was then heading, it seemed to him, was the best method of unifying the party; the Democrats could only win as a united party; the reforms he was pushing through were the only way of drawing back into the party the young, the women, the farmers, even the Wall Street brokers."

Whether college students and white-collar Democrats would splinter off to form a third or fourth party is hard to say. Political opinion was divided in 1970 and 1971, when the controversy in the elite press was at its height. The McGovernites pushed the argument among their fellow New Politics activists. In the October 1970 issue of *The New Democrat,* the house organ of the New Politics movement, Richard Wade contended:

> [I]f there is no change in the Democratic Party by 1972, there indeed will be a fourth candidate nominated by a fraction of disillusioned delegates from the regular convention joined by those who felt excluded altogether. The result would be an easy Nixon-Agnew victory, the shattering of the political structure, and the continued minority rule of a divided and distraught nation.... I think the greatest energy should be applied to the opening and revitalization

of the Democratic Party. Those who worked so hard for Kennedy and McCarthy have earned a voice in the party. They ought to continue the job in the months ahead and then, perhaps, nominate the man who now best embodies that effort, the Senator from South Dakota.

After broaching the fourth-party topic, the group discussed the campaign's strategy for the primaries and caucuses. They concluded that, because of the campaign's meager funds, McGovern should focus on a handful of state primaries rather than all twenty-three. But if he won a few key primaries, he could clean up in the caucus and convention states. According to Hart, "the most convincing argument for the party regulars, the center, would be organizational strength—victories in the middle and later primaries and superior numbers of people in the caucuses in the non-primary states."

What the group did not mention was the most obvious fact of all: As chairman of the commission that produced many of the primaries and caucuses, McGovern knew the shape of the nomination track better than anyone else.

—ᴍ—

THE CONVENTIONAL WISDOM about George McGovern is that he won the party's nomination by knowing the new nomination rules better than his rivals. In truth, McGovern did more than use the new rules to his benefit. Had he run under a democratic nomination process, he would have lost. This tabulation of primary and caucus votes in 1972 underscores the point:

	Percentage of Vote	Total Votes
Humphrey	26.5	4,051,340
McGovern	25.8	3,950,394
Wallace	23.6	3,612,650
Muskie	11.9	1,824,948
Others	12.2	1,853,373

McGovern's aides recognized all along that the new activist system would help him significantly. Eli Segal certainly knew.

After resigning from the McGovern Commission in mid-1970, Segal worked as the general counsel for the Senate Select Committee on Nutrition and Human Needs, which McGovern chaired. On July 21, 1970, Segal wrote McGovern a half-page memo in which he urged the senator to lobby the DNC to implement the reforms. As Segal noted, "I remain convinced that this project is valuable for at least two reasons: first, *the actual implementation of the reforms would make the nomination of a liberal candidate more likely;* second, the identification with party reform gives you a catalyst to reach party leaders unhappy with your outspoken position on controversial issues." (Emphasis added.) McGovern heeded the advice, buttonholing DNC officials and not stepping down as commission chairman until January 1971.

How could McGovern have won the party's nomination under a system that supposedly had been democratized? He won partly because his aides discounted his numerous defeats in state primaries, such as Michigan and Pennsylvania, spinning those losses as inconsequential. He won partly because of the multi-candidate field, in which he emerged as the most electable liberal. But he also won partly because of his overwhelming victories in the states without primaries—the caucus and convention states. As John G. Stewart, communications director for the DNC from 1970 to 1972, concluded, "In many ways" the 1972 Democratic race was "a reversal of 1968: Hubert Humphrey was forced to stake his candidacy on his showing in the primaries, while George McGovern was cleaning up in the convention states."

McGovern cleaned up in the non-primary states by employing well-designed blitz tactics. Where big-city and state bosses had relied on working-class and white ethnic patronage workers to identify and bring voters to the polls, McGovern relied on volunteers. Most were not traditional Democrats. Rick Stearns, the coordinator of McGovern's operation in the caucus and convention states, described his initial efforts in Kansas: "We ... collected every sympathetic list we could—student directories, the Women's Caucus, the ACLU, Unitarians, the New Democratic Coalition, Methodist Church voters, and so on."

Of course, in 1968 Eugene McCarthy had sought out the same types of volunteers. Where McGovern differed is that he cultivated the activists systematically. He spent much of his time in 1971 wooing individual activists in several non-caucus states. In an unpublished manuscript, Stearns described the campaign's efforts in Iowa:

> Our principal organizing weapon was a list of computerized contributors gathered by our direct-mail apparatus, listing the names of some 125 Iowa Democrats. Selecting one at random in Des Moines—Chris Froisheiser, a twenty-five-year-old insurance agent—we called him, gave him a list of fourteen other Des Moines names and asked him to organize a meeting on the following night.
>
> We met in the basement of Froisheiser's apartment complex. Thirteen of the fourteen attended. Among them was a former precinct committeeman who had been a candidate for Polk County Chairman. Deciding that this was as much experience as we were likely to find, he was named temporary state coordinator, while from the remaining thirteen, the Greater Des Moines McGovern for President Committee was created.
>
> That night we slept on Froisheiser's floor. The following day Pokorny and I split the remaining list by zip codes. Gene went north, I south, meeting two days later in Iowa City. By then we had a statewide organization, albeit skeletal, but with at least one contact in each major county or city. When I returned to Des Moines, a month later, this time to the basement of a downtown church, 175 people were waiting.

Stearns used the same strategy in the Vermont caucus. "The open and poorly attended caucuses of Vermont will favor candidates with a strongly motivated following," he reasoned. "With careful organization a good McGovern showing at the state convention can be made." Theoretically, Muskie should have won Vermont easily because he came from Maine. Instead, McGovern won nine of the state's twelve delegates.

Stearns also used the strategy at the Utah state convention. He had predicted that "an active liberal-student coalition which took control of the 1970 state convention will be back in force in 1972." McGovern faced long odds in Utah. Governor Calvin Rampton had been a conservative member of the McGovern Commission and had endorsed Muskie for president, and the state's voters were conservative. The odds didn't matter. McGovern won eleven of the state's nineteen delegates.

McGovern also recognized the debt he owed to the activist nomination system. Early on the morning of Friday, July 14, the third session of the convention in Miami Beach, he paid tribute to the nominating process he helped create. In the original text of the speech, after saying that he accepted the party's nomination, McGovern explained his view of how he won:

> My nomination is all the more precious in that it is a gift of the most open political process in all of our political history. It is the sweet harvest of the work of tens of thousands of tireless volunteers, young and old alike, funded by literally hundreds of thousands of small contributors in every part of this nation. Those who lingered on the brink of despair only a short time ago have been brought into this campaign, heart, hand, head and soul, and I have been the beneficiary of the most remarkable political organization in the history of this country.

—⚏—

In May 1971, McGovern attended a reception in Washington for Fred Dutton's new book, *Changing Sources of Power: American Politics in the 1970s*. Handed out at the signing was a two-page summary of its major points: "Four Major Presidential Candidates in the '72 and '76 General Elections"; "The Sharp Erosion of the Major Parties"; "The 18 to 34 Year Old Group's Critical New Potential"; "First-Time Voters as a Massive New Factor"; "The Likely Greater Turn-Out of Younger Voters Just Ahead"; and "The Politics of the New Generation of Voters." On May 20, 1971, Dutton dashed off a handwritten note to McGovern, thanking him for attending the reception and telling him of his whereabouts in the next few months. In the postscript, Dutton gave McGovern an enticement to read the tome thoroughly: "The book really tells of your natural constituency." McGovern said later, "[Dutton] mentioned that concern to me, and I thought it made a lot of sense."

Gary Hart viewed McGovern's coalition similarly. As he wrote of the campaign in June 1971, "we were constructing a

McGovern coalition of the Kennedy-McCarthy activists, the young, minority groups, antiwar organizations, women and others whose commitments to the principles of the Democratic Party generally outweighed the voice they had exerted in its affairs."

McGovern also spoke about the need to build a new political alliance along the lines of Dutton's Social Change coalition. At Hunter College in New York City on December 9, 1971, McGovern said,

> I think we can build a different majority. It is not a majority that will welcome, or even tolerate, the bombing and burning of helpless Asians so long as the cost is reduced. It is not a majority so unthinking that it can be led around by rhetoric, or so uncaring that it can be undivided on matters of style from its common interests in matters of substance.
>
> Instead, it can be constructed from small businessmen who know that appointing William Rehnquist, having the FBI investigate Daniel Schorr, or locking up youthful pot-smokers, does nothing about the heroin enslavement that accounts for a major share of robberies, about the proliferation of handguns that has made us all fear for our lives, or about the other real causes of crime in this country.

McGovern was not dismissive of blue-collar Democrats. In the summer or fall of 1970, he requested that the research arm of the Library of Congress present a summary of recent books and magazine articles about "the political and social attitudes of the blue-collar worker." But like Dutton, he did consider the interests of traditional Democrats secondary to those of his new base. "The young, the black, and the poor provide the core with which I'd begin," he told Milton Viorst of *Playboy* magazine in a mid-1971 interview. "But no one is going to be elected President with that coalition alone. I want to develop programs that have broad appeal for workingmen and women, organized and unorganized. As we move along, I also want to speak out on the concerns of women. And I intend to focus on the problems of rural America as well as of the cities."

In his 1968 campaign, McCarthy had placed the interests of young people, activists, and doves above those of Catholic and blue-collar Democrats. His rationale had been that in a general election, any Democratic nominee would win the votes of Catholics and working-class whites against Nixon. McGovern thought that he differed from McCarthy in that he actually cared about traditional Democrats too. McCarthy, he said to Viorst, "somehow addressed himself to the issues that were compatible with the interests of the middle class. He lacked empathy with the guy at the bottom."

At the same time, McGovern and McCarthy held a similar political philosophy, a belief that government's primary task was to liberate individuals. During a press conference at the Capitol to announce his candidacy for the presidency, on January 19, 1971, McGovern sounded the theme of secular liberation:

> Americans have never believed that simply to talk about problems was to solve them. We need action, and I intend action.
>
> But surely our failure to act must also reflect a larger loss of spirit and confidence—almost as if citizens felt that the conditions and quality of their lives was beyond their influence. And it is this, in my judgment, that is the heart of the matter. From participatory democracy to women's liberation and citizens' conservation councils, we see an increasing assertion of the individual, a desire not simply to have things done, but to do them.
>
> We want to matter as individuals—all of us. The task of future leadership is not to rule people's lives. It is to change the institutions of society so the citizens may shape their own lives.

McGovern's emphasis on individual liberation and his focus on a new political constituency in the early 1970s were significant: In the cultural revolution, he decided to ally with secular Americans rather than traditionally religious Americans.

He might have gone the other way. The son of a Wesleyan Methodist minister, McGovern and his siblings read Scripture every day before school, and they attended evangelistic meetings where preachers talked about damnation and salvation. After the war, McGovern became a student pastor with a Social

Gospel orientation at a Methodist church in suburban Chicago. McGovern did reject parts of his Christian faith. When his unmarried fifteen-year-old daughter became pregnant in 1966, he and his wife allowed her to procure an abortion. However, McGovern was ambivalent about abortion and skeptical about drugs.

Despite his reservations about the cultural revolution, McGovern needed to represent the New Politics constituency that supported it. His overarching goal was to end the war immediately. To that end, he needed to hold campaign events at campuses and cocktail parties before factories and industrial plants.

Consequently, McGovern endorsed much of the New Left's cultural agenda. On abortion, he argued that the matter should be left to the states rather than the federal government. Regarding drugs, he argued for decriminalizing the use of marijuana but maintaining laws against hard drugs such as cocaine, heroin, and LSD. On amnesty for draft resisters, he argued that if elected he would, after removing American troops from Vietnam, grant amnesty to those who had resisted military conscription. As for amnesty for deserters, he said that if he were elected, they would be evaluated on a case-by-case basis.

McGovern took a position on cultural issues that placed him to the left of his Democratic rivals. By way of comparison, Ed Muskie staked out much more conservative social positions. While touring the nation's campuses, Muskie received, in the words of the *New York Times,* only "average grades." At a rally on February 3, 1972, at the University of Wisconsin, Madison, he expressed skepticism about legalizing pot and had a cloud of marijuana smoke blown in his face. "Mr. Muskie's remarks were continually interrupted," the *Times* reported, "by shouted obscenities ... [and] mock expressions of sympathy." On visits to the Madison campus and to Wisconsin State University in Eau Claire, Muskie stood firm on his principles. He refused to give amnesty to draft evaders and, as a man who believed in the "value of human life," he supported abortion only if necessary to save the lives of mothers.

McGovern realized that his social liberalism might alienate traditional Democrats. In one typical passage in his autobiography,

Grassroots, he summarized his exchanges with university students about abortion with a wounded, slightly indignant tone: "No, I would not recommend the intrusion of the federal government into this highly sensitive area. It did not seem to me to be an issue that should be involved in a presidential campaign. Recognizing the depth of public feeling on the matter, it was my view that the federal government should not tamper with existing state law, that any remedy should come through action at the state level."

In fact, McGovern failed to recognize the depth of public feeling about abortion, amnesty, and drugs. His positions were to the left of the public in general and traditional Democrats specifically. As a result, McGovern consistently ran behind his top rivals among Catholic and working-class Democrats.

In the New Hampshire primary in March, McGovern's appeal to working-class and Catholic Democratic voters was minimal. He carried working-class wards only in those parts of the state that were within the circulation area of the *Manchester Union Leader,* whose publisher, William Loeb, subjected Muskie to unrelenting criticism. As Lanny Davis explained in *The Emerging Democratic Majority*, Loeb's attacks prompted many blue-collar Democrats to defect from Muskie to Mayor Sam Yorty of Los Angeles and Representative Wilbur Mills of Arkansas, two conservative Democratic presidential candidates. Overall, McGovern rarely won more than a third of the vote in the state's blue-collar Democratic neighborhoods.

In the Wisconsin primary in April, McGovern's support among traditional Democrats improved only slightly. He did win five of the state's seven congressional districts. But the *Washington Post,* Theodore White, Rowland Evans and Robert Novak leaped to the conclusion that McGovern was picking up steam among Catholics and blue-collar workers. In fact, Lanny Davis showed that McGovern did not do well among those groups for a Democratic presidential candidate. His percentages in working-class neighborhoods "rarely went over 35 or 40 percent, and were usually in the low and mid-twenties." For example, he won the Fourth Congressional District, which encompasses Milwaukee, with only 27 percent of the vote. In most of the ethnic working-class wards of Milwaukee, he rarely got more than 20 to 25 percent of the vote. McGovern won the state not because of strong support among traditional Democrats, but because in a five-candidate race he received sufficient backing among his natural constituency of students, upper-class reformers, and antiwar Democrats.

In the Nebraska primary in May, McGovern's appeal to Catholic Democrats was average. He had to endure subtle attacks from Humphrey for his positions on cultural issues. For instance, at a Catholic school in Omaha, Humphrey said by way of comparison, "I do not favor national legislation to abolish state abortion laws and I do not favor abortion on demand." The McGovern campaign responded by handing out leaflets to parishioners at nearly every Catholic church in Omaha detailing McGovern's legislative record and showing pictures of him with Kathleen Kennedy, daughter of Bobby Kennedy. McGovern did carry rural counties with large German-Catholic populations, but his success may have resulted from his South Dakota background. As the *New York Times* concluded, "[Humphrey's] charges obviously hurt, particularly in conservative urban Catholic areas of the kind the South Dakotan has been trying to convert. He lost nearly 2 to 1 in Catholic south Omaha's four wards."

McGovern and several of his aides were under no illusion about his support among Catholic Democrats. On June 15, staff members Gerry Cassidy and Kenneth Schlossberg sent McGovern a three-page memo about the "Catholic vote." It painted a dreary picture of the candidate's strength among this historic Democratic constituency. "The DNC's old-time reliance on simply thumping the economic issue and relying on the unions won't be enough," they wrote. "Your situation, heading a newly reformed party, may add particularly difficult problems to this issue." On July 21, Cassidy and Schlossberg followed up with an eight-page memo to Frank Mankiewicz, a senior McGovern aide, in which they emphasized the negative impression caused by the McGovern Commission's informal quotas:

> The lack of ethnics (and old people) at the convention was obvious and well perceived. We have already heard disturbing questions

about, "If quotas are good for the young and the black, why not for the elderly and the Polish?" In fact, the campaign made every effort to appeal to the special concerns of the black voter, therefore why not make a similar effort to appeal to the Catholic-ethnic? Why is home rule for D.C. more worthy of special concern and a campaign pledge than aid to parochial education?

Cassidy and Schlossberg also stressed that the McGovern coalition might alienate Catholic and blue-collar Democrats:

> The heavy emphasis in the press during and since the convention on voter registration of youth as a secret key to your victory in the fall contains what we see as a very dangerous side-effect—the appearance of deliberately dividing the electorate into "us" and "them." The "us" being the accepted McGovern constituency— the young, the black, the poor, the women's libbers, etc.—and the "them" being the rest of white middle-class working America, including Catholic-Ethnic America.... *The New Majority* may constitute the winning edge but without the rest of the normal Democratic constituency—or at least a healthy portion of it—the winning edge may just well end up the losing edge. By unduly dwelling on the "top" of our coalition, we risk further aggravating social tensions in the foundations of our necessary support and having the house fall down.

In fact, Cassidy and Schlossberg concluded that Nixon was wooing Catholic voters more effectively than McGovern. As they pointed out, Nixon supported aid to parochial schools, stressed his personal opposition to abortion, and tried to reduce crime. "[T]he battle for the Catholic-ethnic vote will largely be one of demonstrating understanding and concern for them. They are the whites left behind in our cities, they are cops, they are the blue-collar workers. They are looking for someone to listen and respond. Right now Nixon seems to be doing more of both for them."

McGovern agreed with this analysis. Over the week of Labor Day, while eating lunch with Theodore White in Albuquerque, McGovern confessed that his campaign was struggling with Catholics and working-class voters. "Our main problem is the blue-collar Catholic worker," he said. Summarizing McGovern's thinking, White wrote, "His record in the primaries, he said, had been 'erratic' in those factory towns. 'You just didn't know what would reach them.'"

In the hope of returning Catholics to the Democratic fold in November, McGovern put two Catholics on the Democratic ticket (Senator Thomas Eagleton of Missouri and, after he was dropped, Sargent Shriver). He made amends with Mayor Daley, whose Illinois delegation had been bounced by the Credentials Committee at the convention. And he endorsed an income tax credit for parents who send their children to parochial schools. The campaign, however, put very little money behind reaching blue-collar ethnics. Schlossberg and Cassidy had asked for a budget of $250,000. They received $12,000. (By contrast, the Nixon campaign spent $2 million.)

McGovern also tried to make amends with other traditional Democrats. In August, he flew to the LBJ Ranch in Texas to seek the endorsement of the former president, and he lobbied George Meany, the AFL-CIO president, to support the ticket. Neither effort succeeded. Johnson, who had prevailed upon an aide to write a long, negative paper about McGovern's professional career, supported the ticket in the most desultory way possible, sending a letter to the local paper without mentioning McGovern by name. The AFL-CIO, in a dramatic break with precedent, remained neutral in the 1972 presidential contest.

McGovern's strategy to keep traditional Democrats in the fold collapsed.

On Election Day in November, McGovern lost overwhelmingly among Catholics. Nixon carried 59 percent of the Catholic vote, the same percentage that Humphrey had won four years earlier. As the historian George Marlin noted, Nixon's total represented a new record for a Republican presidential candidate.

McGovern also lost overwhelmingly among working-class whites. Blue-collar workers gave 55 percent of their vote to Nixon, up from 41 percent in 1968. Indeed, the shift in voting among Catholic and blue-collar Democrats was historic. A full 37 percent of Democrats cast their ballots for the Republican candidate. As White noted, "The Democratic defection in 1972

is without precedent—in neither of his huge victories did Eisenhower win more than 23 percent of Americans who claimed to
be Democrats; and in Johnson's huge landslide, only 20 percent
of the Republicans defected."

Traditional Democrats deserted McGovern in November for
many reasons. They opposed his proposal to give every American
a grant of $1,000 a year; they detested his support of forced bus-
ing; and they ridiculed his dumping of Eagleton from the ticket,
especially after he had said that he stood behind the Missouri
senator "1,000 percent." Democratic strategists acknowledged
that McGovern's support for the New Left's cultural agenda dam-
aged his candidacy. Charles Guggenheim later noted,

> McGovern came on as a new person talking about populist issues,
> and populist issues attracted that group very much. But then, I
> think, when [Senator Henry] Jackson began to go on about the
> three A's—acid, abortion, and amnesty.... McGovern felt that
> Nebraska was where it began. After the Wisconsin primary, some
> people thought that McGovern was really going to be a threat....
> The underside was more abhorrent to the blue-collar vote than to
> any other group in the American electorate.

Ben Wattenberg said that the election was the "equivalent of
a referendum" on the cultural revolution. "If there was going to
be an election on something in this country, this was a pretty
good thing to have an election on," he said. "And the American
people voted 'no' on what the New Politics was all about." Wattenberg noted that Gallup took a poll that found McGovern to
have *lost* support after the Democratic convention—the only
time in polling history that a nominee had lost ground.

Representative James O'Hara of Michigan, the chairman of
the *other* Democratic reform commission, agreed that McGovern had lost the election at Miami Beach. McGovern came to be
identified, he said, with the counterculture. "The American people made an association between McGovern and gay lib, and
welfare rights, and pot-smoking, and black militants, and
women's lib, and wise college kids, and everything else they saw
as threatening their value systems," he said. "I think it was all
over right then and there."

Historians and journalists often describe the New Deal coalition as internally inconsistent, representing groups with many divergent interests, such as Southern whites and Northern blacks or Catholics and Jews. But internal inconsistency also defined the Social Change or McGovern-Dutton coalition. As the election results indicated, few Catholic and blue-collar Democrats wanted to be in the same party with college students, liberation-minded feminists, and upper-class reformers. And these traditional Democrats certainly did not want to sit in the back of the Democratic train while college students, doves, and secular white-collar workers sat in front.

McGovern's coalition was exposed as no more than a minority alliance, unable to unite the interests of the New Politics constituencies with the New Deal ones. More broadly, McGovern's 1972 campaign was the third main result of the McGovern Commission: The new activist system had nominated a Democrat who got crushed in a general election.

EIGHT

Blue by You

George McGovern's victory in the 1972 California primary was more than a wake-up call to the traditional Democratic leadership. It was an alarm bell. *The Democratic Party is being taken over by the party wreckers!* So the party regulars changed their tactics accordingly. Instead of letting the secular liberals sneak into the conductor's booth, they announced that the activists were attempting to hijack the Democratic train.

The sense of panic was widely shared. No less a consensus politician than Hubert Humphrey hit an uncharacteristically dark note. In a statement for a Platform Committee hearing in June 1972, he warned that a "single, narrow, ideological, social or political elite" threatened to capture the Democratic Party. "[W]e must remember," he wrote, "that the strength of the Democratic Party since the days of Franklin Roosevelt has resided in our ability to put together coalitions which form majorities, to convince a majority of Americans that we are the party which represents the average American working family."

George Meany, president of the AFL-CIO and a proud Irish Catholic, was not one to blab to the press. For years, he had kept his doubts about and criticisms of the national party off the record. But in 1972, he went public. Besides storming out of the Miami Beach convention and criticizing McGovern as an apologist for Communism, Meany assailed upscale social liberals. At a convention of the United Steelworkers of America in September

1972, he said that the Miami Beach convention had been a "classy convention of the elite," attended mainly by "gay liberationists and people who want to liberalize abortions."

Another party regular who disdained the secular liberals was Robert Strauss, the treasurer of the Democratic National Committee. Strauss, a gentlemanly sort, did not air his criticisms publicly. He just kept the activists at arm's length. While McGovern was accepting the party's nomination, Strauss was pouring drinks for himself in a trailer outside the convention hall. When McGovern made his only campaign appearance in Dallas, Strauss was out of town.

In spurning the youthful activists and defending the traditional Democratic Party, Strauss was no Johnny-come-lately. Robert Strauss was born in a small town in West Texas in October 1918. Although raised in a nonpracticing Jewish household, Strauss had little in common with secular liberals. After graduating from the University of Texas at Austin, he worked for Lyndon Johnson's successful 1937 congressional campaign. His political interests were those of the business class. After purchasing a law firm and three television stations in Dallas, he became a millionaire. His closest political friend was Governor John Connally, who served as secretary of the Navy in the Kennedy administration, governor of Texas, and secretary of the Treasury under Nixon.

Strauss accepted the job as treasurer with the national party in early 1970 on one condition: Lawrence O'Brien would become the party chairman. Strauss did not know O'Brien well; their contact had been limited to the fall 1968 campaign, when O'Brien was DNC chairman and Strauss was Humphrey's campaign chairman in Texas. But Strauss knew that O'Brien, as a former Johnson and Kennedy aide, was a party regular, not a reformer.

Strauss's colleagues viewed him as a loyal, faithful Old Politics liberal. "Any man who would become the treasurer of a party that was over nine million dollars in debt," O'Brien commented, "was obviously a good Democrat." Jean Westwood, whom McGovern had chosen to replace O'Brien, said that Strauss was as much a symbol of the conservative Democratic establishment as she of the McGovern forces.

Yet Strauss was more than a traditional Democrat. He was one of the party's most competent and trusted leaders. At the beginning of his term as treasurer, the party had a debt of $9.3 million. Two and a half years later, he had cut the debt in half. At the convention in Miami Beach, AFL-CIO leaders approached him about raising money for Democratic congressional candidates. Four months later, he had raised millions of dollars, enabling the party to pick up two seats in the Senate and surrender only twelve in the House.

After the national ticket was clobbered in November, leaders of the AFL-CIO got behind Strauss again. He was their choice to replace Jean Westwood as DNC chairman.

AFL-CIO leaders did not choose Strauss in order to maintain the status quo in the party. Bringing back a conciliator like O'Brien, who had ruled in favor of McGovern on the question of the California delegation's credentials at the convention, was out of the question. They chose Strauss to help them wrest back control of the party machinery. Their goal was counterrevolutionary: they wanted New Deal Democrats to displace New Politics Democrats.

Perhaps the most forceful counterrevolutionary was Al Barkan, Meany's chief political deputy. By driving out the pro-abortion and pro-pot advocates, Barkan believed, the Democratic Party could once again become the political home of millions of working-class voters who had deserted the party in 1972. "It was a zero sum game for him," said Mark A. Siegel, executive officer of the party's three reform commissions.

Strauss never said whether he agreed with the counterrevolutionaries, but he acted as if he did. After becoming chairman, he hired Robert Keefe, a deputy to Barkan, as DNC executive director.

Ken Bode expected Strauss to turn back the clock on the reforms and purge the young secular activists. In a memo written shortly after Strauss won the party chairmanship, Bode ridiculed Strauss as a Southern bumpkin and brute: "Robert Strauss met with the National Steering Committee of the New Democratic Coalition on Sunday, December 10, as, 'mah furst public meeting with any group since becomin' yure charmin.'

The leaders and officers of the NDC seemed genuinely moved by the gesture. Strauss, speaking in code, explained to them that they should hunker over and prepare for a fuckin'."

Bode's fear was not misplaced. Party regulars continued to wield clout. Mayor Daley was still in charge of the Cook County Democratic Party; John Bailey was still boss of the Connecticut Democratic Party; Jacob Arvey was still a DNC committeeman. Former Johnson and Humphrey aides had founded the Coalition for a Democratic Majority, an organization dedicated to reviving most of the New Deal coalition. And the AFL-CIO remained a major player in party affairs. As late as 1973, David Broder of the *Washington Post* wrote, "the leaders of organized labor are more deeply involved in the affairs of the Democratic Party than ever before in its history."

In theory, party regulars could have regained control of the national machinery. After all, the various wings of the party toppled one another with regularity. After the 1948 convention, the Northern Catholic bosses had wrested control from Southern state chairmen. After 1968, secular professionals had overthrown the bosses.

If anyone could eject the seculars from the conductor's booth and install the regulars, Strauss could. In many ways he was a natural successor to David Lawrence and John Bailey. He was an experienced political broker. A successful business lawyer, he had founded the powerful law firm of Akin, Strauss, and Gump. He exuded confidence and know-how. "I've got a proven record," he said. "As Dizzy Dean said, 'It ain't bragging if you can do it.'" He was gracious, charming, and mannerly.

So what prevented another leadership change after 1972? The chief obstacle was a practical one: the legacy of the McGovern Commission. Although the commission had expired before the 1972 convention, its work continued to influence the party in three ways.

First, the McGovern Commission had convinced many elite passengers on the Democratic train to support the activist nomination track. A good example was Americans for Democratic Action, the venerable political organ of the party's citizen-intellectual wing. ADA endorsed the commission's guidelines in the strongest terms possible. In a report titled *Let Us Continue,* the group did not level one criticism at the reforms and rules changes. "The Guidelines," ADA wrote, "have reinvigorated the party, engaged the enthusiasm of thousands of new Democrats and set a context for a strong and winning party."

Second, the McGovern Commission had laid a booby trap to protect the activist nomination track: It had established informal quotas for presidential delegates. Any effort to eliminate the quotas was portrayed in party councils and in the media as discriminatory, as an effort by old white men to exclude women and people of color. Sissy Farenthold, president of the National Women's Political Caucus, argued, "It is crucial that the Democratic Party not over-react to the defeat of the national ticket" and "exclude women, minorities, youth, and rank-and-file working people."

Third, the McGovern Commission had strengthened the grip of activist conductors. By helping McGovern win the party's nomination and become the party's titular head, the commission gave him authority to name a new DNC chairman, which he exercised the day after the Miami Beach convention. In September 1972, Jean Westwood created a new reform body: the Commission on Delegate Selection and Party Structure. It was chaired by Barbara Mikulski, a city councilor in Baltimore. Of its fifty-one members, the majority favored the McGovern Commission's guidelines. Among the commissioners were not only Ken Bode and Phyllis Segal, but also Sarah Kovner, the national treasurer of the New Democratic Coalition, as well as Joseph Zazyczny, a city councilor in Philadelphia and a pro-McGovern white ethnic.

Consequently, the regulars could not regain control of the party levers. Too many secular professionals had lodged themselves in the conductor's booth. For example, Strauss had narrowly defeated Westwood, winning by four and a half votes out of two hundred cast. Fulfilling Barkan and Meany's dream of a workingman's Democratic Party was impossible.

To the extent that Strauss had a plan to revive the national party, it was for New Politics and Old Politics Democrats to share power. "I want to create a climate where all sides begin talking to each other," he said the day after being elected DNC chairman. He also nodded in the directions of both camps. At his first press conference as chairman, Strauss pleased the party reformers by saying, "Anyone who expects me to turn my back on the reforms is in for a rude shock." Several weeks later, he pleased the regulars by saying, "Not all change is reform, and not all reform is functional."

In other words, Strauss sought to mediate the dueling visions of Al Barkan and Fred Dutton. His path for the Democratic Party was evolutionary, not revolutionary or counterrevolutionary. Control of the party machinery would be shared between secular activists and traditional Democrats. The presidential nomination system would be shared among voters, activists, and politicians. The coalition would assign equal weight to the interests of secular professionals, feminists, Catholics, and blue-collar workers. The party would fight hardest to reduce economic inequality but would not forget the goal of individual liberation.

In many ways, Strauss succeeded. First, he weakened the grip of secular activists over the party machinery. His initial step was to add twenty-two members to the Mikulski Commission, most of whom were traditional Democrats. Strauss contended that the commission lacked enough representatives from the state parties. He was bitterly opposed by Bode and other secular professionals, who argued that his move violated the DNC's charter. But Strauss won the day. His last step was to announce that the Democratic National Committee possessed the authority to review and revise the Mikulski Commission's proposals. In other words, party regulars, not reformers, had veto power over the commission.

Strauss restored a voice to politicians in the nomination system. He persuaded the Mikulski Commission to reinstate ex-officio delegates, who were usually politicians and state party leaders. His work had been sponsored by Old Politics Democrats, such as Penn Kemble of the Coalition for a Democratic Majority. This group had argued that bringing back ex-officio delegates would "reduce the class bias in the party's nomination process: the impact of the more affluent, educated activists who have the time and the means to participate more effectively in so-called grass roots processes of our political parties."

Strauss helped build a broad electoral coalition. Gone was talk of building a Social Change coalition. In its place was talk of a Broad Coalition. "We saw once again that we are the Party of the old and the Party of the young, the Party of white people, black people, Spanish speaking people, Native Americans and European ethnic Americans," the authors of the final report of the Mikulski Commission wrote in December 1973. Strauss, in his address at the midterm convention, boasted that the convention showed that the party "has reestablished our great coalition of working families, minorities, labor, the farmer, and the businessman."

Strauss helped unite Democrats around a core economic message. Although his effort was aided by the fact that the country was in recession in 1973 and 1974, he focused national leaders on the issues that united the party (economic), not those that divided it (social). His triumph came at an unprecedented midterm convention in early December 1974 in Kansas City, Missouri. When the 1,900 Democratic delegates and party leaders assembled to approve a party charter, they debated nothing having to do with abortion, homosexual rights, or gun control. Instead, they passed an eight-point program that urged Congress to enact an expanded public-service jobs program, tax cuts for the poor and the middle class, and mandatory energy conservation measures.

The epitome of Strauss's middle way was his compromise over delegate quotas. Feminists insisted that the informal quotas be retained. "The Party would be committing a grave error in the hysteria of the moment to throw out the baby with the bath water," Phyllis Segal wrote to Mikulski in early 1973, "and it is therefore important to introduce some rational thought to the discussion of 'affirmative action' to encourage reasonable representation. *Our goal should not be to destroy Guidelines A-1 and A-2, but to make them work properly.*" (Emphasis in the original.) Party regulars argued not only for abolishing the quotas, but also against affirmative action for demographic groups. "Democracy cannot be accomplished by fiat," wrote the Coalition for a Democratic Majority. "If certain groups in the Democratic electorate are underrepresented in Party councils, those who would increase their representation must persuade other elements in the Party to help them achieve a greater role."

Between those two positions, Strauss claimed the middle ground. He convinced the commission to strike down the informal quotas. "Damn, that's good news," he exulted after the vote on October 23, 1973. "It's another constructive step forward." Yet he lobbied successfully on behalf of affirmative action. With an assist from Democratic governors, in December 1974 he pushed through a requirement that the states "encourage full participation by all Democrats, with particular concern for minority groups, native Americans, women, and youth ... as indicated by their presence in the Democratic electorate."

As a result of Strauss's efforts, the national Democratic Party enjoyed a rare period of harmony. At no time was this more apparent than on the first day of the mini-convention in Kansas City. After the delegates enacted the eight-point economic plan, Jesse Jackson threw his arms around Richard Daley. The next evening, after George McGovern delivered the keynote address, Strauss held aloft the 1972 nominee's right arm.

—ᴍ—

EIGHT DAYS BEFORE the Iowa caucus in 1976, Jimmy Carter was inside the dark wood-paneled basement of Holy Spirit Church in Creston, a farm town populated largely by German Catholics. Carter, a one-term governor of Georgia, had arrived on New Year's Day with one personal aide and negligible press coverage. While he was greeting potential voters downstairs after the morning Mass, a young woman approached him. Would he support federal legislation along the lines of the abortion ban that had been passed in his native state and was struck down by the Supreme Court in *Doe v. Bolton?* Carter paused and lowered his normally soft conversational voice to a near-whisper. "Under certain circumstances, I would," he replied.

Critics accused Carter of being "fuzzy" on the abortion issue, of playing both sides of the fence. And they were right. Following the game plan laid out by Richard Scammon and Ben Wattenberg in *The Real Majority,* Carter finessed the social issue. He never unequivocally supported any effort to overturn *Roe v. Wade* or *Doe v. Bolton.* He also never supported government funding of abortion. Yet Carter's personal view of abortion was quite pro-life. When a feminist-minded administration official in 1977 attacked his position on abortion, he returned her memo with his response penned in the margins: "My opinion was well defined to U.S. during campaign. My statement is actually more liberal than I feel personally."

Carter faced a unique political challenge: to win the votes of Catholics, evangelicals, and feminists. Partly because of Robert Strauss, each constituency was still part of the Democratic coalition. The party included almost as many white conservatives (19 percent) as white liberals (22 percent). Democratic presidential candidates still stumped at Knights of Columbus halls, the church basements of white Baptist denominations, and VFW lodges.

If balancing such divergent interests sounds like an impossible task, it wasn't in 1976. The political environment was much different from today. Battle lines in the culture war had yet to be drawn; the situation was fluid. Social conservatives still had a presence in the Democratic Party. Jesse Jackson delivered an eloquent pro-life speech at the March for Life, while Senator Ted Kennedy of Massachusetts voted for a constitutional amendment to overturn *Roe v. Wade* and return the issue of abortion to the states. And social liberals still had a presence in the Republican Party. Nelson Rockefeller, a former governor of New York who had signed a major pro-choice bill into law, was the vice president, while President Ford had not raised a fuss over Medicaid funding for abortion.

In the primaries, Carter sought to appeal just enough to Catholics and evangelicals that he didn't lose feminists. His strategy in the Iowa caucus was a classic example of finessing an issue.

To Catholic audiences, Carter conveyed the impression that he was the most pro-life Democratic candidate. When a local

Catholic newspaper sent him a questionnaire about his position on abortion, he answered that under certain circumstances he might accept a "national statute" restricting abortion. In the basement of Holy Spirit Catholic Church in Creston, his answer in support of the old Georgia law had even greater significance. That statute had permitted abortion only in grave circumstances, in which the unborn infant threatened the mother's life or health or had been conceived as a result of rape or incest. Even then, the woman had to receive permission from a hospital board. Considering that roughly 95 percent of abortions are performed for other reasons, it is fair to say that the law extended general legal protection to unborn infants.

To feminists, Carter conveyed the impression that he supported a woman's right to choose. Pro-life activists in Iowa repeatedly asked him whether he supported a constitutional amendment to overturn *Roe.* He never said he supported such an amendment. When the woman in Creston asked him about the old Georgia law, he lowered his voice and gave a nonspecific answer.

Carter's strategy worked. His chief competitor had been Senator Birch Bayh of Indiana, a favorite of organized labor and feminists. Bayh had won a straw poll at a candidates' rally in Sioux City. But in the last two weeks of the campaign, he was heckled, taunted, and harassed by right-to-life activists for his support of *Roe.* Bayh finished a distant third in Iowa, and his campaign never recovered. Another of Carter's competitors had been the 1972 vice-presidential nominee, Sargent Shriver, a favorite of Catholics. But Shriver also opposed a constitutional amendment to overturn *Roe,* undercutting his support among his natural constituency. He finished sixth in Iowa, and his campaign never got on track.

In contrast to Bayh and Shriver, Carter won social conservatives without losing social liberals. A feminist who was a county leader for Carter, after overhearing his remarks in Creston, told the reporters Rowland Evans and Robert Novak, "I'm terribly disappointed in him, but I'm still for him." Pro-lifers supported him too. A pro-life Catholic organization in Dubuque listed Carter as their favorite candidate in the state. A politically active priest based in Des Moines campaigned for him across the state. At the January 19 caucus, Carter received 28 percent of the total vote, more than twice as much as his nearest rival.

Carter's strong showing in the Iowa caucus was a key ingredient in his winning of the party's nomination. He struggled in the second half of the primary season, losing several big states; and political observers agree that if he had finished poorly in Iowa, he would not have become the Democratic nominee. As Scammon and Wattenberg had predicted, finessing the social issue could work.

In the general election, Carter continued to finesse the social issue, but slightly differently. He appealed more to Catholics and evangelicals than to feminists.

Many Catholics had expressed outrage at the party platform's opposition to a constitutional amendment to overturn *Roe.* The church hierarchy, still shocked that the Supreme Court had eliminated legal protection for unborn infants, mobilized accordingly. Archbishop Joseph Bernardin of Cincinnati, the head of the National Conference of Catholic Bishops, blasted the party platform as "irresponsible" and "morally offensive in the extreme." On the eve of the Democratic convention, ten thousand people rallied under a blazing sun in Central Park and marched to Madison Square Garden to urge the party to oppose the abortion plank. On the same evening that Carter accepted the party's nomination, a pro-life Democratic candidate, Ellen McCormack, criticized him on primetime television for supporting the party's platform stand, while one of her delegates warned that "the Democratic Party is in danger of becoming the party of abortion." The priest chosen to give the closing benediction at the convention backed out, citing Carter and the party's stand on abortion.

Carter's staff came to a realization: The campaign had a "Catholic problem." Solving it became an obsession inside the campaign. Two Catholic staff members were hired, including an aide to the National Conference of Catholic Bishops. The monthly mail was monitored as to whether more constituents supported or opposed Carter's stand on abortion.

To grasp the breadth and depth of the Catholic problem, Carter's strategists commissioned two Democratic strategists who had worked with Catholic candidates. Adam Walinsky, a speech-writer for Robert Kennedy in 1968, wrote a long, eloquent memo that framed the Catholic problem in historical context:

> The 1960's were the time when the Democratic Party finally fell to the "reformers"—to the professionals, the young, the black, the Puerto Rican, the women as interest group—which had been locked in combat with Tammany since the creation of the first city machines. Why and how that happened is a subject for another rainy day. What is relevant here is that under the impulse of pros-perity, leisure, war, and communications, the machines—which is to say, the institutional structure that had always succored the immigrants within the Democratic Party—collapsed and lost their influence before their job was done. The result was a time warp that was and remains enormously destructive to the Democratic Party, and to our politics generally.
>
> It is true that the immigrants, by the 1960's, were demonstrably better off than the racial minorities whose plight was virtually the exclusive focus of government policy during the decade.... But this economic and educational progress has not brought with it the social and political recognition that such achievement, born of bit-ter struggle over so many years, might have been expected to bring. So we had the spectacle in 1972 of a Democratic Presidential can-didate promising to appoint another black to the Supreme Court, promising to appoint a Mexican-American to the Supreme Court, but never even acknowledging the fact that for all their achieve-ments, there has never been an Italian on the Supreme Court, never been an Eastern European (other than a Jew) on the Supreme Court.

Carter's domestic policy adviser, Stuart Eizenstat, acted upon Walinsky's remarks. In September 1976, Carter was scheduled to speak before an Italian-American organization. Eizenstat urged the candidate and his top strategists to make the speech the equivalent of John F. Kennedy's famous speech before the Southern Baptist ministers in Houston in 1960. He added that Carter should promise to appoint an Italian Ameri-can or a person of Eastern or Southern European heritage to the Supreme Court or the cabinet. Carter did so.

In addition, Carter finessed the abortion issue some more. In a near-reversal of his previous stance, he came out *against* the party's plank on *Roe v. Wade*. "It would be inappropriate for any citizen to be deprived of a right to seek an amendment to the Constitution and I think it's inappropriate for the Democratic Party to seek to obstruct a change in the Constitution," Carter said in an interview with the National Catholic News Service in mid-August. The fact that he opposed the platform highlights the extent to which he wished to placate Catholics. After all, his two top domestic aides, Eizenstat and Joseph Duffey, had written the platform language.

This time, Carter's straddling of the abortion issue did not work immediately. Catholic leaders demanded that he endorse a constitutional amendment to overturn *Roe* or extend most legal protections to unborn children. Reporters continued to write stories about Carter's "Catholic problem." And the letters about his stand on abortion ran 9 to 1 against abortion. As late as August 23, an aide to campaign manager Hamilton Jordan wrote to his boss, "Our 'signals' to the urban ethnic Catholic voters are still being perceived as weak."

Looking to finesse the abortion issue again, Carter called for a meeting with Church leaders. He met with six bishops at the Mayflower Hotel in downtown Washington on August 31. Speaking off the cuff and in an amiable tone, Carter said that he wished to have "an intimate personal relationship" with the prelates. He restated his position on abortion, including his disavowal of the party's platform stand on the issue. After stressing the similarity of their views on many social issues, such as health care and housing, Carter concluded his presentation believing that he had found common ground with the bishops.

Archbishop Bernardin, who coined the phrase "seamless garment of life" to describe the Church's support for human life at all stages of development, became known as a Church official who soft-pedaled the abortion issue. At the August 31 meeting, he left no doubt about the importance he assigned to the rights of unborn infants. Reading from a prepared statement, the archbishop stressed the prelates' insistence on a constitutional amendment that "will give the maximum protection possible to the unborn. As Bernardin explained, "If there is agreement that abortion is a moral evil because it violated a person's most basic right, then the only logical conclusion is that something must be done to correct the evil; and the only remedy is a constitutional amendment.... Indeed, without such a remedy, the effort to promote other human life causes for individual and social betterment, about which we are all so concerned, is seriously weakened."

After Bernardin read his statement, one bishop asked Carter if he would support any constitutional amendment to curb abortion. Carter said that he would not flatly oppose any such amendment, and perhaps someone might just come up with wording that he could endorse. After the meeting adjourned, Bernardin came away feeling that Carter had moved toward the side of the bishops. He told reporters, "Governor Carter did tell us that if acceptable language could be found, he would support a constitutional amendment."

Carter never did so. At a presidential debate on October 22, he ruled out support for any constitutional amendment on abortion. Catholic bishops expressed "disappointment."

Carter continued to straddle the issue, disappointing not only Catholic leaders but also feminists and secular liberals.

Catholics for a Free Choice, an organization with close ties to Planned Parenthood, had asked to meet with Carter several times. On September 1, the group's legislative director, Virginia Andary, wrote to Carter saying that the organization "was deeply disappointed that you have not met with us nor responded to our request for a meeting to discuss the Catholic lay person's feelings about abortion. This is especially distressing in light of your recent meeting with the National Conference of Catholic Bishops." Carter never met with Catholics for a Free Choice.

Eight days later, three feminist-minded Carter aides wrote a short, impassioned memo against the Hyde amendment, designed to stop Medicaid from funding abortions:

> If this amendment passes, irregardless [sic] of what the Supreme Court has said about a woman's right to an abortion, we will be forced back into the days of poor women trying to abort themselves

with hangers and sticks and bottles or anything else they can get their hands on. I don't know if you have seen a woman die from trying to abort her child but I have and believe me it is not a pleasant experience.... Now if this amendment passes and it is laid at JC's doorstep, it is going to be awfully hard to get women to work or vote for Jimmy Carter no matter what happens.

Carter did not heed the feminists' warning. His position that government should not fund abortion never wavered.

Carter had good reason to oppose legal abortion in most cases: His position, far from hurting him politically, was helping him. His top pollster, Patrick Caddell, had surveyed voter attitudes to abortion in a dozen states. "Often overshadowed by other issues, such as Vietnam, Watergate, and now the economy," Caddell wrote in his seven-page memo, "abortion remains a potentially explosive issue in some areas of the country." He found that opposition to abortion was most intense in the Midwest: a quarter to a third of voters would not vote for a candidate who supported abortion. By contrast, in only two Northeastern states was voter intensity on the side of pro-choice candidates. Caddell concluded, "any impact that abortion has usually helps the candidate who opposes abortion rather than supports abortion."

As in the Democratic primaries, Carter's strategy of finessing the abortion issue succeeded.

As late as August, Carter was viewed as the more socially conservative candidate. President Ford's strategists had commissioned a poll after the Democratic convention that asked about perceptions of candidates and issues. The results were surprising: Voters saw Carter as much more conservative than Ford on questions about marijuana, abortion, and pornography. "Essentially, [Carter] was seen as an economic liberal and a social conservative—uniquely so," recalled Ford's top pollster, Robert Teeter. "When you looked at the difference between Ford and Carter on the economic issues, it was about what you'd expect—the traditional party difference. But when you looked at them on the social issues, the difference was great, and Carter was seen as more conservative."

Carter failed to maintain that public perception. In mid-August, Ford endorsed a constitutional amendment to overturn *Roe* and return the issue of abortion to the states. Around the same time, news that Carter had granted an interview to *Playboy* magazine had leaked to the press.

Even so, Carter accomplished his goal: to win the votes of social liberals and social conservatives. He won 48 percent of those who were opposed to abortion for any reason and 54 percent of those who thought abortion should never be forbidden. He won 54 percent of the Catholic vote, the highest share a Democratic nominee had received since Humphrey and a percentage that none have equaled since. And he won 55 percent of the vote among those making $15,000 to $29,999 a year.

As president, Carter continued to finesse the social issue.

In the summer of 1977, House and Senate conferees sought a compromise over the Hyde amendment. At a July 12 press conference, Carter left no doubt where he stood. The federal government "should not finance abortions except when the woman's life is threatened or when the pregnancy was the result of rape or incest," he said. "I think it ought to be interpreted very strictly." In December, he signed the amendment into law.

The wording of the regulations was left to the former DNC general counsel Joseph Califano, who headed the Department of Health, Education, and Welfare. But Califano, having been heckled by feminists for his opposition to abortion, was in no mood to write the regulations. So he assigned the task to three HEW lawyers, all pro-choice. The guidelines they drew up were loose: Women who said they had been the victims of rape or incest had up to sixty days to report the incident, and they need not report it personally. Carter was not pleased. He believed that abortion doctors could easily evade the law's provisions. When Califano called to tell him about the regulations, Carter disavowed the language. "I think that might permit too much of a chance for abuse and fraud," Califano recalled the president saying. "I want to end the Medicaid mills and stop these doctors who do nothing but perform abortions on demand all day." After Califano failed to implement his request promptly, Carter called the HEW secretary from

Camp David in April 1978 to change the regulations. Califano complied, and Medicaid funding of abortion was cut 98 percent.

Running for re-election in 1980, Carter attempted to finesse the abortion issue again. His campaign aides believed that, while neither social conservatives nor social liberals would endorse his centrist position, most of the American public would do so. Robert Maddox, the administration's liaison to religious groups, wrote in a 1980 memo:

> Generally speaking, I think we ought to seize the initiation on these moral issues. The President's positions are right on target to reach the people who live on the broad, middle ground from which we must garner the bulk of our support. In a careful but vigorous way, we need to meet the President's detractors head on. We will not get the ultra-conservatives but we can do all we can to blunt their attack by energetically "speaking the truth is love."

But this time, Carter's centrist position on abortion was repudiated. At the 1980 convention in New York, the Democratic Party adopted what can only be described as a pro-abortion plank. Gone was the mild language that opposed a constitutional amendment to overturn *Roe*. In its place the party endorsed not only abortion rights, but also taxpayer-financed abortions: "[T]he Democratic Party … opposes restrictions on funding for health services for the poor that deny poor women especially the right to exercise a constitutionally guaranteed right to privacy."

Carter opposed the plank and reiterated his opposition to the overwhelming majority of cases in which unborn infants are aborted. In response to a questionnaire from Intercessors for America, a nondenominational evangelical group, he wrote that legal abortion should be permitted only "in the cases of rape, incest, or when the life of the mother is threatened."

The fact that Carter could not finesse the issue of abortion this time shows how secular the Democratic Party had become. It was one thing when Robert Strauss was unable to eject secular liberals from the conductor's booth. But it was another when the president, the leader of his party, was unable to stop secular liberals from steering the party toward the destination of human liberation.

Why was Carter no longer able to straddle the cultural divide? The conventional answer is that social conservatives bolted the Democratic Party, leaving feminists in charge of the party platform. Appalled at Carter's refusal to support a constitutional amendment to overturn *Roe,* the Christian right followed the lead of the Reverend Jerry Falwell and aligned with the Republicans.

It's true that Carter's relations with evangelicals in 1980 were poor, as his aides were well aware. In the summer, the campaign had dispatched Roosevelt Grier, the former football player and bodyguard of Robert Kennedy, to meet with evangelical leaders on the West Coast to gauge their level of support for the administration. Grier's trip was not encouraging. "It was ... evident to Mr. Grier," wrote one Carter aide, "that a substantial number of evangelicals were turning to Governor Reagan because he is saying what they want to hear."

But the conventional wisdom is overly simplistic. The defection of social conservatives to the GOP was caused by push *and* pull factors. Many evangelicals *did* feel the pull of the Moral Majority. But many Catholics felt *pushed out* by secular liberals in general and feminists specifically.

Catholic Democratic leaders were outraged at the party's plank on abortion. The Carter campaign was deluged with calls and letters in protest of the plank. A letter to Carter from Bishop Elden Curtiss, Diocese of Helena in Montana, conveys the flavor of Catholics' distress:

> I write to you today to ask that you reject the pro-abortion plank of the Democratic national platform.
>
> I realize that oftentimes those who draw up the platform are not the same ones who are left to defend it publicly.
>
> The Democratic platform has many planks that cover basic issues of human rights. This is in keeping with the spirit and thrust of Catholic social teaching. Yet this one plank is in stark contrast since it calls for the denial of the most basic human right—life itself.
>
> In light of this basic discrepancy, I ask you to examine your conscience carefully, as one who stands for basic human rights in our society. And I ask you to reject publicly this one plank of the Democratic national platform.

The anger of Catholic Democrats was misdirected, however. Instead of aiming fire at Carter, they should have targeted leaders of the National Women's Political Caucus, the National Organization for Women, and the National Abortion Rights Action League. They were responsible for moving the party's plank on abortion to the left.

At the Platform Committee hearings in June 1976, Carter's lieutenants insisted that the platform, as in 1972, avoid any mention of the issue. But when feminists threatened to bring the abortion minority report up for a vote at the New York convention, Joseph Duffey and Stuart Eizenstat responded by drawing up mild language that opposed a constitutional amendment to overturn *Roe:* "We fully recognize the religious and ethical nature of the concerns which many Americans have on the subject of abortion. We feel, however, that it is undesirable to attempt to amend the U.S. Constitution to overturn the Supreme Court decision in this area."

Yet after the Platform Committee approved the minority report, feminist leaders did not hide their disappointment with the plank. They wanted an endorsement not only of *Roe,* but also of government funding for abortion. And they realized that the abortion plank was more of a symbolic victory than a substantive one. "It worries me because there is nothing that speaks to the whittling away of the Supreme Court decision, the attempts, for example, to cut off Medicaid funds to women who get abortions—a restriction which affects poor women—or those private hospitals which refuse to perform them," said Freddi Wechsler, political action coordinator for the NWPC. "All of those things have nothing to do with a constitutional amendment."

After the 1976 convention, the feminist attitude toward Carter changed from disappointment and worry to distress and fear.

When feminists learned that Carter would approve the Hyde amendment, they were alarmed. A group of pro-choice female administration officials urged the president to meet with them. On July 18, 1977, the two sides met in the White House. By all accounts, the afternoon meeting was a disaster. The women viewed Carter's opposition to abortion as personal and irrational. "People discussed the fact that they would like the President in the future to ask the best experts on the issue for information like he did on the B-1 bomber," one female participant wrote two days later to Margaret Costanza, Carter's liaison to the feminists. "They are concerned that contrary to the B-1 bomber and other issues, here he is legislating his personal views."

By 1980, feminists' relationship with Carter had deteriorated completely. The National Organization for Women came out against his re-election. Bella Abzug, Gloria Steinem, Sissy Farenthold, and even Margaret Costanza endorsed Ted Kennedy.

If feminist leaders had merely protested in the streets or complained to the media, their effort to enact a pro-abortion plank at the 1980 convention would have failed. But by the mid-1970s, feminists recognized that an outsider strategy alone would no longer suffice. So the movement trained or recruited leaders skilled in implementing an insider strategy. And top feminists, like the party bosses of old, knew how to work a back room.

A good example of the growing sophistication of the feminist movement was Koryne Horbal. Unlike Bella Abzug and Gloria Steinem, Horbal got her start in politics not by pushing a left-liberal cause, but by working at the precinct level. In the mid-1960s, she led her neighborhood's opposition to a proposed golf driving range across the street from her home in Minnesota. After her effort succeeded, Horbal ascended the ranks of the Minnesota Democratic Farm Labor Party, rising from Ononaka County vice chairwoman to state chairwoman in 1968. "I'm someone who always likes to know the rules and how things work," she said. "So I like to work behind the scenes." In 1972, Horbal worked behind the scenes to secure passage of Title IX, the federal law that requires colleges to treat men's and women's sports equally.

In 1976, Horbal worked the back rooms to change the Democratic Party's position on abortion. Along with several feminists, she lobbied members of the Platform Committee to approve the abortion plank. "We let the Carter organization know that their own women were supporting our position," she explained, "and that we had the votes to take this issue to the floor of the full convention for debate on prime time."

The feminists' success in enacting the abortion plank in 1976 also stemmed from the near-total absence of an effective opposition. George Meany and Al Barkan had scaled down their efforts in national party politics. Few party bosses remained. As for the right-to-life movement, it had only supporters of Eileen McCormack, a Long Island housewife turned Democratic presidential candidate. Nellie Gray, the longtime leader of the annual March for Life in Washington, was a McCormack delegate, and her comments suggest that pro-life Democrats suffered from a dearth of lobbyists. "In those days," she recalled, "all of us in the pro-life movement were active in three or four things at the same time." Horbal put the matter more succinctly: "I think the difference was that we had feminists not only on the outside, but we had many strong feminists on the inside, who knew how the rules worked. And that's always the most important thing, knowing how the rules work and how the structure works."

Also, the feminist movement was well organized. At the 1976 convention, the umbrella feminist organization boasted fifty staff members and its own newspaper, the *Women's Political News Service*. It also held a fundraiser for 2,500 people at the Metropolitan Opera House.

In addition, the feminists were not above manipulating language. Their main goal was requiring that half of all delegates at the 1980 Democratic convention be females; the feminists recognized that they had no chance to override the Mikulski Commission's recommendations for the 1976 convention. They packaged their proposal not as a 50–50 quota for females, but rather as a way of ensuring "equal representation" for males and females alike. "Instead of selling it as a quota, we sold it as a democratic concept," acknowledged Joanne Howes, a board member of the National Women's Political Caucus, adding with a chuckle, "Maybe this was a semantic argument.... It was a matter of getting the right language."

Feminist leaders expected the Rules Committee in June 1976 to adopt their equal-representation plank. But Carter's lieutenants, as well as Bob Strauss and Mark Siegel at the DNC, lobbied the committee to defeat the proposal. Unbowed, top feminists urged Carter to accept equal representation on reform

commissions and convention committees, such as Rules and Credentials. Their argument was not a hard sell. For decades, the
members of the Democratic National Committee had been split
equally between male and female. On July 11, 1976, at the
Statler Hotel in Manhattan, Carter agreed to endorse 50–50
quotas for commissions and convention committees.

The feminists had won more than a symbolic victory. They had
established the principal that the national party should operate
with equal numbers of men and women. "It was a matter of making people feel comfortable" with the concept, said Howes. The
next logical step was to apply the equal-division rule to delegates.

The feminists also sold the concept to other members of the
Democratic coalition. They talked with black leaders, such as
Richard Hatcher, the mayor of Gary, Indiana, and Hispanic representatives. And feminist leaders shrewdly decided that Mil-
dred Jeffrey, the chairwoman of the National Women's Political
Caucus, should be the public face of the equal-representation
clause. A confidante of UAW leader Walter Reuther and a member of the Lawrence Commission, Jeffrey was respected by every
wing of the party.

Highlighting the extent to which they acted like party insiders, feminist leaders maneuvered around the regular channels to
enact the hard quotas. They never made a case to the media or
the public. They never lobbied the party's latest reform panel,
the Winograd Commission, which was headed by Morley Winograd, the state chairman for Michigan. Instead, they lobbied the
members of the DNC. And the DNC approved the hard quotas
in December 1978 at the mini-convention in Memphis. Mark
Siegel, a member of the Winograd Commission, was shocked
that the feminists had won so complete a victory. "I was sort of
taken aback by it," he recalled, "because we certainly had the
votes not to go on record in favor of 50–50."

The 1980 convention in New York represented a complete
rout of traditional Democrats. The forces of the Old Politics had
been barred from the conductor's booth. As Theodore White
reflected, "The rules, refined again and again refined, divided
Americans by sex, race, origin, and surnames, effectively turning the Democratic Party into the party of quotas."

More than a decade after hijacking the party machinery, secular professionals were in the saddle. And none were more powerful than the feminists. Women filled half the slots, while secular feminist organizations controlled the delegates. The National Organization for Women boasted 200 delegates. The National Women's Political Caucus had 400 delegates. By contrast, the four major trade unions had 300 delegates.

Carter forces continued to oppose proposals in favor of abortion and gay rights, but they never stood a chance. "We were dealing with forces completely outside our control," said Tim Kraft, head of the Carter organization.

Seculars had swamped the regulars. By a margin of 2 to 1, the delegates passed Minority Report no. 11, endorsing not only abortion on request but also taxpayer financing of abortion. In addition, the delegates adopted a so-called "freedom of sexual preference" plank. And they approved a platform that promised to withhold money and technical assistance to candidates who opposed the Equal Rights Amendment.

Bella Abzug knew that quotas had changed the party. "Our ten-year campaign for equal numbers of men and women had been completely won at last, and it had been won because we had succeeded in greatly increasing the number of women delegates," she reflected. "By winning political power within the party, women had forced the members to address our concerns. No matter where they stood on candidates, the women delegates were united on equal representation and our other issues. The increased presence of women was changing not only the face, but the structures and policies of the Democratic Party."

—⁂—

THE NIGHT THAT he won the 1992 California Democratic primary, Bill Clinton felt a rare trace of despair. The normally ebullient governor of Arkansas was with his wife, Hillary, in their hotel suite at the Biltmore in Los Angeles. They were watching the election returns on their television set, and the big story in the media had nothing to do with Clinton clinching the party's presidential nomination. It had to do with Ross Perot, the homespun billionaire who was mounting a third-party presidential bid. Not only was Perot on the verge of overtaking Clinton for second place in the national polls, he was the first choice of voters in Democratic primaries.

"Our campaign had to regain momentum," Clinton reflected. "We decided to reach specific constituencies and the general public directly, and to keep pushing the issues." In other words, he decided to move to the political center, where the great mass of voters resided. Like most presumptive and actual presidential nominees, Clinton understood that after winning the party's nomination he needed to move away from his party's liberal base.

Clinton had distanced himself from union leaders. He had come out for the North American Free Trade Agreement, which unions believed would result in jobs being shipped to Mexico. And he had distanced himself from economic liberals. Central to his campaign was a promise to cut taxes for middle-class families.

Now, after the California primary, Clinton had two more chances to distance himself from unpopular Democratic interest groups.

His first chance came when he was invited to attend a Rainbow Coalition event. The host was Jesse Jackson, the very symbol of the post-civil-rights movement that had alienated many whites. On June 13, Clinton took advantage of his opportunity. The rap artist Sister Souljah had said that gang leaders should consider killing whites as well as blacks. Clinton denounced her remarks as racist. "If you took the words white and black and reversed them," Clinton told the crowd, "you might think [former Klan leader] David Duke was giving that speech."

Clinton's second chance came when Governor Robert Casey of Pennsylvania asked to deliver a pro-life speech at the Democratic convention. Such a speech normally would not have been a big deal, especially if it had been delivered during the afternoon, when few reporters or television viewers paid attention. But this one would have been different. Casey's speech was sure to alienate feminist leaders, representatives of the countercultural forces that had turned off religious and working-class voters. Yet their anger and dismay would have helped Clinton.

Clinton would have been more likely as a candidate to woo the Reagan Democrats that had deserted the party in the 1980s. Both Clinton and Ron Brown were well aware of this history. In 1980, Clinton had served as a floor whip for Carter opposing the feminist minority resolution in favor of federally funded abortion. (If women were seeking abortions as a matter of personal preference rather than health reasons, Clinton told one friend, why should taxpayers bear the cost?) After winning back the governor's mansion, Clinton moved to the center on the issue, signing legislation in 1985 that banned third-trimester abortions, and opposing government funding of abortion.

In 1984, Clinton led the Arkansas delegation to the Democratic convention in San Francisco. The party's nominee was former vice president Walter Mondale, the son of a United Methodist minister and a protégé of Hubert Humphrey. Clinton recognized that, although Mondale was an upright man, Republicans scored political points at their convention for characterizing party leaders as "San Francisco Democrats," an allusion to the city's large homosexual population.

In 1989, forty-eight House Democrats wrote to Brown urging that the party platform drop its language in support of government-subsidized abortion. "A good case can be made," they wrote, "that the last three presidential elections have turned, at least in large part, on the loss of traditional Democrats who have broken with the party over so-called social issues, particularly abortion."

In May 1992, Casey appeared at the Platform Committee hearings in Cleveland to make a similar argument. His speech pointed to exit polls of 100,000 voters on the night of the Bush-Dukakis election in 1988: According to an ABC News report, "Despite all the TV ads and speeches on prison furloughs and the Pledge of Allegiance, few votes cited those as key issues. The number one issue? Abortion! Cited by nearly one-third of voters interviewed by ABC News. And those who cited abortion went for Bush."

Clinton certainly understood the importance of downscale social conservatives. He wrote in his memoirs that he was "inclined to let Casey talk, because I liked him, respected the convictions of pro-life Democrats, and thought we could get a lot of them to vote for us on other issues." And by letting Casey speak, Clinton could have built his reputation as a repairer of the nation's cultural breach. He viewed himself as a consensus politician, a latter-day Bobby Kennedy who could unite the country around universal values. "Much of my public life," he wrote, "was spent trying to bridge the cultural and psychological divide that had widened into a chasm in Chicago." Clinton's political track record suggested as much.

Clinton had gained national attention as the chairman of the Democratic Leadership Council, an organization dedicated to the principle that the party's liberal interest groups held too much sway. He called himself a "New Democrat," which meant partly that he eschewed class warfare in favor of national unity. He spoke about the need for the Democratic Party to make a "new covenant" with the American people.

If anyone could have brokered the competing interests, Bill Clinton could. He seemed empathetic. Whenever he sought to relate with another person, he bit his lower lip. He told the voters, "I feel your pain." Clinton was well positioned in the party to devise a truce between feminists and Casey. He was close to the intellectuals and the New Politics activists in the party; he had served as co-chairman of McGovern's 1972 campaign in Texas and attended the annual Renaissance Weekend in Hilton Head, South Carolina, with his fellow meritocratic elites. And he was close to Southerners, having been elected governor of Arkansas five times. In short, Clinton was, as even his critics conceded, a master politician. "There was no question," wrote the journalist Richard Reeves, "that Bill Clinton was ... the best politician of his generation."

Yet Clinton and Brown denied Casey's request. Brown never responded to a July 2 letter that Casey addressed to him. Although Brown tried once to reach Casey over the telephone to settle the matter, he failed to follow through. "It was getting old, really," Brown told reporters. On the first day of the convention, July 13, Governor Ann Richards of Texas, the convention chairwoman, received a hand-delivered letter from Casey asking for a chance to speak. Richards also never responded to Casey.

Why did Clinton and Brown prevent Casey from addressing the delegates?

For years, Democratic officials claimed that there was an easy answer: Casey had failed to endorse Clinton or the Democratic ticket. "He was denied access to the microphone because he had not endorsed Bill Clinton," Brown said in December 1992. "I believe that Governor Casey knew that. I had made it clear to everybody. And yet it still got played as if it had to do with some ideological split. It had nothing to do with that."

Brown's answer was deceptive. It's true that Casey had not endorsed Clinton specifically or the Democratic ticket in general. But neither had Kathleen Brown, the lieutenant governor of California, yet she was allowed access to the microphone.

In 2004, Clinton offered a variation of the Casey-didn't-endorse explanation. He claimed that Casey had been excluded in the interests of party unity:

> In 1972 and 1980, Democrats had been crippled by showing the American people a divided, dispirited, undisciplined party. I was determined not to let that happen again. So was DNC Chairman Ron Brown. I was inclined to let Casey talk.... But Ron was adamant. We could disagree on the issues, he said, but no one should get the microphone who wasn't committed to victory in November. I respected the discipline with which he had rebuilt our party, and I deferred to his judgment.

(When I asked Hillary Clinton in July 2006 about why Casey had been excluded, she referred me to her husband's autobiography.)

Clinton's answer, too, was deceptive. The 1972 and 1980 conventions had been divisive affairs because the race for the party's nomination was seriously contested. In 1972, McGovern's nomination was in doubt as late as the third day of the convention and was assured only when the DNC chairman ruled in his favor on the dispute over the California delegation. In 1980, Carter was the party's presumptive nominee, but he had suffered through two days of Ted Kennedy trying to snatch the nomination away from him. The 1992 convention, by contrast, was a placid affair. The only disputes were whether Casey would be allowed to speak and whether Clinton's rivals, such as Jerry Brown, would endorse him before his acceptance speech.

In truth, the exclusion of Robert Casey had nothing to do with party unity or his failure to endorse the ticket. The reason was ideological: Casey was pro-life. A top DNC official with first-hand knowledge of the Casey affair admitted as much in a 2006 interview. "They didn't want him to speak," the official said, "because he was pro-choice—I mean pro-life."

Clearly, Clinton believed he needed to pander to secular feminists. The events of Tuesday, July 14, throw this fact into relief. Clinton made exactly one public appearance that day: He addressed a gathering of the National Women's Political Caucus. "It makes a difference," he said, "whether the president believes in a woman's right to choose, and I do." As for Casey, it was the day he *would* have addressed the convention.

The 1992 convention was not the first time that Casey had been excluded from reaching a larger spotlight. In 1966, when he ran for governor of Pennsylvania, his first stop was the office of David L. Lawrence, the aging power broker of the state delegation. Accompanied by the Lackawanna County chairman, the brash thirty-four-year-old state senator received an earful from Lawrence. "Your candidacy makes no sense," Casey recalled Lawrence telling him. "You're too young. You're not identified with any statewide issue and, besides, you're Catholic."

In other words, David Lawrence had excluded Casey for a pragmatic political reason. He didn't think Casey could win. (He was right; although he endorsed Casey later, Casey lost the May primary.) By contrast, Bill Clinton excluded Casey for an ideological reason. He pandered to the secular feminists and liberals in the party. As Casey reflected, "Often, it seemed as if the national Democratic Party was little more than an auxiliary of the National Abortion Rights Action League. I was living proof of this division."

The fact that Bill Clinton could not broker the interests of pro-life Democrats and secular feminists is significant. Even someone called "the greatest politician of his generation" could not loosen the grip of the secular liberal conductors. Indeed, no individual—not Robert Strauss, not Jimmy Carter, not Bill

Clinton—could stand in their way. So fast was the Democratic train hurtling that it simply ran them down.

⸺⚏⸺

THE PRESIDENTIAL ELECTIONS of the 1990s represented a change for the national Democratic Party. Unlike the case in 1972 and the 1980s, the nominee's secular liberalism did not help sink him in November. Not only did Bill Clinton win twice, he also won among working-class and Catholic voters twice.

Clinton was under no illusion that his secular liberalism had helped him politically. "I expected to be weaker in some parts of America, because of my positions on the cultural issues—guns, gays, and abortion," he wrote of the 1996 race. Even so, Clinton realized that secular liberals and feminists held veto power on several issues. Besides signing executive orders that provided federal funding of abortion overseas and permitted homosexuals to serve in the military, he vetoed legislation to ban partial-birth abortion and helped prevent Casey again from addressing the national convention in 1996.

But on other cultural issues, Clinton recognized that adhering to secular liberal orthodoxy invited disaster. Moving to the center was essential. He signed an executive order that allowed schools to issue uniforms to their students; signed into law the Defense of Marriage Act, which opposed gay marriage; and ran ads on Christian radio stations that emphasized his opposition to homosexual marriage.

Noting these and other trends, many political commentators concluded that the national party had all but abandoned secular liberalism. In 1996, E. J. Dionne Jr. of the *Washington Post* wrote, "It was clear that the Democrats had substantially transformed themselves from the days when they were charged with being the party of 'acid, amnesty, and abortion,' no small achievement."

In reality, Clinton was the exception that proved the rule. Only the greatest politician of his generation could win the support of upscale secular liberals while minimizing his losses among downscale social conservatives and Catholics. The two subsequent Democratic nominees demonstrated this point.

The first textbook example was the candidacy of Vice President Al Gore. In his rhetoric and many of his economic positions, Gore ran as a populist liberal. His campaign theme was "The People Against the Powerful," and he endorsed universal health care. On cultural issues, Gore ran as a secular-libertarian kind of liberal. Not only did he support legal abortion in all circumstances, he also ditched Clinton's slogan that abortion should be "safe, legal, and rare." He supported domestic partnership benefits for homosexual couples and many gun regulations.

Many political scientists expressed certainty that Gore would win the election. Their political models, which were based on the state of the economy as well as Clinton's high job-approval ratings, showed that Gore would win between 53 percent and 60 percent of the popular vote.

After Gore lost, Stanley Greenberg wrote an astute election postmortem that attributed the nominee's defeat to "the cultural minefield." Greenberg was not alone in reaching this conclusion. The national press corps, after virtually ignoring for decades the rise of the secular left in the Democratic Party, awakened to it, too. "Voter Values Determine Political Affiliation," read a March 2001 headline in the *Washington Post.* The story noted that while Gore won 17 out of 25 of the nation's most affluent counties, he lost in poor states such as West Virginia and in 9 of the 10 poorest counties in Kentucky. "Battles over abortion, gun control, and other cultural values are dramatically reshaping the voting behavior of the American electorate, turning longtime working-class white Democrats into Republicans," reporter Thomas Edsall concluded.

Some Democrats sought to moderate the party's stand on cultural issues. Democrats for Life of America, an organization that had been revived in 2002, called for opening up the party to cultural conservatives:

> If the national Democratic Party is to avoid falling into a semi-permanent second-class status, it must stop this hemorrhage of pro-life supporters. It must stop asking people to choose between their moral beliefs and their party. At a minimum, it will have to adopt

a "big tent" strategy; it will have to welcome pro-life people into its ranks. In practice, this means it will occasionally have to support pro-life legislation (e.g. the partial-birth abortion ban), and it will have to give serious consideration to putting a pro-life candidate on the national ticket.

But as in 1992 and 1996, the national party excluded pro-life Democrats again. Seventeen House Democrats in April and May 2003 wrote to the DNC chairman, Terry McAuliffe. Their request was reasonable: Have the DNC link its Web site to that of the DFL. After all, the DNC provided links to 261 organizations, including the U.S. Forest Service and the Oneida Indian Organization. But the request was rejected. McAuliffe wrote in June that the DNC opposed using the party's Web site to promote an organization "whose purpose is to reverse the current platform and/or to enact legislation that contradicts this platform."

The party's presidential candidates also failed to heed repeated warnings against alienating conservative voters. The first time that all six of the party's 2004 candidates appeared together was at an event honoring the thirtieth anniversary of *Roe v. Wade.* On January 21, 2003, more than 1,500 abortion-rights stalwarts packed the Omni Shoreham Hotel in Washington. Kate Michelman, the president of NARAL Pro-Choice America, introduced the candidates as they emerged from a curtain behind stage.

The candidates did little to refute Casey's claim that the national party was hardly more than a NARAL auxiliary. The flip-flopping of House minority leader Richard Gephardt on the abortion issue is a classic example. Before his first presidential run in 1988, Gephardt had been a pro-lifer. Besides having a pro-life voting record of 91 percent from the National Right to Life Committee, he had sponsored a Human Life Amendment, which sought to extend constitutional protection to unborn infants. Yet once Gephardt mounted his presidential bid, he switched his position on abortion. (At one debate in 1988, Gephardt's flip-flop was hypocritically attacked by Senator Al Gore, whose NRLC voting record was 84 percent.) To the star-studded audience at the Omni Shoreham, Gephardt said that he had undergone a gradual "change of heart and mind.... [M]y eyes were opened ... by friends and colleagues and strangers, women I didn't know and would never meet again, and by members of my own close family."

Gephardt's explanation was misleading. His change of heart and mind had a different source: the realization that upscale secular voters dominate Democratic caucuses and primaries. The people who vote in Democratic primaries and caucuses are simply different from those who vote in general elections. They are similar to air travelers—educated and affluent. By contrast, the people who vote in November are similar to train travelers—less educated and less affluent. In the 2004 Iowa caucus and New Hampshire primary, about 56 percent of Democratic voters had earned a four-year college degree or more. Yet in November 2000 and 2004, only 42 percent of all voters had similar credentials.

John Kerry, a consistent supporter of legal abortion, made a point of appealing to secular liberals and feminists. Eight months before the Iowa caucus, the senator from Massachusetts announced that if he were elected, his nominees to the Supreme Court would have to endorse *Roe v. Wade*. When reporters asked him whether this was a litmus test, Kerry acknowledged that his comments could be interpreted as such. "If some people want to call it a test, they can call it a test," he said. "The bottom line is I want someone who will understand that right and uphold it." (The candidates' determination to enforce the abortion litmus test took on a farcical quality. Representative Dennis Kucinich, who had earned a perfect score from right-to-life groups before he ran for president and switched his position, announced that he "absolutely would appoint a homosexual judge," including "any lesbian, bisexual, or transgender person—just as long as they'd be willing to uphold *Roe v. Wade*.")

After clinching the party's nomination in the spring, Kerry campaigned as if Catholics and downscale social conservatives did not matter. In August, voters in Missouri voted overwhelmingly for a state amendment to ban homosexual marriage. Bill Clinton advised Kerry to endorse a constitutional amendment banning gay marriage, according to *Newsweek* magazine. Kerry declined. "I could never do that," he told an aide.

Kerry's strategy for winning over affluent voters succeeded. Of the nation's 25 wealthiest counties, 16 went for Kerry. Among professionals, his support was 56 percent.

But Kerry, like every socially liberal Democratic nominee except Clinton, failed to attract the support of white Catholic and downscale social conservatives. Stanley Greenberg wrote a post-election analysis that blamed Kerry's defeat, like Gore's, on cultural polarization. Likewise, William Galston and Elaine Kamarck, two respected Democratic thinkers, wrote a major report in October 2005 that underlined the numerical weakness of Fred Dutton's Social Change coalition. They pointed out that in 1976,

> Jimmy Carter eked out a victory with only 51 percent of the moderate vote because he won nearly three in ten conservative voters. In 2004, John Kerry won 54 percent of the moderates and still lost by 3.5 points because he won a much smaller share of conservatives. With three conservatives for every two liberals, the sheer arithmetic truth is that in a polarized electorate effectively mobilized by both major parties, Democratic candidates must capture upwards of 60 percent of the moderate vote—a target only Bill Clinton has reached in recent elections—to win a national election.

After the 2004 election, many Democrats concluded that the party should no longer shut out culturally conservative Democrats. At a meeting of America Votes, a coalition of liberal activist groups, Kerry said that the national party needed to rethink how it presented itself to voters on issues like abortion, and that pro-life Democrats should be embraced. Hillary Clinton moderated her rhetoric about abortion. In January 2005, she said that "abortion in many ways represents a sad, even tragic choice to many, many women." In July 2006, she said that if Robert Casey Jr., son of the late governor, wished to address the national convention about abortion, she would support him. "Of course," she said. "We're a big tent party." Her husband wrote in his mega-selling autobiography that "if we [Democrats] want to be competitive in the so-called red states, we have to engage in a serious debate on the cultural issues."

The rhetoric suggested that secular liberals and feminists would share the conductor's booth with culturally moderate and conservative Democrats. But feminists shot down any such plans. Karen White, the national political director of EMILY's List, dismissed Kerry's remarks that he had lost partly because of his failure to move to the center on cultural issues. "You don't just throw out words or issues to come up with an excuse for why you lost," she said.

Former Indiana representative Tim Roemer, a respected member of the 9/11 Commission, ran for chairman of the DNC. His platform was national security, a moderate pro-life position, and a return to traditional Democratic values. Roemer lost his bid because he was pro-life. "I had some pretty piercing and nasty opposition research done on me in the DNC race that I don't think the Republicans had done quite so well in six of my races for House of Representatives," Roemer said in a 2006 interview.

Roemer lost to Howard Dean, former governor of Vermont, who in his 2004 presidential candidacy had emerged as a hero to secular liberals. Dean, too, had emphasized the need to reach out to culturally conservative Democrats. Yet his comments in an early 2007 interview suggested that the party had no intention of moving to the middle on cultural issues. "We're never going to convince them [socially conservative voters] on civil rights for gay people or abortion rights," he said.

National Democrats had the chance to move away from the most unpopular items on the secular left's agenda. In April 2007, the Supreme Court upheld federal legislation banning partial-birth abortion. The decision was highly popular. Nearly seven in ten Americans supported banning the procedure, which had been likened to infanticide.

But the leading Democratic presidential candidates blasted the Court's decision. Hillary Clinton said, "This decision marks a dramatic departure from four decades of Supreme Court rulings that upheld a woman's right to choose and recognized the importance of women's health." According to John Edwards, the vice-presidential nominee in 2004, "This hard right turn is a stark reminder of why Democrats cannot afford to lose the 2008 election. Too much is at stake—starting with, as the Court made all too clear today, a woman's right to choose." Senator Barack Obama of Illinois commented, "I strongly disagree with today's Supreme Court ruling, which dramatically departs from previous precedents safeguarding the health of pregnant women." To these presidential candidates, aligning with ordinary general-election voters did not matter; aligning with Democratic primary and caucus voters did.

Democratic politicians are well aware of the power held by the party's upscale, socially liberal primary voters and activists. Although reporters continue to write story after story about the influence of money in politics, national Democrats recognize that the party's primary voters and delegates wield more clout than its donors.

John Breaux, a former senator from Louisiana, certainly does. In January 2002, I asked Breaux whether he might run for president someday. He would have made an appealing candidate. Besides being down-to-earth and well spoken, Breaux possessed exactly the center-right credentials the party needed. But he saw no way that a pro-life Democrat such as himself could get nominated.

"You can't get through the nomination process," he said simply. "I think you could win the general election but not the primary." Asked why, Breaux elaborated: "Because the majority of the people at the convention would not vote for you. They wouldn't do it."

What about the role of big-money donors, such as Planned Parenthood or EMILY's List?

"I don't think the financial factor has been the big difference," he said. "I think it's just who goes to the convention."

Toward a
New People's Party

Should the Democratic Party be revolutionized again? Reforming the party wholesale certainly would not hurt it politically. The Democratic Party—specifically, its national or presidential wing—has been in the minority since the McGovern Commission rules changes were enacted. It's true that the party's nominee won the popular vote in 2000 and lost by only three million votes in 2004. but a loss is a loss. In the world of sports, the top coaches don't explain away defeat; they acknowledge it and change accordingly. If the national Democratic Party were a sports team, it would be known as a losing franchise. It's not simply that the party has lost seven of the last ten presidential elections. Only one Democratic nominee since 1976 has won at least half of the popular vote. (By contrast, three different Republican nominees have done so.) One of the party's most influential political consultants, Robert Shrum, owns a 0–8 win-loss record in presidential elections. Not since the era of 1896 to 1928, when Democrats were assembled in a coalition forged by William Jennings Bryan, have the party's presidential candidates lost so badly and so regularly.

Of course, the way the Democratic Party picks its presidential nominee has always been flawed. The King Caucus system of 1800 to 1816, in which the Republican and Federalist members of Congress met to decide who would be their respective nominees, solidified the support of Washington-based party leaders behind one candidate, but it failed to win the backing of local and state political leaders, as well as most voters. The boss system of 1828 to 1968 produced nominees that usually were popular among voters—especially working-class and religious voters—and in most wings of the party, but it did so by undemocratic methods. The activist system of 1972 to the present has expanded voter participation in the selection process, but it has produced nominees who are unpopular among the majority of general election voters, and has retained some of the undemocratic features of the boss system.

Efforts to fix these defects of the activist system, which the McGovern Commission created, have failed with one exception. The Mikulski Commission (1973–76) achieved the twin goals of making the party's nomination system more democratic and helping produce a nominee who won in November. The commission also replaced the soft quotas with an affirmative action requirement for women, minorities, and young people as delegates—a factor that helped Jimmy Carter get elected. Since then, party reformers have scrapped the goal of making the nomination process more democratic. Instead, they have tried to improve the party nominee's chances of winning in November. Most notably, the Super Tuesday contest of primaries and caucuses in seventeen Southern and border states was intended to move the party away from the Northeastern, liberal wing of the party and toward the Southern, moderate and conservative wings. But the reformers' efforts were to no avail.

Worse, party officials have created undemocratic procedures. At the 1980 convention, feminists succeeded in passing hard quotas for female delegates, requiring that half of the delegates be women. In the early 1980s, the Hunt Commission designated certain party officials as super-delegates, equal to about a fifth of the convention's delegates. As a result of these rules changes, secular professionals have tightened their grip over the party machinery. They now are the Democratic Party establishment— the new elite that replaced the old elite. But they have not moved the party closer to the views of white working-class and white Catholic voters, let alone built a majority coalition.

What the Democratic Party needs is not more reforms of the activist system. The party needs a new nomination system altogether: one that keeps the best part of the boss system—picking nominees who can win in November rather than passing various ideological litmus tests—and discards its worst part—choosing nominees by undemocratic methods. Achieving this new nomination process *is* possible.

Although the demise of the boss system seems inevitable in retrospect, it did not appear that way to the band of mostly young reformers from the McCarthy campaign. As the events in Connecticut and Chicago described in this book illustrate, their efforts lacked support from other Democratic presidential candidates and even from McCarthy's top advisers. They were operating out of moral conviction—and future reformers will need to do the same.

To create a new People's Party, the Democratic nomination system should repose power, to the fullest extent possible, in the people. This was the animating vision of Iowa's Harold Hughes. The kingmakers in this system would not be party leaders, politicians, or activists. They would be ordinary American voters, the ones who decide elections. Bringing this state of affairs about is not impossible. It requires undertaking five reforms.

First, all state caucuses should be abolished. The main problem with caucus elections is the amount of time and effort they require of voters. Those who attend caucuses have to do more than show up and vote; they have to spend at least an hour and often several hours sitting through a meeting before declaring their support for a candidate. Another problem is that caucuses are nighttime-only affairs. Unlike primaries, when voters can cast their ballots from morning until night, caucuses occur for only a few hours in the evening. Another problem is that voters don't cast their ballots in secret but rather must declare publicly for a candidate. "Caucuses empower the, uh, more of the mobilized militants of Republicans and Democrats," said Curtis Gans, director of the Committee for the Study of the American Electorate.

As a result, few voters participate in caucuses. In the famous Iowa caucus, only 5 to 10 percent of registered Democratic voters participate. Of the state's 500,000 Democrats, only 61,000 turned out in 2000; and only 122,000 showed up in 2004, when the Democratic field was wide open. What's more, comparatively few working-class Democrats vote in the Iowa caucus. In the 2004 caucus, 42 percent of Democratic voters had less than a four-year college degree. By contrast, 58 percent of all voters in the 2004 general election had earned less than a four-year college degree. That percentage gap of 16 points favors college-educated voters over their working-class counterparts.

Instead of caucuses, the Democratic Party should require that all state parties hold primary elections. In primaries, voters have a chance to cast their ballots all morning and afternoon, and frequently in the evening. They can also vote in secret rather than in public. Not surprisingly, voter turnout is always much higher in primaries than in caucuses.

Second, independents should be allowed to vote in all state primaries. "We need to recruit more people and recruit more independents," former DNC chairman Don Fowler said, after noting with a trace of impatience in his voice, "we're not the majority party anymore." But in many states, party regulations exclude independent voters from casting ballots. Of course, the Democratic primaries should not be opened up to Republican voters, who don't have the Democratic Party's best interests at heart. But by excluding independent voters, state Democratic officials force their candidates to appeal to the most ideological and activist-minded types of voters.

The 2006 Senate election in Connecticut was a classic example of the perils of excluding independent voters from participation in a primary. Democratic activists in the state and around the country were furious with Joseph Lieberman, a three-term senator, for supporting the war in Iraq and President Bush's handling of it. Even though Lieberman was the party's vice-presidential nominee in 2000 and an admired figure in both parties, liberal activists threw their support behind Ned Lamont. In the state's Democrats-only primary, the activists' opposition to Lieberman was enough to deny him renomination as the party's candidate for the Senate; Lamont defeated Lieberman 52 to 48. But three months later, in the general election, Lieberman ended up defeating Lamont handily as an independent candidate. Lieberman's victory wasn't the result of a sudden rapprochement with antiwar activists; he continued to support the war. His victory stemmed from the fact that the influence of the activists was severely diluted in the general election, when independents are allowed to vote. Among independent voters, Lieberman won a majority.

At a DNC meeting in Phoenix in December 2004, Don Fowler pushed through a rules change that does open up the nomination process. In sixteen states with no party registration at all, each state Democratic party asked a person wishing to vote in its primary or caucus to attest, usually on a sheet of paper, that he or she is a Democrat; the effect of the state parties' efforts was to limit the elections to Democrats only. Fowler's measure allows independent voters in those sixteen states to cast ballots without having to reveal their partisan preference. Despite this reform, twenty-two state parties prohibit independent voters from participating in their primaries or caucuses. The DNC ought to require states to open up their process to independents.

Third, all quotas for delegates should be eliminated. Quotas are simply undemocratic. They require including certain groups, while effectively excluding others. As Theodore White wrote eloquently of the McGovern Commission's soft quotas, "By insisting on a fixed proportion of youth, for example, and ignoring a fixed proportion of the elderly, it excluded the old. By insisting on a fixed proportion of blacks, Indians, or Spanish-speaking and ignoring, say, Italians, Poles, Irish, Jews, old-stock colonials, it restricted."

Also, quotas are all about securing results for a minority of voters. Indeed, Ken Bode and Fred Dutton acknowledged later that the goal of their soft quota proposal for women and minorities had nothing to do with democracy or expanding voter participation. Their purpose was to achieve a policy result: creating a "loose peace constituency" in the party and increasing the odds of nominating an antiwar candidate in 1972. (Since the 1980s, half of all presidential delegates are required to be women and about a third must be minorities.) The delegate quotas continue to have a political rather than participatory effect. They simply cement the party's ties with feminists and liberal minority activists, the two groups best poised to take advantage of them.

By eliminating hard quotas for minorities and women, Democrats would open up the party in a genuine way. Any registered voter could run for a seat as a delegate. He or she would not be bound by an arbitrary political rule.

Fourth, all super-delegates should be eliminated. The process by which Democratic officials become super-delegates is also undemocratic. Super-delegates are not elected; they don't stand for election as a delegate. Party officials *appoint* them. Thus, super-delegates gain their office by the same undemocratic methods as the party bosses and their cronies.

The McGovern Commission eliminated the modern equivalent of super-delegates by requiring state parties to repeal rules that provided for ex-officio delegates (that is, delegates by virtue of their current or previous office). But subsequent reform commissions essentially put ex-officio delegates back in. Today they represent 20 percent of all delegates to the convention. Although no presidential candidate has needed the votes of super-delegates to win the nomination, that may change in the future. If a candidate wins by the votes of super-delegates, the activist system will be exposed as undemocratic, just like the boss system.

Fifth, swing states should hold the first primaries in the nomination process. The goal of this reform, frankly, would be political: to give the party's presidential nominee the best shot of winning in November. The Democratic nominee would be much more likely to hew to the center of the political road, the spot where elections are won. To that end, party officials should select the five most competitive states in the last presidential election; competitiveness could be gauged by the smallest margin of victory in the previous election.

This proposal will face objections. For instance, this reform is not as democratic as holding a national primary on the same day. In practice, however, a national primary would unduly benefit candidates who are already either wealthy or popular. Then again, a swing-state project is not undemocratic either. All states would have a chance to compete early in the nomination phase, including Iowa and New Hampshire, which had close races in 2000 and 2004.

Even if all five reforms were adopted, the Democrats' nomination system would still bear traces of the activist system. Diluting the power of liberal activists is one thing; eliminating their power is another. For example, turnout in primary elections for decades has been much lower than in general elections. Those who participate in primaries are the most committed and partisan of voters. What's more, college-educated voters are much more likely to participate in primaries than their non-college-educated counterparts.

Even so, a people-dominated system would be more democratic and more likely to produce a successful party nominee. Simply by reducing the power of party activists, white working-class and religious Democrats and independents would have a greater say in selecting the party nominee. And if that occurred, the presidential wing of the Democratic Party could once again boast of being a real People's Party.

Acknowledgments

A lexis de Tocqueville wrote that citizens in a democracy, being independent and weak, would find themselves "helpless if they did not learn to help each other voluntarily." Tocqueville's insight applies equally to my writing of this book. Without the help of others, I would have been like a captain without a journey, chart, ship, or crew.

My father long ago laid out the journey before me. While taking me to innumerable ball games or tinkering around the house, he told me about how the Democratic Party in 1968 first lost its way. His brothers—Tim, Jay, Guy, and Mark—told me the particulars of the story. Also, my mother gave me a general picture of the Democratic Party in the mid-twentieth century from the perspective of ordinary Democrats.

Several mentors made me appreciate that the journey was worth undertaking. The late Michael Kelly reaffirmed my belief in the pre-1968 Democratic Party ("the pre-1968 party," he called it) and hired me as a reporter-researcher for the *New Republic*. His gracious mother, Marguerite, delivered a bold speech at her son's funeral in April 2003, in front of an audience composed heavily of liberal secular professionals, in which she chastised the national Democratic Party for abandoning its moral principles.

My friend Mark Tremmel piloted the book. He shared his insights into and wisdom about politics; shaped and sharpened my arguments; and read, edited, and reread my chapters. Even this description fails to capture the true measure of his contribution. Looking back at my email account, I see that in the last five years he has read or responded to almost two hundred messages, as well as answering scores of my late-night phone calls about politics. Without Mark, this book likely would never have been published.

Many other people, with little expectation of future gain, helped me build the book. Deal Hudson, the former publisher and editor of the late, great *Crisis* magazine, spurred me on to undertake the journey. In January 2002, he suggested that I write an article about pro-life Democrats in Congress. A year later, he served as a key sponsor, writing a letter of reference for me when I applied for the Phillips Foundation journalism fellowship in 2003. Tom Phillips provided the necessary funding to transform the idea of a book into a sailing vessel. When all my savings had run out, his foundation gave me a grant that allowed me to continue my research. And John Farley ensured that I could captain the book. He gave me encouragement, office space, and more than a few laughs.

Several informal advisers helped guide me around various eddies and currents in the story. Ray Flynn, the former mayor of Boston and ambassador to the Vatican, answered countless questions about old-time Catholic Democratic leaders. Rhodes Cook provided invaluable assistance with presidential voting statistics, and—though he likely disagrees with the conclusions in this book—he offered insight into the legacy of the McGovern Commission. Alan Ehrenhalt advised that I consult Rhodes, and also pointed me to several important books about the Democratic Party. Mary Meehan offered her perspective as a former aide to Senator Eugene McCarthy.

Countless people unselfishly served as the crew during the maiden voyage. They told me their life stories and answered my repeated questions, but I was unable to find a place for them in the main text. In western Pennsylvania, I wish to thank Wade Snyder, Mark and Marie Haase, Mark Notarberardino, Veronica Ballard, Kathleen Silvis, Scott Conner, Jerry Bartlow, Tom Goodge and Tom Goodge Jr., and Bill Priatko.

Several interview subjects told me about particular channels and straits in the story. None was more generous, patient, and lucid than the late Austin Ranney, who invited me over to his house in the Berkeley hills and answered my follow-up questions without fail. Also helpful was the late Fred Dutton, who shared two delicious lunches with me at the Prime Rib on K Street. Harold Ickes unselfishly sent me a copy of Eli Segal's influential memo on the party's delegate selection rules in 1968. And after my early-morning flight was canceled, Geoffrey Cowan took time away from his duties as dean of communications at USC to talk with me in the late afternoon. David Mixner, Phyllis Segal, and her beloved late husband, Eli, also sat down with me. Each gave me a lot of time, for which I am appreciative.

Some of the research I conducted was in uncharted territory. For granting me access to private material, I am grateful to George McGovern, to Erica DeVos at the Democratic National Committee, and to the Reverend Thomas J. Donaghy, who conducted scores of interviews in the 1970s with friends, family members, and associates of David L. Lawrence.

Tim Seldes kept the book from sinking. When no other literary agent would commit to me, he did. Also, he and his able colleague, Jesseca Salky, steered me through the rocky shoals of the publishing business. Harry Crocker and Jody Bottum also navigated me away from the rapids of naïveté and despair.

Roger Kimball prevented the book from capsizing. He did more than sign me up. He granted me many extensions for the book and offered invaluable guidance and encouragement.

When the book was cruising on the waters, several friends propelled it along.

Dan Kearns dispelled my illusions about secular liberals. Brian Marchiano and Kevin Sullivan offered me the perspective of general readers. John Gorman read an early draft of a chapter and heard my (often unfocused) descriptions of the book. Steve McCorry provided me with his friendship and the futon in his apartment.

Midway through the journey, a host of researchers, librarians, and archivists helped me chart a more navigable course. Kirk Henderson, a fantastic and affordable researcher based near Atlanta, mined the archives of the Jimmy Carter Library with minimal fuss and maximum results. Donald Ritchie, then the associate historian of the Senate Historical Office, gave me a personal tour of the U.S. Senate Caucus Room. Debbie Miller at the Minnesota Historical Society answered my research requests with humor, professionalism, and promptness. Sarah Haldeman at the Lyndon B. Johnson Library in Austin, Texas, guided me through the former president's seemingly endless files with sure-handedness and dispatch. Randy Sowell at the Truman Presidential Museum and Library in Independence, Missouri, suggested that I read the invaluable *Choosing Truman* and sent me several memos related to the Truman administration and DNC's handling of black voters. Jonathan Stayer at the Pennsylvania State Archives replied to my inquiries about David L. Lawrence with promptness and professionalism. And there was Brother Joseph L. Grabenstein, FSC, of La Salle University. Not only did Brother Joe help me troll through the Donaghy papers in the La Salle University archive, he also supplied me with chips, soda, and classic rock-and-roll songs.

Toward the end of the journey, I received material aid from the staffs of the Library of Congress (home of the Joseph L. Rauh Jr. archive); the Moorland-Spingarn Research Center at Howard University (home of oral history interviews with Aaron Henry, Fannie Lou Hamer, and the Reverend Edward King); and the DePauw University Library (home of the Ken Bode archive).

Several people chipped in with advice about the journey ahead. Mark Barrett sent me a copy of a late 1970s article that discussed forming a new Catholic party in New York. Cori Zarek offered sure-handed counsel about possible copyright violations. And Daniel Hoff provided me with the perspective of a young Democrat today.

Other people neglected to talk with me or grant me access to papers at important times. Ken Bode talked with me once about his role in the McGovern Commission, but he declined my further requests. Considering that Bode was once the dean of journalism at Northwestern University, his failure to cooperate was more than a little puzzling. Erica De Vos granted me access to the DNC files at the National Archives from 2002 to 2005, but she declined to do so in 2006. Their full cooperation would have been appreciated.

After the book reached shore, the staff at Encounter Books ensured that it would not be forgotten. Heather Ohle and her production crew endured my repeated requests to alter the jacket design. And Carol Staswick cleared up many ambiguities and outright confusions in the manuscript.

My wife, Angy, was the chief helmsman of the book. She copy-edited and critiqued many of the chapters, endured my endless stories about an obscure political commission, and offered me boundless love and support. She also gave birth to our beautiful daughter, Grace. I dedicate the book to Angy.

Notes

14 *The white Catholic vote in 2000*—Stan Greenberg and Matt Hogan, "Reclaiming the White Catholic Vote," Democracy Corps, March 29, 2005, p. 1.

14 *"Large sections of downscale America shifted . . ."*—Stan Greenberg and James Carville, "Solving the Paradox of 2004: Why America Wanted Change but Voted for Continuity," Democracy Corps, November 9, 2004, p. 2.

14 *Catholics favored Humphrey over Nixon*—Gallup Poll Presidential Voting Analysis, 1952–1968.

14 *"The Democrats . . . are those 'plain people . . .'"*—Richard M. Scammon and Ben J. Wattenberg, *The Real Majority* (Coward-McCann, 1970), p. 63.

15 *"Catholic voters overwhelmingly . . ."*—George J. Marlin, *The American Catholic Voter: 200 Years of Political Impact* (St. Augustine's Press, 2004), p. xviii.

15 *The white Catholic vote*—"Who Voted: A Portrait of American Politics, 1976–2000," *New York Times*, November 12, 2000, p. WK4.

15 *The working-class white vote*—Ibid.

15 *New Deal coalition*—Theodore H. White, *The Making of the President, 1960* (Atheneum Publishers, 1961), p. 406.

16 *Books cited*—Kevin P. Phillips, *The Emerging Republican Majority* (Arlington House, 1969); Peter Brown, *Minority Party: Why Democrats Face Defeat in 1992 and Beyond* (Regnery Gateway, 1991); Thomas Byrne Edsall and Mary D. Edsall, *Chain Reaction: The Impact of Race, Rights, and Taxes on American Politics* (W. W. Norton, 1991).

16 *"The principal forces which broke up . . ."*—Phillips, *The Emerging Republican Majority*, p. 37.

17 *"Although most Democrats cringe . . ."*—Brown, *Minority Party*, p. 4.

17 *Ken Mehlman's apology to blacks*—Richard Benedetto, "GOP: We Were 'Wrong' to Play Racial Politics," *USA Today*, July 14, 2005. Mehlman's full statement was, "Some Republicans gave up on winning the African-American vote, looking the other way or trying to benefit politically from racial polarization. I am here today as the Republican chairman to tell you we were wrong."

17–18 *Voting trends in Westmoreland County*—For these voting statistics, I am indebted to an incomparable political Web site, Dave Leip's Atlas of U.S. Presidential Elections, www.uselectionatlas.org.

18 *"Urban whites, manual workers, Catholics ..."*—Everett Carll Ladd Jr. with Charles D. Hadley, *Transformations of the American Political System: Political Coalitions from the New Deal to the 1970s* (W. W. Norton, 1975), p. 233.

18–19 *"Ideopolises ... Democrats did best among ..."*—John B. Judis and Ruy Teixeira, *The Emerging Democratic Majority* (Scribner, 2002), p. 74.

19 *Working-class Americans satisfied with circumstances*—David Brooks, "One Nation, Slightly Divisible," *Atlantic*, December 2001, p. 59.

19 *Working-class white vote in 2000*—Thomas B. Edsall, "Voter Values Determine Political Affiliation," *Washington Post*, March 26, 2001, p. A1.

20 *Kerry and Edwards in Greensburg*—David Halbfinger, "In Struggling Communities, Kerry Promises Better Future," *New York Times*, August 1, 2004. According to Halbfinger, "a fiery Mr. Kerry shouted" that President Bush's claim that he improved the economy was deceptive: "Yesterday the president said to America that we're turning the corner, the corner on the economy. Let me ask you: If you're one of those 44 million Americans who doesn't have any health insurance, and you have no prospect of buying it, are you turning the corner? If you're one of those people who has a job that pays $9,000 less than the jobs that are being lost overseas, are you turning the corner because of those?"

20 *Gore and Kerry's voting percentages in Westmoreland County*—See http://uselectionatlas.org/RESULTS/

20 *Social and economic attitudes of various Americans*—Edsall, "Voter Values Determine Political Affiliation," *Washington Post*, March 26, 2001, p. A7.

20–21 *Population and industry in Jeannette*—Terry and Kathleen Perich, *Jeannette*, Postcard History Series (Arcadia Publishing, 2006).

20 *"This town used to be jumping ..."*—Interview with Irmo Antonacci.

21 *Decline of industry in Westmoreland County*—Interview with Tom Balya.

22 *Population of Westmoreland County*—U.S. Census Bureau. See http://quickfacts.census.gov/qfd/states/42/42129.html.

22 *". . . vote against Pittsburgh . . ."*—Interview with Allen Kukovich.

22 *Unions in Pennsylvania*—Barry T. Hirsch, David Macpherson, and Wayne G. Vroman, "Estimate of Union Density by State," *Monthly Labor Review,* July 2001, p. 52.

22 *Casey in Monessen*—Casey, *Fighting for Life,* p. 97.

22 *"No one lives in Monessen anymore"*—Interview with Rosemary Trump.

23 *Union members vote for Clinton*—"Who Voted: A Portrait of American Politics, 1976–2000," *New York Times,* p. WK4.

23 *Decline of union influence*—Interview with Bill Cain.

23–24 *The culture-war thesis*—E. J. Dionne Jr., *Why Americans Hate Politics* (Simon & Schuster, 1991), p. 12.

23–24 *Books cited*—Ronald Radosh, *Divided They Fell: The Demise of the Democratic Party, 1964–1996* (Free Press, 1996); Samuel Freedman, *The Inheritance: How Three Families and the American Political Majority Moved from Left to Right* (Simon & Schuster, 1996); Jules Witcover, *The Year the Dream Died: Revisiting 1968 in America* (Warner Books, 1997); Thomas B. Edsall, *Building Red America: The New Conservative Coalition and the Drive for Permanent Power* (Basic Books, 2006).

24 *Morris and Penn's questions*—See Thomas Byrne Edsall, "Blue Movie," *Atlantic,* January/February 2003. The five questions were: Do you believe homosexuality is morally wrong? Do you ever personally look at pornography? Would you look down on someone who had an affair while married? Do you believe sex before marriage is morally wrong? Is religion very important in your life?

25 *Voting returns in Westmoreland County, 2004 and 2006*— See http://uselectionatlas.org/RESULTS/

26 *". . . We thought it was bullshit."*—Interview with Tom Balya.

26 *"Any public official who says . . ."*—The Most Reverend Lawrence E. Brandt, "Integrity and the Political Arena," Pastoral Letter, Diocese of Greensburg, August 10, 2004.

26 *"We've got a lot of very vocal Catholics ..."*—Interview with Rosemany Trump.

27 *"Guns are a big issue"*—Interview with Debbie Irwin.

27 *Catholic Church in alliance with NRA*—Interview with Rosemary Trump.

27 *"those in the dawn of life ..."*—Humphrey delivered the line before Congress on November 1, 1977.

27 *"His words summed up for me ..."*—Casey, *Fighting for Life*, p. 81.

27–28 *Mayor Tate's questions*—Ibid., pp. 83–84.

28 *Casey's record*—See Nat Hentoff, "Life of the Party," *New Republic*, June 19, 2000.

28 *"the kind of letter they might have sent Lyndon Larouche ..."*—Casey, *Fighting for Life*, p. 186.

29 *"What was going on here?"*—Ibid., p. 190.

Chapter Two—The New Deal Democratic Party

31 *"Hague and Kelly admit publicly ..."*—James H. Rowe Jr. to President Harry S. Truman, "The Politics of 1948," memo dated September 18, 1947, Harry S. Truman Library, p. 13. "The Politics of 1948" is also called "The Clifford Memo," in reference to Truman aide Clark Clifford, or "The Rowe-Clifford Memo." Rowe wrote the bulk of the memo and sent it to Clifford, who submitted the memo under Clifford's name.

31–32 *Background of James H. Rowe Jr.*—James H. Rowe Jr. oral history, September 30, 1969, and January 15, 1970, Harry S. Truman Library. The interviewer was Jerry N. Hess.

32 *"Better education, the rise of the mass pressure group ..."*—Rowe, "The Politics of 1948," p. 13.

32 *"Today the plight of the Irish Democratic bosses ..."*—Samuel Lubell, *The Future of American Politics* (Doubleday, 1951), p. 70.

32 *Bosses ousted Wallace*—See Robert H. Ferrell, *Choosing Truman: The Democratic Convention of 1944* (University of Missouri Press, 1994).

32 *Rowe admitted that bosses ousted Wallace*— James H. Rowe Jr. oral history, September 30, 1969, Harry S. Truman Library.

33   *New York Times profile of Lawrence*—"A Convention Pro: David Leo Lawrence," *New York Times,* August 24, 1964, p. 16.

33   *Harper's profile of Lawrence*—Helen Fuller, "The Man to Watch at the Democratic Convention," *Harper's,* pp. 47–61.

33–34   *Lawrence scared Johnson*—"Random Notes in Washington: Johnson Runs, but Not Too Fast," *New York Times,* February 22, 1960, p. 10.

34   *Johnson on Bailey's image*—Telephone conversation between Johnson and Daley, November 16, 1964, Lyndon Baines Johnson Library, WH6411.21. Johnson had suggested that Larry O'Brien replace Bailey as DNC chairman. But after Daley voiced support for Bailey, Johnson backed down.

34   *White on Bailey*—Theodore H. White, *The Making of the President, 1960* (Atheneum Publishers, 1961), p. 67.

35   *Daley stopped Stevenson*—Ibid., p. 193.

35   *Johnson invited Daley to joint session of Congress*—Memorandum from Cliff Carter to the President, November 25, 1963, the President's Appointment File, 11/22/63–11/30/63, Box 1. Carter also recommended that Johnson invite David L. Lawrence, Mayor Robert Wagner of New York City, Governor Pat Brown of California, and Governor Carl Sanders of Georgia.

35   *Johnson on "the Catholic bosses"*—Lyndon Johnson, *The Vantage Point: Perspectives of the Presidency, 1963–1969* (Holt, Rinehart & Winston, 1971).

36–39   *Lawrence prepared Pennsylvania delegation*—For details of Lawrence's maneuvering inside the caucus room, I relied on Kermit McFarland, "State Throws 4 Convention Votes to Wind," *Pittsburgh Press,* July 14, 1948. For the Pennsylvania bosses' decision to support overwhelmingly the Truman-Barkley ticket, see McFarland and Frank M. Matthews, "State Pledges 70 of 74 Votes to President," *Pittsburgh Post-Gazette,* July 14, 1948.

36–37   *Lawrence backed civil rights plank early*—"50 Top Democrats Back Rights Plank," *New York Times,* July 5, 1948.

37 *Platform Committee rejected strong civil rights plank*—See Frank M. Matthews, "Draft Skirts Racial Issue," *Pittsburgh Post-Gazette*, July 13, 1948.

37–38 *Humphrey's fears over strong civil rights plank*—Hubert Humphrey, *The Education of a Public Man: My Life and Politics* (Regents of the University of Minnesota, 1991), p. 76. For details of the infighting between the South and intellectuals over the strong civil rights plank, also see Robert Mann, *The Walls of Jericho: Lyndon Johnson, Hubert Humphrey, Richard Russell, and the Struggle for Civil Rights* (Harcourt, Brace & Co., 1996), esp. ch. 1; *The Last Campaign: How Harry Truman Won the 1948 Election* (Random House, 2000), esp. chs. 12 & 13; and Carl Solberg, *Hubert Humphrey: A Biography* (W. W. Norton, 1984), esp. Prologue.

38 *Pennsylvania delegation "divided"*—McFarland, "State Throws 4 Convention Votes to Wind"; and Matthews, "State Pledges 70 of 74 Votes to President."

38 *Myers' stand on civil rights plank*—See John E. Jones, "Myers Has Faith in Civil Rights Plank," *Pittsburgh Post-Gazette*, July 17, 1948.

38 *Truman aide feared Myers' ego*—George McKee Elsey, *An Unplanned Life: A Memoir by George McKee Elsey* (University of Missouri Press, 2005), p. 163.

38–39 *Lawrence and irritated delegates*—McFarland, "State Throws 4 Convention Votes to Wind."

39 *Lawrence's support for Truman*—Fuller, "The Man to Watch at the Democratic Convention," *Harper's*, p. 50. For Lawrence's role in ousting Wallace and picking Truman, see Ferrell, *Choosing Truman*, pp. 76–77, 80.

39 *Associated Press headline*—See "Pennsylvania Group Indorses Truman over Vigorous Protests," *Chicago Daily Tribune*, June 30, 1948.

39 *Lawrence admires Truman's honesty*— David L. Lawrence oral history, June 30, 1966, Harry S. Truman Library. The interviewer was Jerry N. Hess.

40 *"You got me in all this trouble. . . ."*—"The Reminiscences of Joseph M. Barr," August 1974, Oral History Collection of

La Salle University, pp. 6–7. The interviewer was Thomas J. Donaghy, FSC.

40 *Lawrence's previous stance on civil rights*—"The Reminiscences of Andrew Bradley," August 1, 1974, Oral History Collection of La Salle University, p. 7.

40 *Lawrence's statement on civil rights*—See Michael P. Weber, *Don't Call Me Boss: David L. Lawrence, Pittsburgh's Renaissance Mayor* (University of Pittsburgh Press, 1988), pp. 280–81. Lawrence delivered the speech quoted herein at the fortieth annual conference of the National Urban League in Grand Rapids, Michigan.

40 *Alexander urged Myers to back civil rights*—Letter from Raymond Pace Alexander to Senator Frank Myers, May 11, 1948, Harry S. Truman Library, p. 2. The letter can also be found at http://www.trumanlibrary.org/whistlestop/study_collections/1948campaign/largedocs/documents/index.php?pagenumber=2&documentid=8&document-date=1948-05-11&studycollectionid=Election&groupid=

40–41 *Lawrence supported black voters*—"The Reminiscences of Andrew Bradley," pp. 7–8.

41 *FDR to Byrnes*—Ferrell, *Choosing Truman*, p. 30.

41–42 *Curley at 1948 convention*—C. Edgar Brown, ed., *Democracy at Work: Being the Official Report of the Democratic National Convention, Philadelphia, Pennsylvania, July 12 to July 14, inclusive, 1948* (Philadelphia, 1949), pp. 194–95.

42–43 *Curley's career in Massachusetts*—I have relied on Jack Beatty, *The Rascal King: The Life and Times of James Michael Curley (1874–1958), An Epic of Urban Politics and Irish America* (Addison-Wesley, 1992).

43 *Lawrence's morality and career*—See Thomas J. Donaghy, *Keystone Democrat: David Lawrence Remembered* (Vantage Press, 1986); and Weber, *Don't Call Me Boss.*

43 *New type of boss*—See Blanche Blank, "The New-Style Boss," *New Republic,* September 11, 1961, pp. 11–12.

43 *Schlesinger on new type of boss*—Arthur M. Schlesinger Jr., *The Politics of Upheaval* (Houghton Mifflin, 1960), p. 442.

43 *Lieberman on Bailey*—Joseph I. Lieberman, *The Power Broker: A Biography of John M. Bailey, Modern Political Boss* (Houghton Mifflin, 1966).

43   *Lawrence as "dominant factor"*—Joseph H. Miller, "Barkley Seen as Vice President Choice," *Philadelphia Inquirer,* July 13, 1948.

43–44   *Biemiller's account*—Andrew Biemiller oral history, Minnesota Historical Society. Both Carl Solberg and Robert Mann rely exclusively on Biemiller's account: that Bronx boss Ed Flynn lobbied other big-city bosses to support Humphrey's minority resolution. But Biemiller's account is seriously incomplete. It ignores the fact that David Lawrence, Jacob Arvey, and William Green endorsed what became the Humphrey-Biemiller minority report more than a week before the 1948 Democratic National Convention began. See "50 Top Democrats Back Rights Plank," *New York Times,* July 5, 1948. It is difficult not to view this as another instance in which contemporary historians overlooked the achievements of the big-city and state bosses.

44   *Lawrence convinced Myers*—Frank M. Matthews, "State Delegates Go Down Line with Truman," *Pittsburgh Post-Gazette,* July 15, 1948. According to Matthews, "Lawrence and a group from the delegation prevailed upon Myers to drop his personal offense at Humphrey's action and vote for the amendment."

44   *Pennsylvania's crucial support*—Here are four "blue states" that voted overwhelmingly against the strong civil rights plank: Maine (seven nay votes, three yes votes), Maryland (all twenty votes nay), Delaware (all ten votes nay), and Oregon (five yes votes, eleven no votes). *Democracy at Work,* pp. 203–10.

44–45   *Humphrey credited the bosses*—Humphrey, *The Education of a Public Man,* p. 79.

45   *"Solid South" dissolved*—See Richard M. Scammon and Ben J. Wattenberg, *The Real Majority* (Coward-McCann, 1970), pp. 175–77.

45   *Philadelphia Inquirer headline*—Joseph M. Miller, "Big-City Groups Win Party Rule from Deep South," *Philadelphia Inquirer,* July 15, 1948. Miller was referring to the bosses in particular. "The big-city organizations of the Democratic Party yesterday repudiated the 'deep South' by

forcing through the National Convention a liberalized civil rights program," he wrote in the lead.

45–46 *Adlai Stevenson*—For details about Stevenson, see John Bartlow Martin, *Adlai Stevenson of Illinois: The Life of Adlai E. Stevenson* (Doubleday, 1976).

46 *"makes a mockery ..."*—Drew Pearson, "Stevenson Used Cards Shrewdly," *Washington Post,* July 24, 1952.

46 *Stevenson at Illinois caucus*—James Reston, "Governor Is Firm," *New York Times,* July 21, 1952.

47 *Jacob Arvey's career*—Charles L. Berry, "Arvey's Career Is Patterned along Horatio Alger Lines," *Philadelphia Inquirer,* July 12, 1948.

47 *Lawrence backed Stevenson*—*Pittsburgh Post-Gazette,* July 16, 1952.

47 *New York Times cited Lawrence*—Reston, "Governor Is Firm."

48 *"If you ever saw a shenanigan organization ..."*—Fuller, "The Man to Watch at the Democratic Convention," p. 51.

48–49 *O'Brien on Lawrence*—Lawrence O'Brien, *No Final Victories: A Life in Politics—from John F. Kennedy to Watergate* (Random House, 1974), p. 79.

49 *Patronage figures*—See Steven P. Erie, *Rainbow's End: Irish-Americans and the Dilemmas of Urban Machine Politics, 1840–1985* (University of California Press, 1988).

49 *Lawrence's patronage*—Weber, *Don't Call Me Boss,* pp. 68–70. Also see Daniel Scroop, *Mr. Democrat: Jim Farley, the New Deal, and the Making of Modern American Politics* (University of Michigan Press, 2006), pp. 138–41.

49–50 *Hawkins on Pittsburgh*—Frank Hawkins, "Lawrence of Pittsburgh: Boss of the Mellon Patch," *Harper's,* August 1956, p. 58.

50 *Lawrence on corruption*—"The Reminiscences of Andrew Bradley," p. 11.

50 *"Too often the liberal fallacy ..."*—Statement of James H. J. Tate to the Commission on Party Structure and Delegate Selection, May 24, 1969, DNC Files, National Archives, p. 6.

50 *"... 'How do you start in politics ...?'"*—Interview with Rosemary Trump.

50 *Bailey was accessible*—Lieberman, *The Power Broker*.

50 *Lawrence's philosophy of government*—Donaghy, *Keystone Democrat*.

51 *Daley as ambiguous figure*—Adam Cohen and Elizabeth Taylor, *American Pharaoh: Mayor Richard J. Daley, His Battle for Chicago and the Nation* (Little, Brown, 2000).

51 *Lemann on Daley's Chicago*—"Machine Man," *New Republic*, July 31, 2000.

51 *Connecticut's Protestants and Catholics*—Lieberman, *The Power Broker*.

52 *"Public commentary became surprisingly bitter ..."*—Ibid.

52 *Connecticut birth control legislation*—Ibid.

52 *Connecticut abortion legislation*—"House Voted Listed on Antiabortion Act," *Hartford Courant*, May 23, 1972, p. 20.

53 *"It wasn't something that was discussed ..."*—Interview with Gerald Lawrence.

53 *Daley's pro-life allies*—Interview with Joseph Scheidler.

53 *"Big-city machines undercut ..."*—Clarence N. Stone, "Urban Political Machines: Taking Stock," *Political Science & Politics*, September 1996.

53 *Pittsburgh's black population*—Weber, *Don't Call Me Boss*.

53 *Lawrence outlaws discrimination*—Ibid.

53–54 *Bailey and the Connecticut legislature*—Lieberman, *The Power Broker*,

54–55 *1952 Democratic National Convention*—Martin, *Adlai Stevenson of Illinois*.

55 *"The first thing I noticed ..."*—Ibid.

55 *Lawrence delivered only 36 votes*—Reston, "Governor Is Firm."

55 *"I have been in politics all my life ..."*—Quoted in Walter Johnson, *How We Drafted Stevenson* (Knopf, 1955), p. 156.

56 *Lawrence's Catholicism*—Donaghy, *Keystone Democrat*. Also see Hawkins, "Boss of the Mellon Patch," p. 57.

56 *Connecticut, Knights of Columbus*—Lieberman, *The Power Broker*.

56 *Lawrence and Kennedy on Columbus Day*—David L. Lawrence oral history, John F. Kennedy Library, p. 2.

56–57 *Lawrence and anti-Catholic prejudice*—Donaghy, *Keystone Democrat*, pp. 9–11. Lawrence ran in a Democratic primary for the post of Allegheny County commissioner.

57   *Popular anti-Catholic feeling*—Paul Blanshard, *American Freedom and Catholic Power* (The Beacon Press, 1949), p. 57.

57   *"I was always fearful of the religious situation . . ."*—David L. Lawrence oral history, John F. Kennedy Library, p. 9.

57   *"Certainly, my brother is not assured . . ."*—Letter from Robert F. Kennedy to David L. Lawrence, December 4, 1959, David L. Lawrence Papers, General File, 1959 Democratic National Committee, Pennsylvania State Archives. I learned about this letter from reading Father Donaghy's *Keystone Democrat.*

57   *"The fact is I was not against . . ."*—Letter from David L. Lawrence to Robert F. Kennedy, November 19, 1959, David L. Lawrence Papers, General File, 1959 Democratic National Committee, Pennsylvania State Archives.

58   *"We are all furious at Governor Brown . . ."*—Rose Fitzgerald Kennedy, *Times to Remember* (Doubleday, 1974), pp. 370–71.

58   *"It would be a fine thing . . ."*—"Lawrence Fights Religion as Issue," *New York Times,* January 31, 1960, p. 48.

58   *". . . a Catholic couldn't be elected president. . . ."*—David L. Lawrence oral history, John F. Kennedy Library, p. 4.

59   *"When I heard that he won by 100,000 . . ."*—Ibid., p. 5.

59   *"Then of course the real climax was in Chicago . . ."*—Frank M. Matthews, "The Problems of a Political Boss," *Pittsburgh Post-Gazette,* January 14, 1963.

59   *". . . I'm going to support Kennedy"*—Fuller, "The Man to Watch at the Democratic Convention," p. 52.

59   *"Now look, Dave . . ."*—"The Reminiscences of Matthew McCloskey," Oral History Collection of La Salle University, p. 3. McCloskey was in the hotel bathroom with Kennedy and Lawrence. After Kennedy won the election, he appointed McCloskey as the U.S. ambassador to Ireland.

60   *ADA letter opposing Johnson*—Samuel H. Beer, national chairman to ADA members, June 30, 1960, Joseph L. Rauh Subject File, Box 86, Mississippi Freedom Democratic Party, General, 1960–61, Library of Congress.

60   *"it just isn't in the works"*—"The Reminiscences of Matthew McCloskey," p. 2.

61 *Southerners on national ticket*—The vice-presidential nomi-
nees were John "Cactus Jack" Nance Garner of Texas
(1932 and 1936), Harry Truman of Missouri (1944),
Alben Barkley of Kentucky (1948), John J. Sparkman of
Alabama (1952), Estes Kefauver of Tennessee (1956), and
Johnson of Texas (1960).

61–62 *Figures on Democratic votes*—See http://uselectionatlas.org/
RESULTS/

62 *The electorate*—Kristi Anderson, *The Creation of a Democratic
Majority, 1928–1936* (University of Chicago Press, 1979).

63 *"Even before the Great Depression ..."*—Phillips, *The Emerging
Republican Majority.*

63 *"While the Republican issue had been ..."*—Scammon and
Wattenberg, *The Real Majority.*

63 *"... the nation no longer has an effective majority."*—Samuel
Lubell, *The Future of American Politics* (Doubleday, 1951).

64 *"We weren't just dealing ..."*—"The Reminiscences of
Carmine DeSapio," Oral History Collection of La Salle
University, p. 8.

65 *Kennedy statement*—"Text of Kennedy Message," *New York
Times,* July 15, 1960.

65 *"Dave, I'll remember ..."*—"The Reminiscences of Walter
Giesey," Oral History Collection of La Salle University,
p. 37.

Chapter Three—The Democratic Bosses: Not By the People

67 *Testimony of Fannie Lou Hamer*—Proceedings of the Democratic National Convention, 1964, Credentials Committee, Atlantic City, New Jersey, August 22, 1964, Joseph
L. Rauh Subject File, Box 29, DNC FIles, Library of Congress, pp. 39–44.

67–68 *On Aaron Henry*—Ibid., pp. 24–25. For an extended
account of Henry's remarkable life, see Nicholas Lemann,
*The Promised Land: The Great Black Migration and How It
Changed America* (Random House, 1991).

68 *"They did not have a black at their entire state convention"*—
"Remarks in rebuttal of Joseph L. Rauh, Jr., Counsel, Mississippi Freedom Democratic Party before the Credentials

Committee of the Democratic National Convention, August 22, 1964," Joseph L. Rauh Subject File, Box 86, Mississippi Freedom Democratic Party, July–August 1964, Library of Congress, p. 6.

60 *E. K. Collins, "because they weren't elected ..."*—Proceedings of the Democratic National Convention, 1964, Credentials Committee, Atlantic City, New Jersey, August 22, 1964, Joseph L. Rauh Subject File, Box 29, DNC Files, Library of Congress, p. 62.

69–70 *"Seat them both ..."*—Anne Cooke Romaine, "The Mississippi Freedom Democratic Party through August 1964," Unpublished M.A. thesis, University of Virginia, 1969, interview with Joseph Rauh, Box 86, Mississippi Freedom Democratic Party, General, 1960, 1961, and 1964, Library of Congress.

70 *"I think it's going to hurt like hell ..."*—Telephone conversation between Johnson and Bailey, August 25, 1964, 9:22 A.M., WH6408.35, Lyndon Baines Johnson Library.

70 *"Eleven and eight, we got 'em."*—Robert E. Baker, "Mississippi Rivals Assure Battle for Convention Seats Compromise Rejected," *Washington Post*, August 19, 1964.

71 *Three-part proposal on MFDP*—By all accounts, Democratic leaders had devised a three-part solution in the morning. See Kevin Boyle, *The UAW and the Heyday of American Liberalism, 1945–1968* (Cornell University Press, 1995), pp. 194–96; Steven Gillon, *Mondale: Portrait of an American Politician* (Harper & Row, 1980), pp. 130–31; Nick Kotz, *Judgment Days: Lyndon Baines Johnson, Martin Luther King Jr., and the Laws That Changed America* (Houghton Mifflin, 2005), pp. 214–16; and Timothy N. Thurber, *The Politics of Equality: Hubert H. Humphrey and the African American Freedom Struggle* (Columbia University Press, 1994), pp. 154–57.

71 *Lawrence entered Shelburne Hotel*—Interview with Gerald Lawrence. My description of the hotel is based on photographs from the time.

72 *"He's enthusiastic about it!..."*—Johnson, Humphrey, and Reuther, August 25, 1964, 2:30 P.M., WH6408.40, Lyndon Baines Johnson Library.

72 *Lawrence never revealed*—I interviewed both Walter Mondale and Bill Moyers, the only two surviving principals in the negotiations. Neither could recall who came up with the idea of a national commission. The only other person in the room who may have devised the idea was Tom Finney, a Johnson aide who later worked for Eugene McCarthy.

72 *"I had great help ..."*—David Lawrence to John Rodin, September 21, 1964, David L Lawrence Papers, General Correspondence, R, 1964, Pennsylvania State Archives.

72 *It was "a 'sweetening' that satisfied ..."*—Godfrey Sperling, "Presidential Discipline Applied," *Christian Science Monitor,* August 27, 1964.

72 *Lawrence called settlement a "turning point ..."*—Tom Wicker, "MS. Delegates Withdrawn, Reject Seating Compromise; Convention Then Approves Plan," *New York Times,* August 27, 1964.

72 *"We certainly do not want the South to leave ..."*—Sally Oleon Shames, "David L. Lawrence, Mayor of Pittsburgh: Development of a Political Leader," Ph.D. thesis, University of Pittsburgh, 1958, p. 105. Shames got the quote from James Helbert, "What the Mayor Doesn't Like about the South," *Pittsburgh Press,* February 3, 1957, p. 17.

72 *Lawrence as mediator*—See Donaghy, *Keystone Democrat,* p. 12.

73 *"The South likes David Lawrence ..."*—Telephone conversation between Johnson and Burke Marshall, June 23, 1964, 3:51 P.M., WH6406.14, Lyndon Baines Johnson Library. Johnson had also considered for the job the mayors of Atlanta and Charlotte, LeRoy Collins, and Hubert Humphrey.

73 *Bailey's Committee Against Discrimination*—"Democratic National Committee Sets Up Committee Against Discrimination," press release, January 21, 1965, DNC Files, National Archives.

73 *Commission charter, "It is the understanding ..."*—Official Report of the Proceedings of the Democratic National Convention, 1964, Democratic National Committee, p. 31.

74 *Bernhard on Johnson and the Lawrence Commission*—Interview with Berl Bernhard.

74 *"Berl was associate director ..."*—Memorandum from McPherson to Johnson, November 26, 1965, McPherson Papers, Lyndon Baines Johnson Library.

74 *"For obvious reasons ..."*—Memorandum, Democratic National Committee, Lawrence Committee, September 9, 1966, DNC Files, National Archives, p. 7.

75 *"The leaders of the 'regular' Democratic Parties ..."*—Letter from Rauh to Lawrence, June 22, 1966, Joseph L. Rauh Subject File, Box 29, Democratic Party, Democratic National Convention, 1968, Library of Congress, p. 2.

75–76 *Six "minimal prerequisites"*—Second Report of the Special Equal Rights Committee, January 1968, DNC Files, National Archives.

76 *Bailey made a suggestion*—Transcript of Special Equal Rights Committee Hearing, October 9, 1967, DNC Files, National Archives.

76 *DNC aides traveled to Mississippi*—Memorandum from Frank R. Parker and Bishop C. Holifield to Howard A. Glickstein, July 12, 1968, DNC Files, National Archives.

77 *Lawrence Commission had taken "significant steps ..."*—Bode wrote an unpublished manuscript in the early-to-mid 1970s about the history of the McGovern Commission. The quotation here comes from "Chapter VI: The McGovern Commission—Interpreting the Mandate," Ken Bode Files, DC 2831, DePauw University Archives, p. 7.

77 State and local parties control the presidential nominating system: Theodore H. White, *The Making of the President*, 1964 (Macmillan, 1965), p. 130.

78 *"The laws have been on the books ..."*—Proceedings of the Democratic National Convention, 1964, Credentials Committee, Atlantic City, New Jersey, August 22, 1964, Joseph L. Rauh Subject File, Box 29, DNC Files, Library of Congress, p. 64.

78 *"I quite agree with Mr. Keyserling ..."*—Arthur Schlesinger Jr., "Correspondence," *New Republic*, November 3, 1958, p. 6. Also see Schlesinger, "Death Wish of the Democrats,"

New Republic, September 15, 1958; and Leon Keyserling, "Eggheads and Politics," *New Republic,* October 27, 1958.

79 *"I decided that the rules were rigged ..."*—Interview with Geoff Cowan.

79 *Challenging the regular party was absurdly difficult*—For a description of the Connecticut Democratic Party's laws for challengers, I am indebted to Lewis Chester, Godfrey Hodgson, and Bruce Page, *An American Melodrama: The Presidential Campaign of 1968* (Viking Press, 1969), p. 395.

79 "He never seemed to be going anywhere in particular ....": Joseph I. Lieberman, *The Power Broker: A Biography of John M. Bailey, Modern Political Boss* (Houghton Mifflin, 1966), pp. 4–5.

79–80 *"... Who's Grabowski? Bailey's man."*—Ibid., p. 4.

80 *Bailey as King John—The Presidential Nominating Conventions 1968* (Congressional Quarterly Service, 1968), p. 127.

80 *"... will not yield fair representation."*—Joseph Lieberman, *The Legacy: Connecticut Politics, 1930–1980* (Spoonwood Press, 1981), p. 128.

80 *Cowan gathered his fellow aides*—Byron E. Shafer, *Quiet Revolution: The Struggle for the Democratic Party and the Shaping of Post-Reform Politics* (Russell Sage Foundation, 1983), pp. 14–15.

81 *"All state delegate selection systems ..."*—The Democratic Choice: A Report of the Commission on the Democratic Selection of Presidential Nominees (1968), p. 5.

81 *"... negative votes at the district caucuses"*—The Presidential Nominating Conventions 1968, p. 123.

82 *"The at-large delegates do not represent ..."*—Ibid., p. 101.

82 *The rules were "far from perfect"*—Ibid., p. 131. Richard Hughes made this comment during the second half of ABC's "Issues and Answers," a news program from the time.

83 *McCarthyites and the Rules Committee—The Presidential Nominating Conventions 1968,* p. 115.

83 *Cowan and the minority report*—Interview with Geoff Cowan. He and Simon Lazarus III drafted the language for the minority report.

83 *The language of the minority report—The Presidential Nominating Conventions 1968,* p. 198.

84   *"the reverse of the peace-plank operation"*—Chester, Hodgson and Page, *An American Melodrama,* p. 551.

84   *"aren't worth the gunpowder . . ."*—Ibid., p. 554.

84   *You've got to stop the kids . . ."*—Ibid., p. 551.

84   *"Everybody votes with the chairman . . ."*—Shafer, *Quiet Revolution,* p.36. Also see Letter from Geoff Cowan to Theodore White, August 1,1969, p. 8, private papers of Geoffrey Cowan.

84   *"Nobody understood what the voting was about . . ."*—Shafer, *Quiet Revolution,* p. 557.

84   Harold Hughes, *"build the selection process for 1972 . . ."*—*The Presidential Nominating Conventions 1968,* p. 147.

Chapter Four—A Small Group of Men

87   *"excited as hell"*—Byron E. Shafer, *Quiet Revolution: The Struggle for the Democratic Party and the Shaping of Post-Reform Politics* (Russell Sage Foundation, 1983), p. 40.

87   *"It marked the climax . . ."*—Lewis Chester, Godfrey Hodgson and Bruce Page, *An American Melodrama: The Presidential Campaign of 1968* (Viking Press, 1969), p. 572.

87   *"I went from being anti-Vietnam . . ."*—Shafer, *Quiet Revolution,* p. 40.

88   *"I had found in one state . . ."*—Interview with Eli Segal.

88   *"Do you know what it's like . . . ?"*—Interview with David Mixner.

88   *In 1968 "the system was actually working . . ."*—Richard C. Wade, *New Democrat,* October 1970, p. 6.

89   *"Although the selection process . . ."*—Eli Segal, "Unfair Methods of Delegate Selection for the 1968 Democratic National Convention," private papers of Harold Ickes, p. 2.

89   *"As delegates assemble . . ."*—*The Democratic Choice: A Report of the Commission on the Democratic Selection of Presidential Nominees* (1968), p. 13.

90   *". . . a democracy of individual participation"*—James Miller, *Democracy in the Streets: From Port Huron to the Streets of Chicago* (Simon & Schuster, 1987), p. 333.

90   *"full-scale structural and institutional reform . . ."*—Shafer, *Quiet Revolution.*

90   *". . . the 'good old boy network' . . ."*—Ibid., p. 80.

91 *"There's a large Klan there . . ."*—Segal was referring to Okla-homa. David Mixner, *Stranger Among Friends* (Bantam Books, 1996), p. 45.

91 *Segal's Democratic tradition*—Interview with Eli Segal.

91–92 *Segal's political sympathies*—Steven Waldman, *The Bill: How Legislation* Really *Becomes Law: A Case Study of the National Service Bill* (Penguin Group, 1995), pp. 33–35.

92 *"The executive committee was important"*—Shafer, *Quiet Revolution,* p. 8.

93 *"your talk on the organization structure . . ."*—Memorandum from Eli Segal to George McGovern, "Your Statement on the Organization of the Special Committee," Commission on Party Structure and Delegate Selection, DNC Files, National Archives, p. 1.

93 *They needed "a small group"*—Memorandum: "Executive Committee Meeting Minutes, May 26, 1969, Commission on Party Structure and Delegate Selection," DNC Files, National Archives, p. 1.

94 *No proxies or substitutes*—Shafer, *Quiet Revolution,* pp. 93–94.

94 *"There were twenty-eight members"*—Ibid., p. 94.

94 *"In the end, the fact . . ."*—Lawrence O'Brien, *No Final Victories: A Life in Politics—From John F. Kennedy to Watergate* (Books of Canada, 1975), p. 262.

95 *"Confronted with the very serious crisis . . ."*—Chester, Hodgson, and Page, *An American Melodrama,* p. 717.

95 *"I don't think that anyone could have foreseen . . ."*—Ibid., p. 297.

96 *"strong reform elements appear . . ."*—David Broder, "Democratic Reformers Gain Ground," *Washington Post,* March 2, 1969.

96 *"Some see [the commission] as an opportunity . . ."*—Paul Hope, *Washington Star,* February 1969.

96 *"New Democratic Coalition reformers . . ."*—Jack Newfield, "A New Party for '72 Could Get Us Back to '64," *Village Voice,* July 2, 1970.

96 *"Any such attempt would be blocked . . ."*—Richard M. Scammon and Ben J. Wattenberg, *The Real Majority* (Coward-McCann, 1970), p. 189.

105 *"Pena was flown in for this"*—Shafer, *Quiet Revolution,* pp. 145–46.

106 *"In the field of delegate selection ..."*—Transcript of the Commission on Party Structure and Delegate Selection, April 22, 1969, Commission on Party Structure and Delegate Selection, DNC Files, National Archives, pp. 34–37.

107 *"...changing the guard ..."*—Ibid., p. 10.

107 *Casey's testimony*—Transcript of the Commission on Party Structure and Delegate Selection, May 17, 1969, DNC Files, National Archives, pp. 170–91.

107–8 *Shapp's 1966 victory*—Robert P. Casey, *Fighting for Life* (Word Publishing, 1996), pp. 79–80.

108 *"Don't kill the machine"*—Transcript of the Commission on Party Structure and Delegate Selection, May 17, 1969, DNC Files, National Archives, p. 175.

108 *"... discrimination in reverse"*—Ibid., p. 187.

108 *Caucuses are "inferior"*—Letter from William J. Boyd to George McGovern, "Response to Letters from Intellectuals," Commission on Party Structure and Delegate Selection, April 1969, Box 2, DNC Files, National Archives.

108 *"Although I have long been a critic ..."*—Letter from Clarence A. Berdahl to George McGovern, "Response to Letters from Intellectuals," Commission on Party Structure and Delegate Selection, Box 2, DNC Files, National Archives.

109 *"I don't care who does the electing ..."*—*The Democratic Choice.*

109 *"If someone thinks ..."*—Written testimony from James H. J. Tate, Commission on Party Structure and Delegate Selection, May 17, 1969, DNC Files, National Archives, pp. 7–8.

110 *Boss system fails to "bridge that gap"*—Commission on Party Structure and Delegate Selection, June 7, 1969, DNC Files, National Archives, pp. 14–15.

111 *"Your job is not simply ..."*—Testimony of Donald O. Peterson, Commission on Party Structure and Delegate Selection, April 22, 1969, DNC Files, National Archives, pp. 149–53.

111 *A call for quotas*—Testimony of Paul Schrade, Commission on Party Structure and Delegate Selection, June 21, 1969, DNC Files, National Archive, pp. 60–82.

112–19 *Austin Ranney in Washington*—Except where noted, all details come from interviews with Ranney.

113–14 *"This may not be the appropriate time ..."*—Transcript of Commission on Party Structure and Delegate Selection, November 19, 1969, DNC Files, National Archives, Box 5, Side Two, pp. 1–3.

114 *" it was not feasible ..."*—McGovern, ibid., Side Two, p. 3.

114 *"... we would like to at least urge ..."*—Austin Ranney, Ibid.

114 *"To my surprise ..."*—Interview with Austin Ranney.

115 *"Mr. Chairman, I would say that ..."*—Fred Dutton, Transcript of Commission on Party Structure and Delegate Selection, November 19, 1969, DNC Files, National Archives, Box 5, Side Two, p. 7.

115 *"To keep our party moving forward ..."*—Birch Bayh, ibid., Side Two, p. 10.

116 *"Implicit in this discussion ..."*—Fred Dutton, ibid., Side Three, p. 3.

116 *"The 21 to 30 group ..."*—Dutton, ibid., Side Three, p. 11.

117 *Beer was a leading light*—Interview with Samuel Beer.

117 *"Mr. Chairman, I'd like to speak out ..."*—Samuel Beer, ibid., Side Three, p. 4.

117–18 *"The argument is bogus ..."*—Fred Dutton, ibid., Side Three, p. 5.

118 *Vote count on A-1*—Interviews with Fred Dutton and Eli Segal.

118–19 *"I gave Bayh the reasonable relationship language ..."*—Shafer, *Quiet Revolution*, p. 168.

119 *"My opinion was ..."*—Interview with Austin Ranney.

119 *"I talked to Eli, Anne, and Sam Brown ..."*—Interview with David Mixner.

119 *"At the end ..."*—Interview with Joseph Gebhardt.

Chapter Five—Power to the People

121 *Over the weekend of May 10–11, 1969*—Memo from Fred Dutton to McGovern, Hughes, Dodds, Nelson and Segal, "McGovern Commission 'Soup-Up,'" Commission on Party Structure and Delegate Selection, DNC Files, National Archives, p. 1. Dutton typically wrote his political memos on his law office stationery; this letter was an

exception. Knowing Dutton's industriousness and the fact that the letter was received on May 13, I am confident that Dutton wrote this memo at home over the weekend.

121 *Escabeche and sweet-and-sour bean sprouts*—Myra McPherson, "When Cheese Dip Palls, Try Some Fried Parsley," *New York Times*, June 6, 1967, p. 51.

121 *"I like to keep things on a social level."*—See Freddutton.com.

121 *Passage of the nuclear test ban treaty*—Interview with Fred Dutton.

122 *"I believe the overall party reform effort . . ."*—Memo from Fred Dutton to McGovern, Hughes, Dodds, Nelson and Segal, "McGovern Commission 'Soup-Up,'" p. 1.

122 *"What the Commission and staff are doing . . ."*—Ibid., p. 2.

122–23 *"The real need is not just the usual press/TV releases . . ."*—Ibid., pp. 1–2.

123 *"I'm a great believer . . ."*—Interview with Fred Dutton. See Richard Harwood, "Can New Politics Retain Its Luster?" *Washington Post*, May 23, 1968.

123 *"wobbling persistence of the Democratic coalition."*—Frederick G. Dutton, *Changing Sources of Power: American Politics in the 1970s* (McGraw-Hill, 1971), p. 4.

123 *"the coming of age of the World War II baby boomers . . ."*—Penn Kimball, *Bobby Kennedy and the New Politics* (Prentice-Hall, 1966), p. 82.

123–24 *"With the profound alienation . . ."*—Letter from Fred Dutton to LeRoy Collins, April 22, 1969, Commission on Party Structure and Delegate Selection, DNC Files, National Archives, p. 2.

124 *Dutton's suggestions would "prove helpful"*—Letter from LeRoy Collins to Fred Dutton, April 22, 1969, Commission on Party Structure and Delegate Selection, DNC Files, National Archives.

124 *"If you wanted to end the war . . ."*—Interview with Anne Wexler.

125 *"relatively small, but highly determined . . ."*—Robert E. Thompson, "Liberal Democrats Painting Themselves into a Corner," *New York Herald-Examiner*, June 22, 1969.

125 a "black-blue" or "have-not" coalition—Jules Witcover, *85 Days: The Last Campaign of Robert Kennedy* (William Morrow, 1969), pp. 126, 176–82.

126 *"So far in Indiana . . ."*—David Halberstam, *The Unfinished Odyssey of Robert Kennedy* (Random House, 1969).

126 *"It's easy for you to sit back . . ."*—Jack Newfield, *Robert Kennedy: A Memoir* (E. P. Dutton, 1969), p. 256.

126 *Kennedy's support among blacks*—Ronald Steel, *In Love with Night: The American Romance with Robert Kennedy* (Simon & Schuster, 2000), pp. 171–76.

126 *"had swept not only the Negro wards . . ."*—Samuel Lubell, *The Hidden Crisis in American Politics* (W. W. Norton, 1970), p. 235.

126 *"That I have a chance . . ."*—Newfield, *Robert Kennedy: A Memoir*, p. 265.

127 *"The membership of the McGovern Commission . . ."*—Task Force on Party Reform of the New Democratic Coalition, press release, March 2, 1969, Commission on Party Structure and Delegate Selection, DNC Files, National Archives.

128 *"Whether special representation . . ."*—Letter from Dutton to Collins, April 22, 1969, p. 2.

128 *Dutton nearly arrested in Chicago*—Interview with Fred Dutton.

129 *At the side entrance of the Hilton Hotel*—Jack Newfield, *Village Voice*, September 5, 1968, as quoted in Norman Mailer, *Miami and the Siege of Chicago: An Informal History of the Republican and Democratic Conventions of 1968* (Signet Books, 1968), p. 171.

129 *Dutton not a blue-collar Democrat*—Interview with Fred Dutton.

130 *Humphrey tried to recruit Dutton*—Lewis Chester, Godfrey Hodgson and Bruce Page, *An American Melodrama: The Presidential Campaign of 1968* (Viking Press, 1969), p. 528.

130 *Dutton drafts minority peace plank*—Ibid., pp. 528–29. See also Steven V. Roberts, "War Critics Agree on Specifics of Vietnam," *New York Times*, August 16, 1968.

130 *Dutton one of the party's best strategists*—President Johnson to Edmund G. "Pat" Brown, White House 6606.04 12:50 P.M.

130 *Dutton's numerous top jobs*—Interview with Fred Dutton.

131 *Dutton as chief theoretician of the New Politics*—Richard Harwood, *Washington Post,* May 23, 1968.

131 *Dutton sympathizes with the New Politics*—Interview with Fred Dutton.

131 *"Most of them also dispute ..."*—Dutton, *Changing Sources of Power,* p. 45.

131 *"So many really would have clung ..."*—Fred Dutton oral history, John F. Kennedy Library, p. 20. It's worth noting that Dutton gave this interview on November 18, 1969, the day before the epic meeting of the McGovern Commission.

131–32 *Dutton champions elite students*—For the differences among California colleges and universities, see Nicholas Lemann, *The Big Test: The Secret History of the American Meritocracy* (Farrar, Straus & Giroux, 1999), esp. ch. 14.

132 *"I see the kids coming to us ..."*—Nicholas von Hoffman, "Breeding Cop Haters," *Washington Post,* June 2, 1969.

132 *Dutton's $40 million proposal*—William Trombley, "UC Regent Offers Plan to Raise $40 Million," *Los Angeles Times,* September 19, 1967.

132 *"The park is cultural escalation ..."*—Von Hoffman, "Breeding Cop Haters."

133 *"I think it's a healthy thing ..."*—Fred Dutton oral history, John F. Kennedy Library, p. 19.

133 *"the newer political faces are all men ..."*—Metromedia Radio News Presents ... "RFK," Marking the first anniversary of the assassination of Robert F. Kennedy, George S. McGovern Papers, Correspondence, 1969, Box 812, Princeton University Library, p. 9.

133 *"Our primary function was to broaden the base ..."*—Fred Dutton oral history, Lyndon Baines Johnson Library, p. 14.

134 To *"all the young people ..."*—Dutton, *Changing Sources of Power,* pp. 62–63.

134–35 *"The politics of the seventies ..."*—Ibid., p. 20.

135 *"We will formulate criteria ..."*—New Democratic Coalition,

1969, Commission on Party Structure and Delegate Selection, DNC Files, National Archives, p. 7.

136 *"younger voters, black citizens ..."*—Letter from Dutton to Collins, Commission on Party Structure and Delegate Selection, DNC Files, National Archives, p. 2.

136 *The party's coalition needed young people*—Richard M. Scammon and Ben J. Wattenberg, *The Real Majority* (Coward-McCann, 1970); Jack Newfield and Jeff Greenfield, *A Populist Manifesto: The Making of a New Majority* (Praeger Publishers, 1971); Fred R. Harris, *Now Is the Time: A New Populist Call to Action* (McGraw-Hill, 1971); and Michael Novak, *The Rise of the Unmeltable Ethnics: The New Political Force of the Seventies* (Macmillan, 1971).

136 *"The real division in this country ..."*—Newfield and Greenfield, *A Populist Manifesto*, p. 9.

137 *"the prospective political energy ..."*—Dutton, *Changing Sources of Power*, pp. 33–34.

137 *"significantly more social ..."*—Ibid., p. 28.

137 *"The principal group arrayed against ..."*—Ibid., p. 222.

137 *Dutton understood working-class problems*—Ibid., p. 223.

137 *"the beards and the blacks ..."*—Ibid., p. 220.

138 *Figures on young voters*—Ibid., pp. 16–17

138 *The young could go GOP*—Ibid., p. 60.

138 *"a 'union man' not long ago ..."*—Ibid., p. 142.

138 *"wiping out the intermediate power brokers"*—Fred Dutton oral history, Lyndon Baines Johnson Library, p. 8.

139 *"those of us who have spent ..."*—Newfield and Greenfield, *A Populist Manifesto*, p. 206.

139 *"The Irish cop on the low end ..."*—Ibid., p. 11.

139 *"A coalition of blacks and ethnics ..."*—Novak, *The Rise of the Unmeltable Ethnics*, p. 257.

140 *"Though some of the best progressive voices ..."*—Harris, *Now Is the Time*.

140 *"The seventies should witness ..."*—Dutton, *Changing Sources of Power*, p. 226. Dutton uses the term "social-change coalition" only twice, but it encapsulates his vision for the new Democratic Party.

141 *"All economic and education projections ..."*—Ibid., see ch. 2.

141 *"If Negroes have ..."*—Ibid., p. 109.

141 *"The much-publicized women's liberation movement . . ."*—Ibid., p. 154

141 *"Even in traditional economic terms . . ."*—Ibid., p. 159.

142 *"The cultural revolution . . ."*—Ibid., p. 224.

142 *Survey data from 1968*—Ibid., pp. 221–22.

142 *"The racial prospect is still grim. . . ."*—Ibid., see ch. 6.

143 *Dutton grasped the importance of the Catholic vote*—Fred Dutton oral history, John F. Kennedy Library, p. 45.

143 *"the Catholic vote"*—Dutton, *Changing Sources of Power*, pp. 117–19.

143 *Dutton's father was a Catholic*—Interview with Fred Dutton.

143 *"The net effect of these groups . . ."*—Dutton, *Changing Sources of Power*, pp. 117–19.

144 *"They got us in a corner . . ."*—Chester, Hodgson and Page, *An American Melodrama*, p. 581.

144 *"I'm going to get everyone . . ."*—Ibid., p. 585.

144 *"As delegates assemble . . ."*—*The Democratic Choice*, p. 13.

145 *"inadequate state provisions for voting hours . . ."*—Memorandum from Eli Segal to Ken Bode, July 13, 1969, Commission on Party Structure and Delegate Selection, DNC Files, National Archives.

145 *"Democratic Choice" endorses variety of methods*—*The Democratic Choice*, pp. 19–20.

146 *Bickel skeptical of direct democracy*- -Alexander M. Bickel, *The New Age of Political Reform: The Electoral College, the Convention, and the Party System* (Harper & Row, 1968).

146 *Newfield wrote a reverential book*—Jack Newfield, *A Prophetic Minority* (New American Library, 1966).

146 *"Issue-oriented individuals . . ."*—*The Democratic Choice*, p. 14.

146–47 *"I prefer a system . . ."*—Interview with Eli Segal.

147 *Six key victories*—See *Mandate for Reform*, "The Official Guidelines of the Commission." Also, see Byron E. Shafer, *Quiet Revolution: The Struggle for the Democratic Party and the Shaping of Post-Reform Politics* (Russell Sage Foundation, 1983), pp. 541–45.

147 *Segal as change agent*—Interview with Segal. He was friends with Samuel R. "Sandy" Berger, who also viewed himself as a change agent rather than a true believer. See Frank

Ahrens, "The Reluctant Warrior," *Washington Post,* February 24, 1998.

147 *"It has always intrigued me . . ."*—Letter from Eli Segal to Birch Bayh, July 11, 1969, Commission on Party Structure and Delegate Selection, DNC Files, National Archives.

147 *"Party reform is dictated by expediency . . ."*—Letter from Eli Segal to Midge Decter, September 3, 1969, Commission on Party Structure and Delegate Selection, DNC Files, National Archives.

147–48 *Segal not opposed to informal quotas*—Letter from Eli Segal to commission consultants, June 12, 1969, Commission on Party Structure and Delegate Selection, DNC Files, National Archives.

148 *Segal declined to comment*—Transcript of commission meeting, September 1969, Commission on Party Structure and Delegate Selection, DNC Files, National Archives.

148 *McGovern thought he might be the nominee*—George McGovern, *Grassroots: The Autobiography of George McGovern* (Random House, 1977), p. 158.

148 *"It's a whole new ballgame."*—Robert Sam Anson, *McGovern: A Biography* (Holt, Rinehart & Winston, 1971), pp. 258–59.

148 *Guests at California Street dinner*—McGovern, *Grassroots,* pp. 158–59; also see Anson, *McGovern,* p. 259.

149 *". . . to increase my national constituency."*—Letter from George McGovern to Arthur Schlesinger Jr., August 8, 1969, George S. McGovern Papers, Personal Correspondence, 1969, Box 493, Princeton University Library.

149 *McGovern as the "high-risk" candidate*—"McGovern Joins the Race for '72," *Boston Globe,* Commission on Party Structure and Delegate Selection, Container 7, DNC Files, National Archives.

149 *McGovern in New Hampshire*—Associated Press, September 21, 1969, Commission on Party Structure and Delegate Selection, Container 7, DNC Files, National Archives.

149 *McCarthyites distrust McGovern*—Lanny J. Davis, *The Emerging Democratic Majority: Lessons and Legacies from the New Politics* (Stein & Day, 1974), p. 101.

149 *McGovern aware of McCarthyites' anger*—Interview with George McGovern.

149 *McGovern not initially a reform Democrat*—Shafer, *Quiet Revolution,* p. 61.

150 *McGovern, "procedural reforms can never substitute ..."*—Transcript of the Commission on Party Structure and Delegate Selection, April 22, 1969, DNC Files, National Archives, pp. 1–3.

150 *"I think on balance it would serve ..."*—Transcript of NBC's *Meet the Press,* July 6, 1969 (vol. 13, no. 27), Commission on Party Structure and Delegate Selection, DNC Files, National Archives.

150 *McGovern on the military-industrial complex*—Interview with McGovern.

150–51 *McGovern on Woodstock*—Speech to the American Psychological Association Convention, September 3, 1969, George S. McGovern Papers, Speeches-statements, 1969, Box 699, Princeton University Library.

151 *McGovern on "a coalition of conscience"*—Senator George McGovern, "Reconciling the Generations," *Playboy,* January 1970, George S. McGovern Papers, Articles written by and about McGovern, Box 762, Princeton University Library.

151 *McGovern on college campuses*—McGovern, *Grassroots,* p. 159.

151 *McGovern and Lowenstein at NDC convention*—Brochure of New Democratic Coalition, Missouri Chapter, Series 1, Correspondence, 1968–1974, Western Historical Manuscript Collection, St. Louis.

152 *David Lawrence opposes quotas*—"Draft statement for Governor Lawrence," DNC Files, National Archives.

152 *Rauh endorses quotas*—Joseph Rauh, February 1, 1967, Democratic National Convention, Mississippi, 1967–68, Box 29, Library of Congress.

152–53 *Bernhard rejects quotas*—Letter from Berl I. Bernhard to Walter W. Giesey, April 4, 1967, DNC Files, National Archives.

153 *McGovern hints at support for quotas*—McGovern, "Reconciling the Generations."

153–54 *Commission endorses youth vote*—Warren Weaver Jr., "Democratic Reform Commission Asks Full Party Participation for Youths from 18 to 20," *New York Times*, September 25, 1969, p. 27.

154–55 *Bode's background*—See "Choosing Presidential Candidates: How Good Is the New Way?" sponsored by the American Enterprise Institute for Public Policy Research, Washington, D.C., October 18, 1979, John Charles Daly, moderator (American Enterprise Institute, 1980), p. 12.

155 *Segal, Stearns, and Mixner staffed the moratorium*—Interviews with Eli Segal and David Mixner. For Stearns' involvement, see David Maraniss, *First in His Class: A Biography of Bill Clinton* (Simon & Schuster, 1995), p. 170.

155 *Moratorium grows*—David Mixner, *Stranger Among Friends* (Bantam Books, 1996), p. 87.

155–56 *Commission's sorry financial shape*—Memorandum from Bob Nelson to Senators McGovern and Hughes and Mr. Fred Dutton, August 11, 1969, Commission on Party Structure and Delegate Selection, DNC Files, National Archives.

156 *Unable to pay court reporters*—Letter from Robert W. Nelson to Goodale, Friedsam & Lachowski, December 16, 1969, Commission on Party Structure and Delegate Selection, DNC Files, National Archives. The commission paid the court reporters almost six months later.

156 *Segal dubious about commission's prospects*—Letter from Eli Segal to Simon Lazarus, August 26, 1969, Commission on Party Structure and Delegate Selection, DNC Files, National Archives.

156 *"We're not getting anywhere with this war!"*—Interview with Ken Bode.

156 *Bode's dissertation*—Ken A. Bode, "Latin American Diplomats in Washington, D.C.: Backgrounds and Attitudes," Ph.D. thesis, University of North Carolina, p. 206. Bode wrote that his hypothesis about the importance of typological classifications largely "withstood empirical testing."

156 *Bode knew attitudes of the young*—See Kenneth A. Bode and Thomas H. Greene, "A Preliminary Study of Political Information Level and Attitudes among High School Seniors in Ingham County, Michigan," Ken Bode Files, DC 2831, DePauw University Archives.

156 *Women's contingent support for Humphrey*—See Jules Witcover, *85 Days: The Last Campaign of Robert Kennedy* (William Morrow, 1969), p. 429. According to Witcover, Nixon aide Pat Buchanan said on the Sunday before the 1968 election that he worried Nixon would lose because "the bombing halt really had the women moving toward Humphrey."

156–57 *Kirkpatrick on women's attitudes toward the war*—Jeane Kirkpatrick, *The New Presidential Elite: Men and Women in National Politics* (Russell Sage Foundation, 1976), p. 441.

157 *So Bode came up with an idea*—Interview with Ken Bode.

157 *Historians and political scientists have either guessed*—See Kirkpatrick, *The New Presidential Elite,* pp. 83–84.

157 *Commission cites alleged bias*—*Mandate for Reform,* p. 3.

157 *None mentioned discrimination against women*—"Abuses Alleged in Hearings—Most Common," Commission on Party Structure and Delegate Selection, DNC Files, National Archives.

157 *"Can you imagine ...?"*—Walter Goodman, "The Return of the Quota System," *New York Times,* September 10, 1972.

157–58 *"... the antiwar strategy ..."*—Interview with Alex Sanger.

158 *"It was widely believed ..."*—Interview with Austin Ranney.

158 *Cactus Jack's strategy*—See Lubell, *The Future of American Politics* (Doubleday, 1951), p. 14.

Chapter Six—Enter the Sisterhood

161 *Easing into the elevator*—Interview with Doris Meissner.

161 *Weakness of NWPC*—Ibid.

161 *Filed in through the glass doors*—Byron E. Shafer, *Quiet Revolution: The Struggle for the Democratic Party and the Shaping of Post-Reform Politics* (Russell Sage Foundation, 1983), p. 480.

162 *Feminist leaders had previously threatened*—Interview with Doris Meissner.

162 *Abzug's background*—See *Bella! Ms. Abzug Goes to Washington,* edited by Mel Ziegler (Saturday Review Press, 1972).

162 *"I strongly urge the McGovern-Fraser Commission ..."*—Bella Abzug to Don Fraser, Commission on Party Structure and Delegate Selection, Container 76, DNC Files, National Archives.

162   *Background on Fraser*—Interview with Don Fraser.

162–63 *"Thank you so much …"*—Letter from Don Fraser to Bella Abzug, Commission on Party Structure and Delegate Selection, Container 76, DNC Files, National Archives.

163   *"… a prima facie case"*—Shafer, *Quiet Revolution,* p. 481.

163   *"… there wasn't anything like A-2 …"*—Ibid., p. 469.

163   *"a way to seek to reform …"*—Interview with Doris Meissner.

163   *NWPC document, "The Democratic Party has …"*—Commission on Party Structure and Delegate Selection, DNC Files, National Archives.

164   *Feminists were emerging*—See Linda Charlton, "Women March Down Fifth in Equality Drive," *New York Times,* August 27, 1970.

164   *Powerful GOP women*—Interview with Doris Meissner.

165   *Martha Griffiths on House floor*—Hon. Martha W. Griffiths, Extensions of Remarks, *Congressional Record: House,* April 6, 1971, p. 9895.

165   *Phyllis Segal's research*—Interview with Phyllis Segal.

166   *Abzug on Segal*—Hon. Bella S. Abzug, Extensions of Remarks, *Congressional Record: House,* July 19, 1971, p. 25929.

166–67 *Bode's activities*—See Andrew J. Glass and Jonathan Cotton, "Democratic Reform Drive Falters as Spotlight Shifts to Presidential Race," *National Journal,* June 19, 1971, p. 1301.

167   *Auerbach objected*—Letter from Carl Auerbach to Ken Bode, Delegate Selection and Party Organization, 1969–1975, Joseph L. Rauh papers, Box 28, Library of Congress.

167   *Dutton advised NWPC*—Interview with Fred Dutton.

168   *"My brief takes the position …"*—Shafer, *Quiet Revolution,* p. 474.

168   *"I want to underscore …"*—Memorandum from Lawrence F. O'Brien to Democratic Chairmen, et al., December 8, 1971, Commission on Party Structure and Delegate Selection, Container 76, DNC Files, National Archives, p. 1.

168   *"If the Democratic National Convention …"*—Letter from Doris Meissner to Lawrence O'Brien, April 3, 1972, Commission on Party Structure and Delegate Selection, Container 76, DNC Files, National Archives.

168 *"I should be more interested . . ."*—Lawrence O'Brien to Doris Meissner, April 7, 1972, Commission on Party Structure and Delegate Selection, Container 76, DNC Files, National Archives.

169 Steinem *"spoke of councilmen being ousted . . ."*—Germaine Greer, "McGovern, the Big Tease," *Harper's*, August 1972, p. 60.

169 *"We women look at this subject . . ."*—Shirley MacLaine, "Women, the Convention, and Brown Paper Bags," *New York Times*, July 30, 1972. George McGovern confirmed that he met with the women, though he could not recall any particular exchanges.

170 *Abzug sponsors abortion bill*—See "The Nation," *Los Angeles Times*, May 3, 1972, p. B2. Also see Karilyn Barker, "1,000 Vote Drive for Abortion," *Washington Post*, February 14, 1972, p. A12.

170 *"In matters relating . . ."*—*The Official Proceedings of the Democratic National Convention, 1972*, edited by Sheila Hixson and Ruth Rose, p. 310.

170 *Abzug could not find work*—See *Bella!*, esp. ch. 1.

170 *Steinem could not get a job*—See Carolyn G. Heilbrun, *The Education of a Woman: The Life of Gloria Steinem* (Doubleday, 1995), pp. 84–86.

171 *Grasso was a difference feminist*—See Joseph Lieberman, *The Legacy: Connecticut Politics, 1930–1980* (Spoonwood Press, 1981), last chapter.

171 *". . . white, female, middle-class elite."*—See Hon. Bella S. Abzug, Extensions of Remarks, *Congressional Record: House*, July 13, 1971, p. 24788.

172 *Blake survey*—Judith Blake, "Abortion and Public Opinion: The 1960–1970 Decade," *Science*, vol. 171 (February 12, 1971), p. 548.

172 *Women's attitudes on abortion*—Ibid., p. 545.

172 *Abzug on her abortion bill*—See "The Nation," *Los Angeles Times*, May 3, 1972, p. B2.

172–73 *"This minority report . . ."*—Remarks of Jennifer Wilke, *The Official Proceedings of the Democratic National Convention, 1972*, pp. 310–11.

173 *"I do not lightly ..."*—Remarks of Frances "Sissy" Farenthold, ibid., p. 311.

173 *"In the name of moderation ..."*—Remarks of Eleanor Holmes Norton, ibid., pp. 311–12.

173–74 *Califano presides*—Ibid., pp. 3, 310.

174 *"The only ideological base ..."*—Joseph Califano Jr., "Vatican II for a Party," *New Democrat*, February 1971, p. 10.

174–75 *Califano realized his mistake*—Joseph A. Califano Jr., *Inside: A Public and Private Life* (PublicAffairs Books, 2004), p. 258.

175 *They "just lost Michigan today ..."*—Theodore H. White, *The Making of the President, 1972* (Bantam Books, 1973), p. 213.

175 *Abzug loses re-election*—See Myra McPherson, "Everybody Is People," *Washington Post*, April, 1972.

176 *"Catholics don't own ..."*—Letter from Mrs. Norbert Winter to Professor Richard Neustadt, May 20, 1972, Commission on Party Structure and Delegate Selection, DNC Files, National Archives.

176 *Survey on abortion*—Blake, "Abortion and Public Opinion," pp. 541–43.

177 *"The Democratic Party has no place ..."*—Remarks of Eugene Walsh, *The Official Proceedings of the DNC, 1972*, pp. 313–14.

177–78 *"The Catholic-ethnic vote ..."*—Memorandum from Gerry Cassidy and Ken Schlossberg to Senator McGovern, June 15, 1972, George S. McGovern Papers, Princeton University Library.

178 *Abortion plank fails*—David S. Broder, "Display of Unity," *Washington Post*, June 28, 1972.

178 *"We were very afraid ..."*—Susan and Martin Tolchin, *Clout: Womanpower and Politics* (Coward, McCann & Geoghegan, 1973), p. 49.

178–79 *Abzug unhinged*—"MacLaine, Abzug Shout It Out in Hall," *Los Angeles Times*, July 13, 1972.

179 *Steinem livid*—Myra McPherson, "Sisters vs. Sisters," *Washington Post*, July 13, 1972.

179 *Some women dissent*—Shirley MacLaine, *New York Times*, July 30, 1972.

179 *"All women are not in favor of abortion . . ."*—State Caucus Organizing Guidelines, March 1972, Commission on Party Structure and Delegate Selection, DNC Files, National Archives, p. 7.

180 *GOP women back abortion*—See Spencer Rich, "Platform Panel Hears Recital of Nixon Record," *Washington Post*, August 16, 1972.

180 *Sanford understood*—Tolchin, *Clout: Womanpower and Politics*, pp. 56–57.

Chapter Seven—The Emerging Democratic Minority

181 *Gary Hart walked in*—Gary Warren Hart, *Right from the Start: A Chronicle of the McGovern Campaign* (Quadrangle, 1973), p. 70.

181 *Hart had organized Western party leaders*—Ibid., pp. 7–11.

181 *Hart sees no national plans*—Ibid., p. 11.

181–82 *Hart's doubts renewed*—Ibid., p. 12.

182 *McGovern's long shot*—George McGovern, *Grassroots: The Autobiography of George McGovern* (Random House, 1977), p. 155.

182–83 *McGovern's frayed ties with blue-collars*—Robert Sam Anson, *McGovern: A Biography* (Holt, Rinehart & Winston, 1971), p. 266.

183 *McGovern's thin ties with Catholics*—See letter from McGovern to Father James M. Doyle, September 28, 1970, George S. McGovern Papers, McGovern's Correspondence, Box 693, Princeton University Library.

183 *McGovern frets about ties with antiwar activists*—Letter from James E. Solheim to McGovern, July 31, 1970, George S. McGovern Papers, Correspondence, Box 693, Princeton University Library.

183 *War issue loses steam*—Robert B. Semple Jr., "Candidates for Congress Across the Nation Find War a Minor Issue," *New York Times*, October 19, 1970.

183–84 *National recognition minimal*—David S. Broder, "How 'Serious' Is McGovern's Candidacy?" *Washington Post*, January 24, 1971.

184 *"I quite honestly did not ..."*—Hubert Humphrey, *The Education of a Public Man: My Life and Politics* (Regents of the University of Minnesota, 1991), p. 327.

184 *McGovern less liberal than contenders*—See "Pressure Group Ratings, 1961–1971," *Congressional Quarterly*, February 12, 1972, p. 272.

184–85 *Wexler viewed McGovern as too liberal*—"A Talk with Anne Wexler," *New Democrat*, June 1972.

185 Hart still gloomy—Hart, *Right from the Start*, p. 14.

185 *Hart's joke*—Ibid., pp. 14–15.

186 *"Under the old system ..."*—Ken Bode, "Can Reform Change the Nature of the 'Beast'?" *New York Times*, February 6, 1972, p. E5.

186 *McGovern eyes activists*—Anson, *McGovern*, p. 264.

187 *"My one unique position ..."*—Theodore H. White, *The Making of the President, 1972* (Bantam Books, 1973), p. 54.

187 *"The Reform Commission he was then heading ..."*—Ibid., p. 51.

187–88 *"If there is no change in the Democratic Party ..."*—Richard Wade, *New Democrat*, October 1970, p. 6.

188 *McGovern's strategy*—Hart, *Right from the Start*, pp. 16–19.

188 *Vote totals in 1972*—William V. Shannon, "The Legends of George McGovern," *New York Times*, July 2, 1972.

189 *"I remain convinced that this project ..."*—Letter from Eli Segal to Senator McGovern, July 21, 1970, George S. McGovern Papers, Personal Correspondence, 1970, Box 492, Princeton University Library.

189 *1972 was the reverse of 1968*—John G. Stewart, *One Last Chance: The Democratic Party, 1974–76* (Praeger Publishers, 1974), p. 57.

190 *"Our principal organizing weapon ..."*—Lanny J. Davis, *The Emerging Democratic Majority: Lessons and Legacies from the New Politics* (Stein & Day, 1974), p. 166.

190 *Stearns used same strategy in Vermont*—Ibid., pp. 109–10.

190–91 *Stearns at Utah state convention*—Ibid., p. 110.

191 *"My nomination is all the more precious ..."*—See White, *The Making of the President, 1972*, p. 247.

191 *McGovern and Dutton*—Letter and packet from Fred Dutton to George McGovern, May 20, 1971, George S.

McGovern Papers, Correspondence—1971, Box 299, Princeton University Library.

191–92 *Hart endorses "McGovern coalition"*—Hart, *Right from the Start,* p. 77.

192 *"I think we can build a different majority ..."*—"The Young Can Make the System Work," *An American Journey: The Presidential Campaign Speeches of George McGovern* (Random House, 1974), pp. 175–77.

192 *"The young, the black, and the poor ..."*—Milton Viorst, "Playboy Interview: George McGovern," *Playboy,* September 1971, p. 191.

193 *McCarthy downgrades blue-collars*—See Lewis Chester, Godfrey Hodgson and Bruce Page, *An American Melodrama: The Presidential Campaign of 1968* (Viking Press, 1969), Act IV, Scene 1.

193 *McCarthy "somehow addressed himself to the issues ..."*—Viorst, "Playboy Interview: George McGovern," p. 191.

193 *"Americans have never believed ..."*—*An American Journey,* p. 9.

193–94 *McGovern's religious background*—See McGovern, *Grassroots,* chs. 1–3.

194 *McGovern allows abortion*—George McGovern, *Terry: My Daughter's Life-and Death Struggle with Alcoholism* (Penguin Group, 1996), p. 65.

194 *McGovern's social liberalism*—See McGovern, *Grassroots,* pp. 159–60.

194 *College kids lukewarm to Muskie*—James M. Naughton, "Muskie's Grade a 'C' in Politics on Campus," *New York Times,* February 7, 1972.

194–95 *McGovern aware of possible alienation*—McGovern, *Grassroots,* p. 160.

195 *McGovern in New Hampshire primary*—Davis, *The Emerging Democratic Majority,* pp. 134–39.

195 *Media exaggerated McGovern's appeal*—See Don Oberdorfer, "Radical Issue Hits McGovern," *Washington Post,* May 9, 1972. Also see Rowland Evans and Robert Novak, "Humphrey's New Problem," *Washington Post,* May 5, 1977.

195–96 *Percentages in working-class neighborhoods*—Davis, *The Emerging Democratic Majority,* esp. ch. 9.

196 *McGovern among Catholics in Nebraska*—R. W. Apple Jr., "Aftermath of Two Primaries: California Really Counts," *New York Times*, May 11, 1972.

196 "*The DNC's old-time reliance...*"—Memorandum from Gerry Cassidy and Kenneth Schlossberg to George McGovern, June 15, 1972, George S. McGovern Papers, Princeton University Library.

196–97 "*The lack of ethnics (and old people)...*"—Memorandum from Gerry Cassidy and Kenneth Schlossberg to Frank Mankiewicz, July 21, 1972, George S. McGovern Papers, Princeton University Library, p. 4.

197 "*The heavy emphasis in the press...*"—Ibid., p.1.

197–98 "*Our main problem is the blue-collar Catholic worker.*"—White, *The Making of the President, 1972*, p. 419.

198 *Little money toward blue-collar ethnics*—Ibid., p. 426.

198 *Johnson backs the Democratic ticket*—Peter R. Rosenbluth, "Post-Presidential Papers," Lyndon Baines Johnson Library, Box 29.

198 *Catholics vote for Nixon*—George J. Marlin, *The American Catholic Voter: 200 Years of Political Impact* (St. Augustine's Press, 2004), p. 282.

198–99 "*The Democratic defection in 1972...*"—White, *The Making of the President, 1972*, pp. 459–69.

199 "*McGovern came on as a new person...*"—Charles Guggenheim in *Campaign '72: The Managers Speak*, ed. Ernest R. May and Janet Fraser (Harvard University Press, 1973).

199 "*equivalent of a referendum*"—Ben Wattenberg in ibid.

199 "*The American people made...*"—James O'Hara in ibid.

Chapter Eight—Blue by You

201 "*a single, narrow, ideological...*"—Richard Lyons, *Washington Post*, June 25, 1972, p. A1.

201–2 *Meany on "classy convention of the elite"*—Philip Shabecoff, "Meany Criticizes 'Elite' Democrats," *New York Times*, September 19, 1972, p. 38.

202 *Strauss disdained McGovern*—See Joseph A. Califano Jr., *Inside: A Public and Private Life* (PublicAffairs Books, 2004), p. 263; and Theodore H. White, *The Making of the President, 1972* (Bantam Books, 1973), p. 411.

202 *Strauss's background*—See Jon Margolis, "The Master of Mini-convention," *Chicago Tribune,* December 28, 1974, p. 10.

202 *O'Brien backs Strauss*—Lawrence O'Brien, *No Final Victories: A Life in Politics—From John F. Kennedy to Watergate* (Books of Canada, 1975), pp. 275–76.

203 *Barkan as counterrevolutionary*—David S. Broder, "Labor Exerting New Muscle in Democratic Party," *Washington Post,* September 2, 1973, p. A4.

203 *"It was a zero sum game . . ."*—Interview with Mark Siegel.

203 *Bode ridiculed Strauss*—Memorandum from Ken Bode to Files, December 11, 1972, Ken Bode Files, DePauw University Archives.

204 *"the leaders of organized labor . . ."*—David Broder, *Washington Post,* September 2, 1973.

204 *"I've got a proven record"*—Quoted in Margolis, "The Master of Mini-convention."

205 *"The Guidelines have reinvigorated . . ."*—"Let Us Continue: A Report on the Democratic Party's Delegate Selection Guidelines," Americans for Democratic Action, Ken Bode Files, DePauw University Archives, p. 5.

205 *Farenthold feared overreaction*—Eileen Shanahan, "Women's Leader Scores McGovern," *New York Times,* April 19, 1973, p. 28.

205–6 *"I want to create a climate . . ."*—George Lardner Jr., "Strauss Is Confident, Stresses Party Unity," *Washington Post,* December 8, 1972.

206 *Strauss added members to Mikulski Commission*—See, for example, Broder, *Washington Post,* September 2, 1973.

206 *DNC could review proposals*—David S. Broder, "Democrats Jettison '72 'Quota' System," *Washington Post,* October 28, 1973.

206–7 *"reduce the class bias . . ."*—Testimony of Penn Kemble, August 11, 1973, Ken Bode Files, DePauw University Archives.

207 *Broad Coalition*—Commission on Delegate Selection and Party Structure (Mikulski), December 6, 1973, Final Report, DNC Files, National Archives.

207 *Strauss united the party*—See, for example, David S. Broder, "'Crisis' Plan Pledged," *Washington Post,* December 7, 1974.

207 *"The Party would be committing ..."*—Memorandum from Phyllis N. Segal to Barbara Mikulski, Ken Bode Files, DePauw University Archives.

208 *"Democracy cannot be accomplished by fiat."*—"Toward Fairness and Unity for '76," Coalition for a Democratic Majority, Ken Bode Files, DePauw University Archives.

208 *Strauss quotations*—See, for example, Broder, "Democrats Jettison '72 'Quota' System."

208 *Jackson and Daley*—See, for example, R. W. Apple Jr., "Democrats Adopt a Party Charter," *New York Times,* December 8, 1974.

208 I learned about the statement from Jules Witcover, *Marathon: The Pursuit of the Presidency, 1972–1976* (Viking Press, 1977), p. 206. The description of the church basement is based on my visit to Holy Spirit Catholic Church in Creston.

209 *"My opinion was well defined ..."*—Memorandum from Margaret Costanza to the President, July 13, 1977, Margaret Costanza Files, Jimmy Carter Library.

209 *Democrats had white conservatives*—Earl and Merle Black, *Divided America: The Ferocious Power Struggle in American Politics* (Simon & Schuster, 2007), pp. 13–24.

209 *Jackson and Kennedy opposed legal abortion*—Kennedy voted on April 28, 1976, for a constitutional amendment to grant legal protection to the unborn. See *Congressional Record.* Jackson spoke at the annual March for Life.

210 *Carter's pro-life response to questionnaire*—"Questions for Presidential Candidates," Intercessors for America, Jimmy Carter Library.

210 *Georgia statute*—For a description of the law, see Cynthia Gorney, *Articles of Faith: A Frontline History of the Abortion Wars* (Simon & Schuster, 1998), pp. 151–52.

210 *"I'm terribly disappointed ..."*—Ibid.

211 *Bernardin statement*—Marjorie Hyer, "Democrats Hit on Abortion," *Washington Post,* June 25, 1976.

211 *Pro-lifers march in Central Park*—Peter Kihss, "10,000 Antiabortionists Attend a Protest Rally," *New York Times,* July 12, 1976.

211 *McCormack rips Democrats on TV*—David S. Broder, "Carter Sweeps to Nomination," *Washington Post,* July 15, 1976.

211 *The campaign's "Catholic problem"*—See Memorandum from Stu Eizenstat to Vicki Rogers, August 19, 1976; Dick Moe to Stu Eizenstat, September 13, 1976; and Profile of Abortion Mail 8/7–9/16; Jimmy Carter Library.

212 *"The 1960's were the time . . ."*—Memorandum to Governor Jimmy Carter from Adam Walinsky, July 28, 1976, Jimmy Carter Library, pp. 7–8. See also Michael B. Scanlon, "Carter and Catholics: An Action Plan," July 20, 1976.

212 *Eizenstat's memo*—Memorandum from Stu Eizenstat to Governor Carter, et al., September 16, 1976, Jimmy Carter Library.

213 *"It would be inappropriate for any citizen . . ."*—Kenneth A. Briggs, "Carter Campaign Moving to Mollify Catholics after Dispute over Democratic Party's Abortion Stand," *New York Times,* August 26, 1976, p. 20.

213 *Carter aides wrote abortion plank*—Marlene Simons, "Abortion Key Plank with Pros and Cons," *Los Angeles Times,* July 11, 1976, p. E1.

213 *"Our 'signals' to the urban ethnic . . ."*—Memorandum from Tom Tatum to Hamilton Jordan, August 23, 1976, Jimmy Carter Library.

213–14 *Carter's meeting with bishops*—I have relied on Martin Schram, *Running for President: A Journal of the Carter Campaign* (Simon & Schuster, 1976), pp. 250–53, as well as newspaper accounts.

213–14 *Bernardin's statement*—Undated and unsigned copy. Based on Martin Schram's account in *Running for President* and on newspapers, it's clear that this was the archbishop's statement.

214 *Carter snubs Catholics for a Free Choice*—Letter from Virginia Andary to Governor Carter, September 1, 1976, Jimmy Carter Library.

214–15 *"If this amendment passes ..."*—Memorandum from Mary King et al. to Hamilton Jordan et al., September 9, 1976, Jimmy Carter Library.

215 *"Often overshadowed by other issues ..."*—Patrick Caddell, "The Abortion Issue," Jimmy Carter Library, p. 107.

215 *Carter seen as more socially conservative*—Jonathan Moore and Janet Fraser, eds., *Campaign for President: The Managers Look at '76* (Ballinger Publishing, 1977), pp. 120–21.

216 *Carter accomplished his goal*—Maris A. Vinovskis, "Abortion and the Presidential Election of 1976: A Multivariate Analysis of Voting Behavior," *Michigan Law Review*, vol. 7, no. 77, Symposium on the Law and Politics of Abortion (August 1979), pp. 1750–51.

216 *Carter wins Catholic vote*—"Who Voted," *New York Times*, 2000.

216 *Carter criticizes funding of abortion*—Memorandum from Margaret Costanza to the President, July 13, 1977, Jimmy Carter Library.

216–17 *Califano and Carter on Medicaid funding*—See Joseph A. Califano Jr., *Governing America: An Insider's Report from the White House and the Cabinet* (Simon & Schuster, 1981), esp. ch. 2.

217 *"Generally speaking, I think we ought to seize ..."*—Draft memorandum from Bob Maddox to Anne Wexler et al., 1980, Jimmy Carter Library.

217 *Pro-abortion plank in 1980*—Email from Traci Siegel, executive director of DNC Women's Vote Center, to the author, January 28, 2002.

218 *"It was ... evident to Mr. Grier ..."*—Memorandum from Tom Laney to Jane Fenderson, July 18, 1980, Jimmy Carter Library.

218 *"I write to you today ..."*—Letter from the Most Reverend Elden F. Curtiss to President Carter, September 4, 1980, Jimmy Carter Library.

219 *1976 plank*—See, for example, Marlene Simons, "Abortion Key Plank with Pros and Cons," *Los Angeles Times*, July 11, 1976, p. E1.

219 *"It worries me because there is nothing ..."*—Ibid., pp. E1, E9.

219–20   *1977 meeting with feminists*—Memorandum from Jan Peterson to Margaret Costanza, July 20, 1977, Jimmy Carter Library.

220   *Feminists opposed Carter's re-election*—See Bella Abzug and Mim Kelber, *The Gender Gap: Bella Abzug's Guide to Political Power for American Women* (Houghton Mifflin, 1984), p. 81.

220   *Background of Koryne Horbal*—Interview with Koryne Horbal.

221   *"In those days . . ."*—Interview with Nellie Gray.

221   *"I think the difference was that . . ."*—Interview with Koryne Horbal.

221   *Feminists were well organized*—Abzug, *The Gender Gap*, pp. 47–51.

221   *"Instead of selling it as a quota . . ."*—Interview with Joanne Howes.

221–22   *Quotas for commissions and committees*—Abzug, *The Gender Gap*, pp. 47, 51.

222   *"It was a matter of . . ."*—Interview with Joanne Howes.

222   *Feminists sold the concept*—Interviews with Joanne Howes and Koryne Horbal.

222   *"I was sort of taken aback . . ."*—Interview with Mark Siegel.

222   *"The rules, refined again . . ."*—Theodore H. White, *America in Search of Itself: The Making of the President, 1956–1980* (Harper & Rowe, 1982), p. 286.

223   *"We were dealing with forces . . ."*—Tim Kraft, quoted in ibid., p. 339.

223   *"Our ten-year campaign . . ."*—Abzug, *Gender Gap*, pp. 84–85.

223–24   *Clinton's despair*—Bill Clinton, *My Life: The Early Years* (Random House, 2004), p. 540.

224   *Clinton criticizes Sister Souljah*—Ibid., p. 541.

225   *Clinton opposed federally funded abortion*—Ibid., esp. ch. 21.

225   *Casey in Cleveland*—Statement to the Democratic National Committee Platform Hearing, May 18, 1992, Robert P. Casey, Governor of Pennsylvania.

225–26   *Clinton "inclined to let Casey talk . . ."*—Clinton, *My Life: The Early Years*, p. 547.

226 *"There was no question . . ."*—Richard Reeves, *Running in Place: How Bill Clinton Disappointed America* (Andrews & McMeel, 1993), p. xiv.

226 *"It was getting old, really"*—Ron Brown quoted by Jack W. Germond and Jules Witcover, *Mad as Hell: Revolt at the Ballot Box, 1992* (Warner Books, 1993), p. 39.

227 *"He was denied access . . ."*—Ron Brown quoted in Charles T. Royer, ed., *Campaign for President: The Managers Look at 1992* (Puritan Press, 1994).

227 *"In 1972 and 1980 . . ."*—Clinton, *My Life: The Early Years,* p. 547.

228 *"They didn't want him to speak . . ."*—Interview with DNC official.

228 *Clinton at NWPC event*—See, for example, Mimi Hall, *USA Today,* July 15, 1992.

228 *Casey and Lawrence*—Robert P. Casey, *Fighting for Life* (Word Publishing, 1996), p. 79.

228 *Casey equates DNC with NARAL*—Ibid., p. 185.

229 *"I expected to be weaker . . ."*—Clinton, *My Life: The Presidential Years* (Vintage Books, 2004), p. 344.

229 *"It was clear that the Democrats . . ."*—E. J. Dionne Jr., *They Only Look Dead: Why Progressives Will Dominate the Next Political Era* (Simon & Schuster, 1996), p. 98.

230 *Media notice secular left*—Thomas B. Edsall, "Voter Values Determine Political Affiliation," *Washington Post,* March 26, 2001.

230–31 *Democrats for Life statement*—See David Carlin, "A Political Argument from Pro-Life Democrats," www.democratsfor-life.com/political_argu.html.

231 *DNC excludes DFL*—See Mark Shields, "Democrats Doing Worst to Lose 'Catholic Vote,'" Creators Syndicate, July 22, 2002.

231–32 *Gephardt's flip-flops*—See Deirdre Shesgreen, *St. Louis Post-Dispatch,* January 22, 2003.

232 *Kerry's litmus test*—See Thomas Beaumont, "Kerry to Back Only Pro-Choice Justices," *Des Moines Register,* April 9, 2003.

233   Kerry, "I could never do that"—Evan Thomas et al., *Election 2004: How Bush Won and What You Can Expect in the Future* (PublicAffairs Books, 2004).

233   *"Jimmy Carter eked out a victory ..."*—William Galston and Elaine Kamarck, "The Politics of Polarization," Third Way, October 2005.

233   *Hillary Clinton adjusts her rhetoric*—Patrick D. Healy, "Senator Clinton Speaks of 'Common Ground' on Abortion, *New York Times,* January 24, 2005.

233   *"We're a big tent party."*—Interview with Hillary Clinton.

2334   *"... in the so-called red states ..."*—Clinton, *My Life: The Presidential Years,* p. 663.

234   *"You don't just throw out words ..."*—Karen White, quoted by Peter Boyer, "The Right to Choose," *New Yorker,* November 14, 2005, p. 54.

234   *Tim Roemer comment*—Ibid., pp. 56, 58.

234   *Howard Dean comment*—Roger Simon, "The New Dean Political Plan," *The Politico,* March 15, 2007.

234   *Public backs late-term abortion ban*—See, for example, Gallup Poll on May 10–13, 2007, at www.pollingreport.com/abortion.

234   *"This decision marks a dramatic departure ..."*—Hillary Clinton at www.hillaryclinton.com/news/release.

234–35   *"This hard right turn is a stark reminder ..."*—John Edwards at http://hotline.blog/nationaljournal.com.

235   *"I strongly disagree with today's Supreme Court ruling ..."*—Barack Obama at http://hotline.blog/nationaljournal.com.

235   *"You can't get through the nomination process ..."*—Interview with John Breaux.

Afterword—Toward a New People's Party

237–38   *History of nominating system*—See, for example, Austin Ranney, *Curing the Mischiefs of Faction: Party Reform in America* (University of California Press, 1975).

238   *Failure of Super Tuesday*—See, for example, Jack W. Germond and Jules Witcover, *Whose Broad Stripes and Bright Stars? The Trivial Pursuit of the Presidency, 1988* (Warner Books, 1989), pp. 278–92.

239   *"Caucuses empower ...."*—Interview with Curtis Gans.

239–40 *Iowa caucus figures*—Rhodes Cook, *Race for the Presidency: Winning the 2004 Nomination* (CQ Press, 2004), p. 12.

240 *Education level of caucus participants*—"Poll: Who Turned Out," *New York Times,* January 20, 2004.

240 *"We need to recruit more people ..."*—Interview with Don Fowler.

241 *"By insisting on a fixed proportion ..."*—Theodore H. White, *The Making of the President, 1972* (Bantam Books, 1973), p. 41.

Index

Kemble, Penn, 123, 206
Kennedy, John F., 11, 12, 15;
    and Bailey, 34; and Daley, 35;
    on Johnson, 59–60, 65; and
    Lawrence, 48–49, 56–59, 65;
    nomination of, 59; and
    O'Brien, 99; and Southern
    Baptists, 212; and Stevenson
    draft, 55
Kennedy, Edward M. (Ted),
    106, 121, 148; and Carter,
    227–28; feminists for, 220;
    vote against *Roe,* 209
Kennedy, Joseph, 57–58
Kennedy, Kathleen, 196
Kennedy, Robert F., 35, 84;
    assassination, 88, 111; on
    "black-blue" coalition, 125–
    26, 151–52, 182; Clinton on,
    3–4; and Dutton, 8, 130; on
    Johnson, 60; "law & order,"
    92, 126; and Lawrence, 57,
    59; primary victories, 88;
    Segal on, 91–92
Kennedy, Rose, 58
Kerner Commission, 91, 99
Kerry, John, 14, 19–20, 232–33;
    on abortion, 26; and social
    issues, 24
Keyserling, Leon, 78
Kimelman, Henry, 148
King Caucus system, 78, 237
Kirkland, Lane, 96
Kirkpatrick, Jeane, 156–57
Kovner, Sarah, 205
Kraft, Tim, 223
Kucinich, Dennis, 232
Kukovich, Allen, 22, 28

labor unions, 9, 22–23, 223; vs.
    campus youth, 106; and Clin-
ton, 23, 224; and Humphrey,
    94–95; and McGovern, 182–
    83, 201–2, 203; and McGov-
    ern Commission, 94–95, 101;
    and Vietnam, 95
Ladd, Everett Carll, Jr., 18, 20
Lamont, Ned, 240
Laney, Ben, 37
Last Hurrah, The, 32, 56
Lawrence, David L., 7, 31, 33–
    45, 95; and abortion, 53; and
    Casey, 228; Catholicism of,
    56–59; on civil rights, 36–41,
    43–45, 72; and Curley, 42–
    43; on delegate quotas, 152;
    and Johnson, 33–34, 60–61;
    and Kennedy, 48–49, 56–59,
    65; on Mississippi delegation,
    69–70; modest lifestyle, 42–
    43; as negotiator, 51, 72–73;
    patronage jobs, 49; on police
    corruption, 50; political train-
    ing, 43; on racial equality, 53;
    on social issues, 52–53; and
    Stevenson, 47–48, 54–55; and
    Truman, 39–40
Lawrence, Gerald, 53
Lawrence Commission (1965–
    68), 7, 73–77, 90, 152, 222
Lawyers for McCarthy, 81–83
Lazarus, Simon, 156
Lemann, Nicholas, 51
Leubsdorf, Carl, 125
Lieberman, Joseph: on Bailey,
    43, 50, 52, 79; as independ-
    ent candidate, 240–41
Lindsay, John, 184, 186
Loeb, William, 195
Louisiana, 89, 102, 127
Lowenstein, Allard, 8, 101, 131,
    135, 148, 151